Real
Talk

FOR
Real
SISTERS

Real Talk

FOR

Real

SISTERS

*Wisdom and Truth for
Today's Women and Teens*

JUDGE PENNY
BROWN REYNOLDS

*Sparrow***House**
PUBLISHING

Real Talk for Real Sisters
Wisdom and Truth for Today's Women & Teens
Judge Penny Brown Reynolds

Printed Edition ISBN: 9781942545309
Library of Congress Control Number: 2015954834

SparrowHouse
PUBLISHING

NOTE TO READERS

This publication contains the opinions and ideas of its author and contributors.
It is intended to provide helpful and informative material on the subjects addressed in
the publication. It is sold with the understanding that the author, the contributors,
and publisher are not engaged in rendering legal, medical, or health advice, or any
other kind of personal or professional services in this book. Discussions do not create
an attorney-client relationship between the reader and any person, nor is it an offer to
create such a relationship. Laws change over time and vary from state to state. The
reader should consult an attorney or a competent professional to address her particular
situation before adopting any of the suggestions in this book or drawing inferences
from it.

The author, contributors, and publisher specifically disclaim all responsibility
for any liability, loss, or risk, personal or otherwise, that is incurred as a consequence,
directly or indirectly, of the use and application of any of the contents of this book.

C O N T E N T S

SECTION I

DEDICATION

This book is dedicated to my granddaughter,
Pelly-Marie Victoria Armour.

Continue to grow in knowledge and wisdom, and always
remember that you are somebody to love.

To my late mother, Deforest Marie Brown and my
late grandmother, Blanche Rousell Brown:

I am able to pass on wisdom because you gave it to me first.
You live inside of me and now inside of others.

WHAT TO EXPECT

Suppose you had the opportunity to know about a situation before you actually had to experience it. Women want to know the truth about their circumstances so they can decide what is best for them. There is much our mothers never told us, and we had to find out on our own, the hard way. How much better could life be if we could hear the voice of a sister who is not afraid to say what most women are thinking? We've all heard the saying, "If we knew then what we know now," and *Real Talk for Real Sisters* gives the reader this foresight.

I wrote this book through my voice, as I share life lessons that are practical and thoughtful. My book addresses women in an informal, yet authoritative style. A judge rarely comes down from the ivory towers of the judiciary to provide wisdom in such a real way, but I've never done what others do. The current state of the economy has created an environment of fear and discontent in this country. The unknown is what people fear the most. My book tells the truth, empowers, and motivates. It provides a comprehensive, straightforward, down-to-earth look at the truth in various stages of a woman's life. After watching news reports of young teenage girls fist fighting, it became clear to me that the book must include a chapter for teen girls who sometimes display behavior in public that is troubling and painful to watch. Without the necessary guidance at home, our daughters have learned that walking down the street wearing hair bonnets and pajama bottoms is acceptable.

Real Talk has "soul-saving sayings" for women of every age in various life situations. My grandmother and mother gave me these soul-saving sayings. I want you to have them to guide you on your journey. Although these life situations may not be applicable to all, the lessons are transferable to every circumstance.

Real Talk concludes with words of wisdom from sisters who have learned lessons and wish to pass them on. It engages various women, such as the single sister looking for love, telling her how to be satisfied alone. The book also addresses the married sister who is learning the practicalities of a good marriage, the caregiver sister who finds herself taking care of her parents, the promiscuous sister who is looking for love in all the wrong places, and the overweight sister who needs to dig deeper to discover the reasons behind her weight gain. My aim is to express and confirm the challenges women often face, offering guidance about how to overcome them. The book unveils the raw truth that will hopefully be a wake-up call to many women.

My book is unique because it addresses many different women in the areas of their lives that are most significant to them. Not every woman wants to read a book on how to get a man. The reader of this book may be an entrepreneur who is making payroll every week in a male-dominated field, or she may be the only sister in the boardroom and is looking for empowerment and confidence. This book allows the reader to know she isn't alone in what she's feeling and experiencing. Women need to be connected to each other, and *Real Talk* bridges the gap.

The message of the book is simple: *When you know better, you ought to do better.* Readers can decide whether to embrace or reject the advice in this book, but they will never be able to say they were not told.

Real Talk could not be timelier. Now more than ever, people need to hear the truth about how to live a better life. Women are joining the workforce in record numbers, and they need to know what to expect when they get there. Women also need an honest view of the challenges and rewards of motherhood. Finally, women need to engage with a text that provides insight for all relationships and stages of life. The close of each chapter has space for the reader to share her own truth and to write down an action plan to deal with that truth.

Most self-help books render advice to women on specific topics, such as love, health and nutrition, or finance. *Real Talk* is unique because its focus is varied, appealing to women of all ages in all circumstances. At any age, a sister can be ambitious, angry, abused, betrayed, depressed, divorced, homeless, or religious. *Real Talk* gives voice to all of these women by delivering a frank truth that requires reflection about the decisions women make. Many women want to think like a woman, not like a man. They want to be whole and accepted for who they are without having to play mind games. Women want to be free. Women want to be loved. Women want to be respected.

Real Talk for Real Sisters is about us, for us, because of us.

INTRODUCTION

My Truth

"It's not the load that breaks you down,
it's the way you carry it."
LENA HORNE

I love being a woman. I love being a sister-friend to other women. I would not trade being a woman for anything in this life. But—we have issues!

First, I think it's a shame that so many women give other women such a hard time. It's difficult to admit, but to write a book of truth, it's best to begin by stating the truth. Now, let me be clear, I realize this is my truth. I feel confident in telling my truth because of everything I have experienced in my life. I learned a great deal from sitting on the bench for a number of years. While listening, observing, and casting judgment on issues faced by everyday people, I was able to learn a great deal about human nature. The courtroom serves as a microcosm of the reality of life's situations. Beyond my experiences in the courtroom, I am an ordained minister who has traveled and observed women across the country. I have also found myself tackling difficult life situations, all while a television audience showed me solving the problems of the people who had come on my court show looking for justice.

I have seen it all. I've seen the best of womanhood, and I have turned my head in dismay at the actions of what some of us have done to others. I only wish it was a myth that women don't always know how to get along. The truth is, we can be difficult with other women for no good reason. Yes, it is embarrassing to raise this issue, but until we put it on the table honestly, we will never really deal with it. I like keeping it real. Talking about this issue raises awareness and presents an opportunity for correction and healing.

My contention about our behavior toward each other is clearly supported by the tremendous success of the reality shows that often feature displays of unapologetic bad behavior among women. I am done being insulted by these shows when their success proves that the drama resonates with women of all races. Whether I approve of them or not, these sisters have found a way to make money while showing the world their authentic selves. Bottom line: the women on these shows represent many of the personalities and behaviors of a number of sisters. Period! End of the story! Sisters are watching a display of how they behave. We may not want to hear it, but there are many sisters cutting up and saying and acting any way for attention. This is why these television shows are so popular.

The refusal to speak about how we treat each other reminds me of the issue of race. Because race is such an uncomfortable issue for many to deal with, our country refuses to have an open and frank dialogue about it. We skirt around the issue. We deal with it only when some ugly racial matter arises, and, by then, defenses are up, and there is little room for an honest dialogue to take place. We should have regular discussions about race. The day that America decides to have regular, open conversations that listen to all voices will be the day that we can begin the healing of unyielding racial brokenness. The same can be said for relationships between women. We hate talking about it, but to heal and save the next generation, we must deal with this troubling issue.

Let me make this clear, I've had wonderful female friends along my journey. Many of these friends were women in the field of law. These were the sisters who didn't feel as though they had to compete. They had a true knowledge of self and never felt threatened by me or anyone else for that matter. Many of these relationships were not formal mentoring relationships, but I looked up to these women because of their support. Honestly, I never had a woman formally take me under her wing. Perhaps this is why it's so important to me to support other women and young women in particular. I understand that insecure people find it difficult to be supportive and to lift up other sisters. However, even though I understand these reasons, I wish it were otherwise.

It is painful to watch women being oppressed by double standards because of their gender. It hurts even more when unfairness and bias come from other women. Why do we do it? Why can't we go out of our way to be supportive and less critical of other women? Why, as women, do we allow our insecurities to find fault with other women? Why do we find it difficult to help other women? This is disappointing for women, given all the progress we have made.

Politics are often sickening to watch in terms of gender double standards. If a female candidate is strong and assertive, she often turns other women off. Consequently, her advisors attempt to soften her image. On the other hand, if she is feminine and attractive, she is accused of being weak. As women, we hold each other to unreasonable standards. Some of us don't need a reason not to like another sister; we just decide from the moment we lay eyes on her that she is someone we will never like.

We are hard on each other. We easily turn on each other; we refuse to stand up for each other, and we work in underhanded ways. It is not uncommon for sisters to feel as though they get more support in the workplace from men. We don't spend enough time mentoring younger women. There are those of us who love being the only woman at the top. We do everything in our power to undermine and stop the progress of other women. It will be interesting to see what happens as women run for president of the United States. Will the media discuss their hairstyles or their clothes? I look forward to the day when a woman is in the White House, as her image will mean so much to young girls. We should critique these women candidates on the facts and their platforms, not their appearance or demeanor. The mainstream media is guilty of focusing on issues that are irrelevant when it comes to women running for office.

We need to be loyal to other sisters. On many levels, we are all the same. We must learn to be supportive of each other.

The mistreatment of other women is often the result of women who are unhappy themselves. Many of us are wounded and carry baggage from our past. We are often broken and tend to treat others how we feel about ourselves inside. Life may not have turned out the way we expected. Somewhere along the way, we stopped dreaming and believing in endless possibilities. Some of us are petty. When women are petty, it likely means that deep within, they feel small and inconsequential. Many of these women are in such pain that they don't know any other way to live. They live on the dark side of life. To find the true happiness we all deserve requires a great deal of soul searching and reflection. Reflection can help women escape the trap of negativity and nastiness.

We really have only a few years to get it right. Time passes so quickly, and we don't spend enough time living in the now. Living in the present allows us to see the destructiveness and futility of acting ugly toward each other.

As I begin to reflect on my life, I ask myself almost daily where the time went. I think back to that little girl who dared to dream, even when everything around her tried to discourage those dreams. In my case, however, my dreams did come true. In fact, I could never have imagined how great my life could have turned out. It just goes to show that if we truly believe that anything is possible, and we work hard and stay committed to that belief, our dreams are certainly attainable.

At some point in my life, I had to embrace my past and accept that it has shaped who I am. I am the first to admit that life is not easy. I have watched women who are under pressure fall back on childhood coping methods. When we were children, we learned how to use a number of coping mechanisms. For me, it was perfection. I don't know any woman who could say that she has lived a perfect life. If she steps forward, I would love to meet her. Living a perfect life somehow implies that one must be perfect. Perfection is toxic in life because it is unattainable. Growing up, I lived my life striving toward perfection. Subconsciously, perfection was a way of correcting all the wrong things that surrounded me. However, I was never happy, as there is no way to achieve perfection. Something would always go wrong.

As I grew into myself, I came to an understanding that if I was ever going to be happy, I had to let the quest for perfection go. I embraced excellence instead. It was a far easier standard to adhere to. My evolution began when I decided it was more important to become a whole person. Being whole has allowed me to feel complete, content, satisfied, and, most of all, free. I love living, and I love and appreciate life. I give to others what is inside me. I want to see other women have joy and come into their own.

Being whole has many advantages. You learn to let things go. You don't let just the little things go; you also let the big things go. The first thing to let go of is the past. You let go of the judgment, the shame, the blame, the pain, the doubt, and the hurt. You live through the pain, and you move on. You don't hold on to it any longer than necessary. You realize that you cannot solve every problem in the world. You cannot save everyone. You learn to accept that doing your best is sometimes as good as it gets.

Being whole means there is nothing or anyone you have to have in this life. You are able to walk away from whatever does not bring you joy. It is acceptance of who you are, including your faults and flaws. Being whole gives peace of mind and requires you to let the drama go. It allows you to keep it real. You face reality not by making excuses, but by determining your priorities and what is important in life. You learn how to say no. You face life with courage and strength and acceptance of others, even when you don't allow them into your private space. Being a whole woman is living a life that is strategic and victorious so you have a positive outcome no matter what challenges you face. You don't care as much about what others say about you. You know in your heart that, at the end of the day, everything is going to be all right, one way or another. Whole women do not give up. We get tired. However, we are strong and never give up.

I have learned a lot along the way. Sure, my mother and grandmother shared a great deal of their wisdom with me, but not nearly enough to prepare me for the hardships that were to come. The tears I cried could have filled a river. The years of daily stress should have taken me out a long time ago. But, somehow, I continued to emerge stronger, wiser, and filled with complete and utter hope for a tomorrow that was better than the present day I was living. It all came with the beauty and majesty of the aging process.

I can share that I've had better days than most, but when the days were tough, they were really tough. As I have passed fifty (gently, of course, because I'm *finally* embracing my age), I've learned a great deal. I have made countless mistakes in my life. There was so much about life I didn't know. There were people I naively trusted. And there were so many lonely nights when I didn't know if I could face the dawning of the next day. Had I known then what I know now, life would have been so much easier. Life really does get better with time. You come to understand that all things really do work together for good in the long run. Sometimes it just takes a while.

When I was younger and made mistakes, I would talk to my mother about whatever was bothering me. She calmly said to me, "Penny Marie, don't be so hard on yourself. When you know better, you ought to do better. Until you know, you will never grow." She said this all the time. I got tired of hearing her. She seemed calm about it. I took her calmness to be weakness. It was foolish thinking on my part. Calmness represents control and true power. Drama, anger, and yelling are not signs of being in control. Those are methods of weakness. As much as I understand this, I still find myself occasionally journeying to the dark side. Admittedly, this is when I allow myself to be misled by people who seem to enjoy bringing out that side of my personality.

As a teenager, how could I appreciate my mother's profound words? I wanted her to tell me something else. I didn't want to hear, *When you know better, you ought to do better.* Later on in life, I understood what she meant, especially when it came to my selection of men.

I knew what I wanted in life. I dreamed of having a career that would change the lives of people. I wanted to matter as a grown-up. I dreamed of a wonderful life with a house and a husband. I wanted to have financial security, but I wasn't looking for the man to provide it. I wanted a man who would both adore me and protect me. My expectations were high, and I started to believe they were unrealistic. Instead of sticking with my hopes and dreams, I compromised to feel loved and to have companionship. That was a big mistake. I selected men who treated me in the worst possible way. I eventually got it right, but it came only after my heart had been broken many times.

My husband never got to meet that young me. I am his wife, and I love him dearly, but I have been through a lot and have the emotional scars to prove it. I sometimes wonder what my life would be like with him if he had met and married that young woman who was so trusting and open. We have a good life. I will not compromise on anything less. He knows that, and somehow it keeps things just where they need to be. Not perfect, but it's where it needs to be.

I watch other women go in and out of relationships, always

selecting the same kind of toxic guys. I see so much of myself in these women. They will continue to do this over and over again until they come to know that they deserve better than what they are allowing in their lives.

Once I knew better and learned the lessons, I was able to finally grow. I was able to move from a place of stagnation and allowing others to mistreat me. It was a dark place where I never seemed to matter. I was always fighting with others in an effort to matter. I was always in some kind of debate or altercation. When a woman is surrounded by people who constantly take and never give anything, it is demeaning and exhausting. It does not bring out the best in a person. It is a one-sided relationship, and that never feels good. I learned that it was fine to allow myself to grow into the knowledge that life could be filled with calmness and inner peace. I had to learn to find peace of mind. I had to learn to be happy without having to have a man in my life. I started to matter to me. I slip every now and again, but remember, I gave up perfection long ago.

Nothing will ever change in your life until you see things for how they really are. Women are good at manipulating reality. Nothing really changes. We manipulate ourselves into living in denial. It's all done in the mind. We refuse to see what is really reflective of what is going on. We make tons of excuses in our minds to justify people not treating us right. Somewhere, deep down inside, we believe we can't do any better.

Sometimes we even carry this denial into our careers. Although we're more qualified than others and work twice as hard, we never stand up for ourselves and demand to be treated with the same respect. We continue to do the same jobs for less money than our male counterparts. It's easy to believe there is nothing you can do to change your situation. In other words, we allow this mistreatment to occur.

Every time we place ourselves in places of inequality, it takes something away from our spirit and our sense of self-worth. We are the only ones who can change the fairness of life. We get to be the great equalizer and bring the justice into our lives that we so desperately seek. Many of us are in bondage because we allow ourselves to be oppressed. We want fairness to drop from the sky. We end up resenting life when fairness does not magically occur.

No matter how hard I tried, I never did better in my life until I learned these lessons and took matters into my own hands. I had to be willing to take risks. I had to learn to ignore the opinions of those who didn't mean me any good. I had to be willing to bring equality to my own life. The saying is true that a person will continue to repeat mistakes until she learns the lessons. Whatever is not fair or just in your life, you have the power to change it. Growing into your womanhood helps you be able to take back your life.

I never appreciated how much wisdom my mother and grandmother shared with me. It became obvious there was a whole lot more my mother could have shared about life, about men, about other women, about being a woman, giving birth, motherhood, love, sex, romance, God, finances, and much, much, more. There is much I wish I had known. Don't get me wrong, I know that the best lessons come from living through experiences, but it sure would have helped to know what was coming. She couldn't do it because she departed this earth far too young. She left my sisters still in their twenties and me needing to hear her voice every day. She was our guiding light. She was a woman of wisdom.

Maybe she didn't get to add to her list of soul-saving mese

sages because her life was cut short. Or maybe there are some things that mothers can't tell their daughters because it may reveal more than any mother would want her child to ever know. Some mothers just don't know how to communicate. Whatever the reason, any true wisdom that is shared from the heart delivers with it a part of an untold story kept in the deepest part of the soul. Some women may have a hard time sharing a piece of themselves, even to their own daughters.

Once, a woman charged me the wrong amount of money to do alterations on a jacket. I was upset and felt cheated because she gave me one price, and when I went to pick the jacket up, she charged more money. I called my mother on the phone to lament about the situation, and she said in her normal, calm voice, "Let it go, baby, you pay to know." She insisted that I wouldn't make the same mistake twice. She explained, "It cost you forty-five dollars to know that you don't want her working on your clothes again." I paid to know. I paid the price to learn that this tailor was not honest.

Years later, I found myself giving the same advice. A friend was going on and on about a woman who offered to do a favor and later decided to change her mind. I listened, and then I said to her calmly, "My mother used to tell me that you pay to know. Now you know, and you can move on and never get her to do anything like that for you again." It seemed like after I said it, she instantly understood the lesson.

I knew in my heart I wasn't merely reciting what I had been told, but it was my mother's voice that was within the grown-up me. What I realized is that my mother lives in those sayings. Those sayings live in me. They have helped shape the woman I have become. Now, I am able to pass these messages on to so many of you, including my own granddaughter, Pelly-Marie.

I am also aware that women have many untold stories. Women carry around secrets that will surely be taken to the grave. The secrets come from the assumption that no one could be as foolish as we had been. No other sister in the world could have fallen so far down as we have or been so stupid or heartbroken. In actuality, our experiences are quite similar. I can't tell you the times I've been in a women's gathering only for the discussion to turn to a shared experience. Something powerful occurs when women talk. Women come together and realize that we are bound by our common experiences.

My book celebrates women, and through its pages, I will share my soul-saving sayings and advice that I learned through my own experiences, witnessed in others, or learned from my mother, grandmother, and aunts. I say what is sometimes unspoken. For some of it, I wish someone had dared to tell me. Remember, these are "my truths." You get to decide for yourself if you want to embrace them or reject them, but you will not be able to say you were never told.

Section
I

Truth to the

Sister

el·der
/ˈeldər/
noun A person of greater age than someone specified.

> *"Aging is not lost youth but a new stage of opportunity and strength."*
> BETTY FRIEDAN

Honestly, who wants to grow old? The truth is, growing older will happen whether you accept it or not. The quicker you can accept it, embrace it, and not be afraid of it, the easier it will be for you to really start the process of living—I mean really living. Women do everything for everyone. We spend the better part of our lives taking care of others. The wonderful aspect of the aging process is you get to embrace you. With each passing year, you have less and less to prove. You really become in tune to what's truly important.

We love saying that fifty is the new forty, or sixty is the new fifty. Really? We will say anything not to be our age. I'm in the fifty club, and although I joined it kicking and screaming, I had to learn that age is not just a number. Getting older means changes will begin to occur, changes no one took the time to sit you down and tell you about. It reminds me of when I had my child. I gave birth to him and woke up the next day and still had a baby bump. It obviously wasn't a baby in there, but no one bothered to share with me that I would have a bump after birth. I was so afraid. I didn't understand why my stomach wasn't flat. After all, I was expecting to go back to my pre-pregnancy size and get my flat stomach back. No one told me—not the doctor, not my mother, not anyone—that I would have a bump after birth.

As we age, our bodies and minds change in ways we are not prepared for. One of the changes that occurs that most women struggle with has to do with going into the pre-menopausal stage. I didn't like the changes to my body. Gone are days of eating what I want. I could eat cereal in bed at ten p.m. while watching the news, or get up and have a midnight snack, and I wouldn't gain a pound. I didn't fully understand that after the age of thirty-five to forty, I had to stop eating as much. I didn't get the lesson until I struggled to get ten pounds off of me. Previously, I could stop eating, drink lots of water, and drop five pounds in a week. When you hit your fifties, with its slowed-down metabolism, it will require that you exercise. I had one problem: I hated exercising. So what was a girl to do? Besides, I had to give up fried chicken and pizza. Well, that wasn't fair. I resisted for as long as I could until half the clothes in my closet no longer fit, and I realized something had to be done. It wasn't really about the weight because the difference in a size 2 and 4 is somewhat of a joke; it was coupled with the other changes my body was undergoing that caused me to resent getting older.

I wouldn't wish menopause on my worst enemy. I heard the stories from many of the women in my church at our Sisters in Faith women's ministry meeting. I sponsored classes on it and brought in experts to talk about it. I had friends who were going through it, but it's not until you have to keep a fan by your bed, go from hot to cold within a few minutes, experience hair showing up in places where it never was before, fighting with fat in your midsection, not being able to sleep at night, losing your sex drive, and when you do try, it begins to hurt—the list could go on and on—I realized that I hated getting older. I talked about it so much that one night my nine-year-old granddaughter who was spending the night came and stood at the foot of our bed. She woke us up to tell us, "Grand-Mama, I'm hot. I'm having a hot flash. I'm hot." She'd heard me talk about it so much that she used the terminology to show me that her pajamas were wet in the back of her shirt, and she was convinced it was a hot flash.

I still don't like the thought of getting older, but one day, I woke up after having a series of losses in other areas of my life and decided I couldn't do anything about getting older, and I needed to take charge of the process. Sure, medicines can help with the night sweats and hot flashes, but I needed to start living a healthier lifestyle. It could no longer be about my nice clothes, great makeup, and keeping my wonderful hairstyles. I had to be healthy on the inside. Once, I had sustained an elbow injury reaching for my purse in the back seat of my car and went to physical therapy for eight months. I hated it, and I felt my body was beginning to fall apart. I realized I had to make a change.

I decided to do what I hated doing. I started exercising. In the first six weeks, I lost no weight. I lost inches. I realized that I had to change my eating habits. After all, too much was at stake. I have only one life to live. I didn't want just a life, I wanted to live. Now, exercise—not occasional walking, but real exercise—is a part of my life. I feel so much better after doing it. I look better, and it was the beginning step to feeling better about getting older. Believe it or not, I feel thirty-something. I look in the mirror, and I never see an older woman. I keep my hair colored, and I keep moving. I dress my age and act my age, but it seems to be getting better with each passing year.

One of the positive aspects about getting older is the wisdom that comes from the lessons we've learned along the way. Life has certainly not been fair to many of us, but with time and getting older, you learn to make the best of it, and you are grateful for the blessings that have emerged from the struggles. One enormous lesson is the power of love. Life is too short to spend time hating anyone. It's better to allow yourself to let stuff go. Love people, even if you have to do it from a distance. You don't have to love what they do, but fill yourself with love. Reconcile with family members where you can. It obviously takes a willingness on their part to do so, but at least on your end, have a mindset that whatever it is you've been fighting about, you don't have to hold any hatred in your heart over it. You don't want to be getting older in life still at war with family members. Even if you don't communicate with them, I'm just advising that you open your heart and love them in spite of the situation.

I love the aspect of getting older where you don't much worry about what others think. There is much power in not caring as much. You don't have to take yourself as seriously. You laugh at yourself more, and you take note of your mistakes but don't live with as many regrets. You really come to a point where you accept yourself for who you are. You don't even have the need to be right as much. You have nothing to prove, so winning the argument doesn't matter. Let others have it. Let them win. So what?

You can make peace with your past because you live your life one day at a time. You may still have goals to accomplish, but now you are doing it for the right reasons. You likely are at a point in your life where your life has meaning. You want to serve and make the world a better place. You can enjoy your children and, especially, your grandchildren.

If you've done right by your finances, you can spend your money on what makes you happy. Hopefully, you are out of debt and can vacation or get the things that help enhance your quality of life.

Health care becomes a bigger issue for you. It will be crucial for you to have access to great medical care. With the Affordable Health Care Act enacted by President Obama, everyone has an opportunity to have quality health care so that everyone can have the opportunity to live a good and healthy life. Thank God for his courage and keeping his promise. His greatest legacy will be that he stood his ground and used the office of the presidency not just as a place to make history but to change the lives of people for generations to come. What President Obama did was life and death for many Americans.

Getting older allows you to be yourself. You get to define what you want to be. If you don't like your wrinkles, do something about it. If you want plastic surgery, and you can afford it, by all means get it. Do what you need to do to stay positive about yourself. You now understand that you don't look for others outside of you to love you. You love yourself, so you can now care for yourself.

You no longer have to keep secrets. The older you get, the more you free yourself from all the issues that you were not willing to talk about when you were younger. Every year, you break free. You start releasing yourself, and before you know it, you'll tell it and not give it a second thought. This is why so many people wait to write their memoirs until they get older. It's almost a force of nature that you want to unburden yourself and be free. Barbara Walters wrote her story in her eighties. She admitted to having a love affair with a married black congressman. After she told it, no one, including me, thought any less of her. In fact, I liked her more. I admired the fact she didn't leave this world being held captive by a secret. She was in control because she decided when it would be told. She freed herself. I admire freedom.

Forgiveness is a great part of getting older. People always say forgiveness is not about the other person, it is about us. It's really true. Forgiving someone is healing. It releases a hold that is put on your spirit. It unburdens you. Forgiveness takes the darkness away.

Getting older doesn't stop anything. It enhances life. You know so much now. You know what's really important. You should continue to dream. Find the miracles in the ordinary. Live every day as though it's your last. Smile and laugh at least once every day. Be funny and enjoy life.

Never think about dying, but rather, concentrate on living. Don't live life being afraid. By now, the worst of everything that could happen to you likely has already occurred. Even if bad things come in the future, because you've gone through so much in the past, you are well-equipped to face any challenge that may be ahead of you.

When you begin to think about it, getting older isn't as bad as it may have seemed. It's really about attitude and how you decide to see things. After all, you can't stop it, so why not just enjoy the ride?

YOUR TRUTH

How did this chapter speak to you?

_____

_____

_____

_____

_____

_____

_____

_____

_____

_____

_____

_____

_____

_____

_____

_____

YOUR TRUTH

What is your truth?

_____

_____

_____

_____

_____

_____

_____

_____

_____

_____

_____

_____

_____

_____

_____

_____

YOUR TRUTH

Plan of action to deal with your truth:

_____

_____

_____

_____

_____

_____

_____

_____

_____

_____

_____

_____

_____

_____

_____

_____

CHAPTER

2

Truth to the

Sister

am·bi·tious
/am'biSHəs/
adjective Having or showing a strong
desire and determination to succeed.

*"The desire to reach for the stars is ambitious.
The desire to reach hearts is wise."*
MAYA ANGELOU

You are the sister who everyone says always wanted to be somebody. You may have been told you think really highly of yourself. I love to tell those folks that if you don't think a lot of yourself, who will? If you are like me, my ambitious spirit has been with me since I was a child. Although I am the poster child for being a dreamer, I believe that an ambitious sister does more than just dream. Deep in her soul she understands that she was born to succeed. She has visions of where she sees herself, and she does what she can to make her visions become reality.

I have been around women who are afraid to admit they are ambitious. She may admit that she is a go-getter and feel proud to succeed, but she is reluctant to call herself ambitious. She may be concerned with the way others see her. It seems to her that if a man is ambitious in the workplace, he is rewarded, whereas she may be seen as bossy or pushy.

You should be proud to say to the world that you are ambitious, particularly if being ambitious is who you really are. We have been restricted as women from being our authentic selves. Out of convenience, we fit into the standard mold while life continues to pass us by.

As an ambitious woman, it will be important that you begin to visualize yourself at the level you want to be. If you can't see it first, no one will be able to see you in the role. I dreamed of being on the bench while I was a law student. I remember reading the court decisions and pretending I was the judge and analyzing how I would rule. While in the courthouse, I would see myself in the black robe and presiding from the bench. The same thing occurred when I decided to go on television. I watched television, and I could see myself doing it. Now, remember, dear sister, you can't sit around all day seeing yourself as a clothing designer or teaching in a classroom and believe that, magically, it will come to pass. My point is you must first see the vision before it can ever be a reality.

You move from seeing the vision to believing the vision is possible. Because of fear, many women—not you—will never realize their full potential because they don't believe it is possible to make their visions a reality. You must believe with all your heart that the desires of your heart are indeed attainable. I understand that you have been denied many opportunities and that you may have gotten to the point where you are tired or afraid to dream because you hate being disappointed. It may be that you are afraid to fail.

You have to remember that the best things in life often do not come easy. You have to work for it, dream it, envision it, and never give up, no matter how many people tell you no. By the way, speaking of people, surround yourself only with likeminded ambitious people. You can't be successful being with negative, do-nothing people who are holding on to your coattails to ride on your glory and hard work. Ambitious people attract all kinds of people. Oftentimes, we attract people who get close to us to get what they want. They believe that what we have, they deserve to have. They don't want to work for it, but they want what we have. They want the hookup without ever working for it. They see you as their opportunity to help their dreams come true because, if you are an ambitious sister like me, you do not have a problem supporting others in their dreams. We share information and provide advice without looking for anything in return because we believe there is enough of everything for everyone. You are the type who must be careful not to allow others to use you.

Although you may not be willing to admit that you are ambitious, others know in fact that you are. You may also find yourself dealing with other sisters who are ambitious and selfish, not humble like you. These sisters are to be watched. They are the ones with the ability to help out another sister, but instead, they hold back so they can remind themselves they have "power." I guess that is what they are thinking. I know this for sure, a woman like this fears you. She is afraid you are everything that she is not. She cannot wrap her brain around the idea that certain things come so easily for you. Secretly, she wants to have many of your attributes. The way it sometimes works, this person, this sister, will get you to trust her, but all the while she is only near you to keep an eye on you, learn from you, and make certain you don't get ahead of her. Watch her and just understand that she is incapable of being a true sister-friend because of her selfishness and insecurity. You can never trust her.

After you have your vision, and you believe it can come true, as an ambitious sister, you must take action toward your goals and aspirations. You need to put it in writing with an attainable timetable. Get to know people who are like you and who want to support you. Ambitious sisters expect to succeed. Even when things do not go their way, they rarely will characterize the disappointment as a failure. You should regroup, come up with another plan, and keep it moving.

No one will hand you your dreams on a silver platter. The days of the hookup are just about gone because people look out only for themselves. If you want something, you have to make it happen yourself.

An ambitious sister works on aspects of her dream, her vision, her desires, or her goals every day. She walks in excellence and competes only with herself to be the best. Ambitious sisters want to get ahead in life. Ambitious sisters are leaders, and they do so to serve. They commit to service to contribute to the world. Ambitious sisters are concerned about making life better for family and the community.

An ambitious sister does not waste time trying to hurt another woman, or anyone for that matter. She has no time for drama and avoids it whenever she can. This sister is above the foolishness of the workplace and feels significant in her role.

If you are like me, you are oriented on results. I am miserable if there is no progress or change in a situation or circumstance I am working on. I have no problem walking away from a situation and going where my talents and gifts can be better appreciated and valued. If no one appreciates the value of who you are, an ambitious sister knows her place in life. You do not need permission from anyone to be your true, authentic self.

I want you to understand that as an ambitious woman, you will face many obstacles. You are a threat because you are not afraid to think outside the box. People are afraid of change, and you represent change. Just know that opposition comes with the territory, depending on where you are operating. You also come up against a system that favors males, as women make less than their male counterparts do. You can fight the system, or you can find your way around it and continue on the path you have envisioned for your future. It isn't fair, but no one promised life is always fair.

Although it may not seem logical, be careful about the advice you receive. Bad advice can derail your goals. To be ambitious may necessarily require you taking risks. Well-meaning people will likely advise you to proceed with caution, which may cause you not to take opportunities that belong to you. Advice is good, but it shouldn't be considered by itself. Listen to that small voice within you. The more you can learn to listen to your own voice, the more independent you will become.

Develop a tough skin and stop taking things personally. The world is not against you. Learn from each and every situation. Learn from people—good and bad. You can't succeed in life needing the approval of others. Don't burn bridges, and do your best to treat people right. Stop doubting yourself and stop being afraid. Fear blocks every desire you have from coming true.

Be proud to be ambitious, but make certain you are ambitious for the right reasons. You don't have anything to prove to anyone. Accept that you are enough.

YOUR TRUTH

How did this chapter speak to you?

_____

_____

_____

_____

_____

_____

_____

_____

_____

_____

_____

_____

_____

_____

_____

YOUR TRUTH

What is your truth?

_____

_____

_____

_____

_____

_____

_____

_____

_____

_____

_____

_____

_____

_____

_____

YOUR TRUTH

Plan of action to deal with your truth:

_____

_____

_____

_____

_____

_____

_____

_____

_____

_____

_____

_____

_____

_____

_____

_____

_____

CHAPTER

3

Truth to the

Sister

an·gry
/ˈaNGgrē/
adjective Having a strong feeling of
or showing annoyance, displeasure,
or hostility; full of anger.

"When there is no enemy within, the enemies outside cannot hurt you."
AFRICAN PROVERB

Been there, done that. Well, I still go there every now and then. Being angry is a normal human emotion. Everybody gets angry. You likely, my dear sister, get angry for a number of reasons. Whether you get angry because someone pushes your buttons or disrespects you; whether you order something online, and the order is wrong; whether they got your order wrong at the drive-thru window at the local hamburger restaurant; you've been put on hold by the telephone company and waited for twenty minutes; your house was burglarized; your children refuse to behave; you were mistreated on your job; or your spouse takes you for granted—all these situations may cause you to become upset and bring out hostility on some level. Obviously, there are a million reasons why you or anyone gets angry.

I have been told anger can be healthy, particularly if it motivates you to stand up for yourself or an injustice. If managed properly, it can prompt you to make positive changes in your life or to a specific situation. In fact, my *SisterTalk Women's Empowerment Conference* was birthed from an angry reaction I had because I felt I had been wronged by other women in my pursuit of a number of ventures and career opportunities. These four women in different situations blocked me from using my gifts and talents when I was either highly qualified or even the best candidate for the position. I was denied access because these women felt threatened by me. After experiencing the injustice of their insecurity, I created a conference that would help other women feel empowered, as it was my way of correcting the injustice other women had done to me. I created a format so thousands of women could be inspired, educated, and enlightened in such a way that they would not feel that for them to shine or to retain power, they had to stop the efforts of another woman from performing and using her gifts and talents. I channeled my anger and hurt into something that will be a legacy of strength and inspiration for years to come.

This advice is not directed to the sister who occasionally gets angry because I believe it isn't a problem to occasionally get upset. However, if you know your anger gets out of control, or you are angry at least once a week for something, or the manifestation of your anger causes you to become another person, there is a problem. You are the "angry sister." We all know one or two sisters who are out of control. It may be hard for you to be honest with yourself and be willing to say that you are an angry sister. Please understand this is not about labels or an attempt to put a label on you. This is about truth, a truth for the purpose of liberation. I want you to gain insight into many of our bad habits that come from years of hurt and pain others placed upon us, and we now channel in the only way we know. We can't improve or solve a situation unless we first recognize it. Therefore, if you are not willing to admit it to anyone else, please be willing to admit it to yourself. It is the only way to attain true liberation. It is the only way for you to be free and to live the stress-free, no-drama life that you deserve.

The great thing about this book of advice is that the reader can go down the list in the table of contents and find a chapter she can identify with, either in the present or in her past. If it gives you any degree of comfort, I stayed an angry sister for a long time. I excelled at masking it until something or someone pushed my buttons. My feelings would boil over like a pot on a stove. I often did it with my family because I felt comfortable enough to do it. I didn't want others to see that side of me, although I often displayed it to others. I am so happy I have been delivered from it for years now.

The interesting fact is I never lost my temper on the bench. I was so honored to be a judge and recognized I had the power in the courtroom. Therefore, becoming angry was unnecessary. Because I am an expressive and direct person, people often mistook my demeanor and passion for anger, when in fact, I loved every single minute of being a judge. Some misunderstood a strong, confident presence for something else. I wasn't about to allow anyone to take me outside of myself while wearing the robe. I was firm and had to get folks straight, but I can honestly say in my heart, I was never angry. It was the role of a lifetime. I had dreamed of it all my life, and no one or no situation was going to take me out of the dignity the position stood for.

After much reflection and being tired of feeling bad within myself, I purposefully searched my heart for the real reasons I was getting so angry. My connection with God was critical in my quest for my truth. It is easy to keep doing things the same way because behavior can become habit forming, and as you and I both know, habits are hard to break. The good news is that any habit can be broken, particularly a behavior that if displayed too often, can be detrimental to your mental and physical being.

You can start by asking yourself what the source of your

anger is. I realize the answer may be complex, but it is the starting point for your reflection. You are likely feeling threatened in some way, or you may be fearful of something. This perceived threat may, as it relates to you, be to your personhood, including your self-image or some aspect of your identity, or it may be a perceived threat to a loved one or your property.

You may have a poor self-image of yourself that was created from childhood. This image may have emerged from being abused as a child, abandoned, bullied, needing love from your parents or other loved ones, or finding that you were not nurtured in the way you needed. So many people today walk around wounded with the scars from childhood. Oftentimes, people reflect their own self-image on others. We are sometimes harder on ourselves than others could ever be. We want so much out of life, and we often work hard to achieve it. If we feel someone is threatening our purpose or not recognizing or respecting who we are, it can cause a rage like no other. I had to learn I don't need the respect of some people because they are too ignorant to comprehend who I really am.

You want to come to an understanding that if your anger is not managed, it can be counterproductive to your life, and it can begin to affect your health. I had to learn how to separate myself from people who did not bring out the best in me. It is as simple as refusing to revisit a restaurant that doesn't give me good service, even if I love the food, so that I can have peace and not find myself angry every time I dine in the establishment. There are people, places, and circumstances you must separate from to get your anger under control.

You need to stop allowing your anger to become out of control and aggressive. It is likely causing health problems, whether they have become manifested or not. For God's sake, stop displaying your anger in front of your children. My granddaughter, Pelly-Marie, would witness her father and me go at it. When she became old enough to tell me, she shared that it made her unhappy and fearful. I realized I had to do something about it. I couldn't pass on to my granddaughter the belief that people argue and fight in the name of love. I cared about my legacy with her and what she was witnessing.

When you are angry, you don't make good decisions. Please stop sending emails, tweets, and texts when you are angry and upset. Give it twenty-four hours and see if you feel the same way before sending a permanent record of an emotion that will likely pass. In that instance, pick up the telephone the next day and deal with the situation with a conversation. In the written form, no one reading your angry communication will likely understand the context. Honestly, you will just look like an out-of-control fool.

When you are insulted, it's natural to feel angry. The urge is to launch into a counterattack to defend yourself and prove you are strong. You are actually stronger when you give the opposite response than what may be justified, and you allow your rage to dissipate. I was involved in a situation where a woman who is pure evil talked to me disrespectfully, and I went to the dark side in dealing with her. Because she lives in the dark side, she was perfectly happy to engage me in her territory. She enjoyed seeing me be aggressive while giving her a piece of my mind. I don't regret telling her what I told her, but I do regret not being in control while I was getting her straight. For months, she went on being her demonic self while I was hurt and regretting allowing her to see me the way she did. She deserved to hear everything I said, but I didn't deserve it. I felt I had grown to a level where I should have known better. Thanks be to God that we continue to be a work in progress. I came to understand she was incapable of respecting me because she had no true concept of what respect really was about. I wanted something from her she could never give. She did not understand, and will likely never understand, the concept of respect.

If you have a shorter fuse than others have, and you hate foolishness, it is more important for you to separate yourself from people who love drama. They thrive on drama, whereas for you, it is toxic. Remember, I am not asking you to suppress your anger. Bottling up your emotions is never good. I am suggesting that you consider letting people go and letting situations go. Forget about it. Just learn to ignore things and avoid the people who bring out the worst in you.

Finally, my angry sister, please remember to delay your response when you can. Give yourself time to deal with situations that displease you and cause you to display rage. Learn to relax and take care of yourself. Remember to take deep breaths. Talk to someone you trust and tell him or her about your feelings. Take a moment to pray and seek guidance from God. Keep busy and never replay the situation over and over in your mind. As long as you allow your anger to control you, you are not free. The goal should be for your liberation, even from yourself.

YOUR TRUTH

How did this chapter speak to you?

_____

_____

_____

_____

_____

_____

_____

_____

_____

_____

_____

_____

_____

_____

_____

_____

_____

YOUR TRUTH

What is your truth?

_____

_____

_____

_____

_____

_____

_____

_____

_____

_____

_____

_____

_____

_____

_____

_____

_____

YOUR TRUTH

Plan of action to deal with your truth:

_____

_____

_____

_____

_____

_____

_____

_____

_____

_____

_____

_____

_____

_____

_____

_____

_____

CHAPTER

Truth to the

Sister

a·buse

ə byo͞oz/

verb Treat (a person or an animal)
with cruelty or violence, especially
regularly or repeatedly.

*"I have learned over the years that when
one's mind is made up, this diminishes fear;
knowing what must be done
does away with fear."*
ROSA PARKS

As many sisters have come to know, abuse can take on many forms. Women who find themselves in abusive situations as adults may have been abused as children or witnessed abuse, but that is not always the case. You could have come from a home where you never witnessed bad behavior or abuse. Anyone can become the victim of mistreatment. Abuse during childhood has implications that can last a lifetime and are passed down through generations, having long-term effects on families and communities. As an adult, admitting you have been abused is difficult, and it can be difficult if you are being abused as a grown woman.

A partner may be abusing you, and you don't know how to deal with it. It can be from insults—calling you out of your name—to constant verbal attacks on your personhood that affect your self-esteem. Abusers use fear and threats to control your behavior. This control sometimes takes place by isolating you from your family, your friends, or any kind of support network. The abuse that is most obvious is the pushing, hitting, pinching, shoving, and all kinds of physical aggression. I listened to it all from the bench.

After being mistreated, you are convinced you are to blame

because you deserve what you are getting. You feel unworthy. You begin to feel hopeless because oftentimes you love someone who is incapable of ever returning the love because of the self-hatred the abuser feels. You make up excuses for him, often thinking that if he could only stop drinking, or if he wouldn't get angry, or if he hadn't lost his job, or even if he had not had a hard life growing up, he would then be the man whom you dreamed of. You just keep hoping for a change. There may be periods of calm, but it always eventually comes back to the same mistreatment of you. He continues with his same abusive behavior. Just when you think you understand what not to do to upset him, you realize anything can bring out the monster in him, including money issues, sex issues, situations with the kids, or employment issues. Anything can bring it out.

In your heart you know who he really is, but you keep daydreaming about a life with a "good man," the one you believe is deep inside him, all while not fully accepting that the man you live with day to day does not match your dream. You fantasize about what could be. Life is a struggle because you're beginning to understand that you cannot love the abusive ways out of him. You just can't. No matter how hard you try. My sister, my dear sister, you are living with someone based upon the potential of the kind of man you believe he can be. Many women fall into the trap of falling in love with potential. The problem is he will never be the man you want him to be as long as he is abusing you. The cost is too high to you. You are sacrificing yourself. Every time you are abused, it takes something away from your soul.

There are some parts in this life you can fix, and there are some that are unfixable. Please understand that I believe people can and do change, but as the victim of someone's abuse, you cannot fix him. You cannot change a person who does not want to be changed. You cannot solve his issues. You cannot repair his brokenness. Besides, it is not your job. It is not your purpose. All you can do is be the best woman you can be and manage to get away from this person so you can be all that God has called you to be. As a little girl, you had dreams. What happened to your dreams? I am sure you never dreamed of growing up only to be abused. No one has the right to hurt you, and no one has the right to take away your dreams and your purpose.

This is hard to say to you, but someone has to tell you. You have taught this person how to mistreat you. You have allowed him to believe that you are not worthy. The first time he got away with the abuse, and you allowed him back, he knew he had your permission to devalue, degrade, and misuse you. An abuser knows when a person has no self-worth. A woman who does not value herself will allow a man or a woman to hurt her the first time and get away with it. The second chance you give is merely an indication to this person that you have invited him or her into your life to control you and to dominate and take away your spirit.

I know all about it. I watched my poor mother be abused. I watched my grandfather hit my grandmother. I watched other women deal with abuse. When I was only fifteen years old, my friend's mother was murdered by her husband. Images of abuse were all around me while I was growing up. When I grew up, I became a victim of abuse myself. It was one of the darkest periods in my life. I can barely remember myself during the time I was abused. It was shameful and a darkness that followed me everywhere I went. How could I have ever allowed it to occur? Who was that woman who let not just one man, but different men over the years, put their hands on me? Who was she? I promised myself as a child I would never allow it to happen. I was repeating the mistakes of everything I saw around me. It was a place of darkness.

I can tell you this: that woman is long gone. I am happy to report that not only is she gone, but never to return. There is not a man walking on two feet on this planet I would ever allow to mistreat me. I will not even allow people to talk badly to me. I think too much of myself to allow it. I have been through too much to ever allow it again. I have been free for over 20 years now. Free to say what I want to say without fear of being hit or beaten. Free to be in a relationship in which when we disagree, the result is not a slap across the face. The change occurred because I changed. I came to know my worth. I came to understand I had to love myself enough to know I didn't deserve abuse from anyone. Once that revelation finally occurs, you will never allow anyone to treat you like that again.

However, I realize I was a different person. I had miniscule self-worth. I wanted to be loved, and I kept picking the wrong men to love me. I didn't understand that the abuser was making a choice to abuse me. I thought it was because he would lose control because something would get him upset, when in fact, the truth is he made a deliberate decision to abuse me to have control over me. Although I appeared to be strong to the world, I lived with a shameful secret: I was being abused. I realized I was living without hope. If I ever was to have a life, I had to leave the situation.

You are the only one who can make that decision for yourself. You deserve better, and if you have children, they deserve better. This is the only life you have to live, and you shouldn't waste it by giving your power and control to someone who does not deserve you. As my mother would always tell me, "You are somebody to love." I do not feel I have the right to tell you to leave. Instead, I want to tell you that you are worthy of better. If you can come to know who you are in this world and that you matter, you will want to leave on your own. You have to understand "You are enough." Yes, you are enough! You don't have to do anything to earn it or change who you are to be it. You are enough just the way you are.

Please know abuse can happen to anyone. For me, in some instances because the abuse was psychological and not always physical, I didn't acknowledge or want to believe it was abuse. I have endured physical abuse as well. The bottom line is you deserve better. You are a grown woman, and you should not have to live in fear or have to deal with someone putting you down and making you feel less than who God created you to be. Just know, this is being done to you for one reason and one reason only: to gain and maintain control over you.

I want you to stop living life on eggshells. You deserve better. If you have children, your children deserve better. I keep repeating this over and over so you can really understand the point. No one can say enough to get you to know you are worthy. I want to rewrite the tape that is playing in your head. The emotional or physical abuse takes away from your self-esteem and your independence. I recognize that you may believe you have no way out, but there is always a way out.

Girl, you need an exit plan. Men who abuse women are crazy, and you have to be careful when you have finally made the decision to leave. Make sure you have made the decision, and don't go back and forth with it. If you're not sure, and you find yourself going back to him after you tried to leave, it can be even harder on you when you return. It can be a matter of life and death.

My comments are designed to speak to your heart. I opened up my heart to share my experiences so you can know it can happen to anyone. The shame is not mine, and it is not yours. The shame of the situation belongs to the abuser. In our society, we keep quiet about things that are wrong because we, as a society, refuse to deal with it. However, a part of being free is I refuse to allow anyone to place shame on me I don't deserve.

I have one last matter I want to share that people are not willing to say. I can stand boldly on this issue because I am a minister. I am talking about the responsibility the church and other religious entities bear in doing nothing to fight against the issue of violence against women. In some instances, the church and its leaders have served as a conduit for the abuse to continue, often using, twisting, and misinterpreting sacred Scripture, telling women to "submit to your husband" and in so doing, you should pray and attempt counseling to deal with the abuse. Some say you should stay in the relationship and work it out because God will somehow see you through. Really?

Hear me loud and clear. What these leaders are saying to you is wrong. We serve a God who wants the best for us and would not want us to be hurt or oppressed in this way. Remember, it is all about power. Women in this society oftentimes are not valued. Not only should you plan to leave the abuser but also plan to leave a place of worship that tells you to submit to abuse and to allow yourself to be less than what God has created you to be. It is shameful and disgraceful that these entities go unchallenged and are allowed to keep many women in bondage. I hope this sets someone free. There is no working it out with him. You can't pray this away. If you believe God can change him, good for you. Get away from him and allow God to do it. But the work belongs to the Lord to do it, not you.

Finally, I want you to understand there is a life on the other side of this turmoil you are living. There is peace on the other side. I rarely look back on those dark days. It serves no purpose. I am a forward-looking sister; that's how I have made it all these years. I journeyed back there for you and told only a little of my story so you can understand my advice is real, and I know how you feel. There is no sugarcoating this. If you stay in an abusive relationship, you die daily, or eventually you die at once. There is nothing but darkness and death in a relationship where you are abused and oppressed.

I want to share what I have witnessed other women do as they have tried to exit a life of abuse. I witnessed from the bench, with women from my church and those seeking spiritual guidance, and with my own family members. Leaving can be treacherous, and you must take care as you proceed. I advise you to contact any domestic violence center or hotline, as they are the real experts on assisting you in getting out of your situation.

As an attorney/retired judge, I must share that the content of this book by its very nature is general, whereas each reader's situation is unique. Therefore, as with all books of this type, the purpose is to provide general information rather than address individual situations, which books cannot do. Be strategic and thoughtful about the best way to proceed. You know him better than anyone else does. Don't be afraid, and trust yourself. No one is going to come and rescue you. Domestic violence experts are ready and willing to assist you, though. I recommend you contact them. Don't take my words out of context and pack up and try to leave your situation without first consulting an expert and creating a life plan for yourself.

The next time he hits you, take pictures of the injuries, just in case you need it to prove abuse. Give them to someone or put them in a place not in your home. Most women stay in these abusive relationships because of finances. If you are working, make sure you put some money aside that has only your name on the account. I have seen some women get post office boxes so their mail or financial statements could be sent without the abuser ever knowing. You know your situation, and this may or may not be the best approach for you.

If you don't work outside the home, try to do something that can generate income. Sell something you make or do something part time while working in the home. You need to come up with an idea to generate income so you can save the money. Be sure to put the money in a safe place that he can never find.

Begin to research a safe place you can go once you leave. The experts will be able to guide you in this area. This is difficult because if you have children, having to live with other people will not be easy. It will require sacrifice, and often this is the hard part. The best advice I can tell you is to try to deal with people who are sincere and understand you really need help. Give a certain time that you wish to live with them, offer to give them money to stay there if you have any, and when the time is done, leave.

The experts will likely tell you that your plan of escape should include securing transportation. It is not necessary, but it certainly could help. Start putting clothing away. You can store belongings at a friend's house or secure storage somewhere. Make copies of important papers and documents including medical records, insurance information, birth certificates, titles, passports, etc. You will need extra keys to the home and cars, and provisions for your children. Know your abuser's schedule and decide when it is a safe time to leave. Think it through and secure the assistance and advice of professionals who can help you transition safely. I keep reiterating the point about securing assistance because you must know you cannot do this by yourself, and because this man could seriously hurt you or your children, it is important for you to be deliberate with each step you make. If you are married, you need to secure good legal representation. Secure the services of an attorney who specializes in family law. You need someone who is a family law expert and is sensitive to what you're going through. If you are not married, it will be easier logistically to leave. No matter what you do, never underestimate that this man has the ability to kill you. This is a critical situation, and I want you to completely understand what you are dealing with.

I cannot promise you an easy transition. To be honest, most things in life are hard. Freedom is never easy to attain. However, once you finally get your freedom, you can begin to heal. You can finally begin to walk toward your destiny and purpose. You were created for a better life. The decision is yours.

YOUR TRUTH

How did this chapter speak to you?

_____

_____

_____

_____

_____

_____

_____

_____

_____

_____

_____

_____

_____

_____

_____

_____

YOUR TRUTH

What is your truth?

_____

_____

_____

_____

_____

_____

_____

_____

_____

_____

_____

_____

_____

_____

_____

_____

_____

YOUR TRUTH

Plan of action to deal with your truth:

_____

_____

_____

_____

_____

_____

_____

_____

_____

_____

_____

_____

_____

_____

_____

Truth to the

Sister

a·dul·ter·y

/əˈdəlt(ə)rē/

noun Voluntary sexual intercourse between a married person and a person who is not his or her spouse.

*"It's time for you to move, realizing that
the thing you are seeking is also seeking you."*
IYANLA VANZANT

I want you to know that being involved in an adulterous relationship is a silent killer. It is destroying the center of your dreams and your aspirations, and has your life on one continuous train that is going nowhere and never will go anywhere. Your future is on hold, and you have completely given your power over to someone who understands your desperate need to be loved. You want to matter to someone so badly that you are willing to accept being in a relationship that is unhealthy and cannot completely develop into anything that is meaningful and blessed. No matter how he makes you feel, the foundation of the relationship is built on a falsity. In other words, it is a lie. It is not real because you do not fully belong to one another.

On the real, it's time to leave that woman's husband alone or stop sleeping around on your man! I'm not judging you because, if truth be told, nearly everyone has slept with someone they had no business sleeping with at some time in their lives, whether the person was married or not. This is not about judgment, but rather about truth and about trying to save you from a life that pulls you down emotionally to a place where you will not know who you are. As a woman, having an affair takes something out of you. The cost is too high to your spirit and your dreams to allow yourself to be in a relationship with a man who has committed himself to another woman. The cost is too high if you are the one who is married, and you are seeing another man. Something somewhere inside you or in your life is broken, and this is not the way to repair the breach.

You do know that men and women are in affairs for different reasons? Whether you're lonely and haven't been able to find a single man to date, whether it started out as a friendship or innocently online and grew to an intimate relationship, or whether you enjoy being with a married man because you don't want commitment, whatever the reason, he wants you for sex, period! It is about his ego. One woman will never be enough for him. You can fall in love all you want, but as long as you are the other woman, that is all you will be, the "other." You're not the first, and you will never be his priority.

Men who cheat on their wives know exactly what to say and do. He will tell you how wonderful you are and that no one has made him feel the way that you do. He will ask you to do things that he will never ask of his wife. You see, it is a way of pleasing him and competing against her when you will never be the better woman. You are the side woman—his side piece. Although there are television series that glamorize the life of the other woman, what it does to the spirit of your womanhood cannot be glowing in any way.

No one will argue that it's not exciting in the beginning. He probably buys you gifts, gives you money, takes you out, or even travels with you. You may spend more time with him than he does with his own wife, but nothing he does or says will ever change the facts that you are not first and that you're not his wife. You can fantasize until the cows come home, but you are fooling yourself to believe otherwise.

I know you're not a bad person. You're good woman. A

woman who, for whatever reason, finds herself in this unfortunate situation. It may have started out as a temporary thing and developed into something more. He found you in a vulnerable state. You developed feelings for him, and those feelings turned into love. One year passed, and then the years kept moving forward. You looked up, and the situation had become a permanent fixture in your reality.

Sometimes things just happen. I know women who have been in long-term relationships with men who are married and even went on to have children with them. I have one friend who fell in love with a married man. He divorced his wife. You would think he would have married her. No. He remarried all right, but he married a different woman, and my friend continued in her role as the mistress with the new wife. By the way, my friend is single. My heart hurts so much for her that she doesn't value herself enough to break away from a man who divorced one woman and married another woman, only for my friend to continue in the relationship with him. A man who would do such a thing is a low-down dirty dog. However, it my friend who troubles me more. It makes me sad because she taught this man how to treat her. She has settled for the bare minimum of life. It breaks my heart.

If you are married and having an affair, you may wish to argue with me and say you're getting what you need from this relationship, even if it's wrong in the eyes of the world and the church. This relationship may be helping you deal with living with a spouse who has long left you emotionally. You and your husband may be living in separate bedrooms and have not had sex in years. You may feel trapped in the shell of a marriage, and this outside affair may be the only thing that is keeping you going. You've made a decision that you can't leave the marriage because of your children, your lifestyle, the investment you've made, or an aversion to starting over. You may even like your spouse as a friend, but there is nothing between you guys on an intimate level. Because of everything you're going through, you feel justified in what you're doing.

All these excuses may sound reasonable to you and may be true, but they are just excuses. Life is too short for you to compromise your character, your worth, and your identity. You long for love, and it's sad you're not with this person in a legitimate relationship. But the truth remains: it isn't real. It's not right, and it will never be right. There can be no freedom when you are running away from a bad situation into one that is not right.

You're not alone. I read a report that suggests more than one third of men and about one quarter of women admit to having had a least one extramarital sexual act. The number is much higher when you consider emotional infidelity. We all know people who are having emotional affairs on Facebook. It's sad because these "virtual" affairs can cause harm in relationships that are already vulnerable on many levels.

Another word of caution—stay away from friends who encourage you to be involved in adulterous relationships. These are not real friends. They may want you to join them in what they are doing, or they want your life not to be whole. "Misery loves company." It's likely that you guys can conspire and do your deeds together. There can be no wholeness in your life, however, with something that is not right.

Many marriages can be repaired. It takes a lot of hard work and counseling. It takes a determination from both parties to want to fix what is broken and bring the intimacy back so you don't feel like you need to go outside your marriage to get what you need. However, getting a lover on the side is not the answer. It may be a temporary fix, but it can't be a lasting life for you. Holidays and important days are all meant to be spent with the people you love. It rarely happens that you and your so-called soul mate will be able to be together on a consistent basis to share in these wonderful moments.

How to get out of it? How do you walk away? How do you just leave your feelings on the table? Well, the first step is to be honest with yourself. You have settled for less, and you must admit it. You must tell yourself you deserve better. You must stop lying to yourself that this is acceptable. It's not acceptable. Be honest about the relationship. Let the shame go. You've done it. When you know better, you ought to do better. You've experienced it, and now you can walk away with lessons learned.

Leaving requires a lifestyle change. You can't be friends with your married lover. You're going to have to let him go. At least if you take the lead, your brokenness will not be as bad as if he dropped you. It will not be easy to walk away, but you must come to the point where you believe it's for the best. Fill your days with other activities so you will not become lonely.

Embark on a pathway of truth. I am not judging you because I do not have the right to do so. I just want you to be all you can be. I want you to know you do matter. You are enough. You are worthy of being first. You deserve better than having to be on the sidelines of life waiting on the phone call to come or waiting to hear when you're going to be together. Trust that you are good enough, and walking away becomes easy.

Don't leave because it is wrong; leave because you are worth more.

YOUR TRUTH

How did this chapter speak to you?

_____

_____

_____

_____

_____

_____

_____

_____

_____

_____

_____

_____

_____

_____

_____

_____

_____

YOUR TRUTH

What is your truth?

_____

_____

_____

_____

_____

_____

_____

_____

_____

_____

_____

_____

_____

_____

_____

_____

YOUR TRUTH

Plan of action to deal with your truth:

_____

_____

_____

_____

_____

_____

_____

_____

_____

_____

_____

_____

_____

_____

_____

_____

Truth to the

Sister

ad·dic·tion

/əˈdikSH(ə)n/

noun A strong and harmful need to regularly have something or do something.

"You are not obligated to win. You're obligated to keep trying to do the best you can every day."
MARIAN WRIGHT EDELMAN

What you do does not have to be who you are! I will be the first to admit I am not an expert in the area of addiction. The goal of this advice to you is to speak to your soul on this issue. For some, you may have not yet admitted you are an addict, while others have been working daily to deal with it. It seems to me that the road to freedom begins by admitting your truth.

I realize that when folks hear the word addiction, they may immediately think of alcohol or drugs. Women, like men, can be addicted to many things. Studies show that alcohol is the most commonly abused substance in the United States. The disease of alcoholism has many causes and treatments available. Many tools are out there for you to get the help you need once you realize you have an issue.

I am simplifying a complicated issue, but from what I understand, many factors contribute to addiction. Depression and anxiety can cause it. When you are alone, you might feel empty or incomplete. You feel that loneliness.

I believe in my heart that you can work on healing. Although it may be a lifetime struggle or commitment, in life, everybody has something. I'm not saying that everybody is addicted; I am just suggesting that life is filled with challenges of some kind. We must persevere and continue moving forward no matter what the challenge may be. Recovery is possible for you. The major component is acceptance that you have a problem and acceptance that you have to decide for yourself that you're worth the fight to reclaim your life and your power.

I realize family and friends have tried to help, and in some instances their well-meaning talks and interventions have made you go in the opposite direction. I'm big on telling people that they can move forward in any situation when they let go of the shame and the guilt. I can't say it enough: "What you do is not who you are." This statement is not an excuse for you not to take responsibility for your actions, but rather it's an affirming statement that lets you know you were created for a purpose. We all make mistakes and are trapped by disease or demons, but we are still worthy of having a life.

If you find yourself afraid or embarrassed to admit you are struggling with addiction, you have to find the will to let the fear go. Tell yourself that you deserve a life with clarity and a life you control. Don't allow this outside thing to control you.

As women, we are wired to be connected. This book is about connecting with other women and giving voice to the issues we face. Connections will allow you to be able to recover from your addiction. Some of you have lost a lot because of it and may feel there is no way to get what you lost back. Perhaps it may not be for you to be restored back to what you had before or who you were before; after all, too much has happened, but you do have an opportunity to move forward and find your new self.

What is critical to understand is that you can't do it by yourself. It is imperative that you get connected with a program or a professional. If possible, stay connected with your family or friends who believe in you and support you. People who kick you when you're down are not healthy for you to be around, but don't expect them to enable you in your addiction. They do you an injustice when they don't stand up so you can continue to see yourself in the mirror of life.

The good news is thousands and thousands of women have recovered. I am a big proponent of twelve-step programs and support groups. There are so many success stories. Just remember life's journey is rarely in a straight line. There is no magical formula to always getting it right. We wake up every morning, and we put one foot in front of the other, and we do the best we can. My philosophy can certainly be applied to someone who is addicted to something. Being your best self requires accountability and responsibility to yourself and to others. Being accountable to yourself is important because when it didn't occur for you in childhood or along the way, you have to step up for yourself. And when you don't have the strength, the willpower, the discipline, or the knowledge to do so, it requires that you seek help.

I make no excuses for people. I just have an open and understanding heart that refuses to be judgmental. Sometimes a woman's addictive behavior is a way of coping with the early childhood scars and traumas from her past or even the challenges she has to face in her current life, including issues of domestic violence, stress at work, and the stress of parenting. It may be difficult to break away from the addiction because of a learned helplessness that was observed as a child and has been passed on to you as woman. Even with understanding the *why*, there is still a way of escape.

Regardless of what your truth may be at this moment, I urge you to believe you are worthy of a better life. Breaking the cycle of addiction is important if you have children. Our children are our cheerleaders, and as parents we have a moral obligation to protect them and give them memories that will allow them to be productive adults. Your children need a chance. However, the reality is that although you love them, their love will not be enough for you to decide the time has come for you to get connected and get started on the road to recovery.

In the end, it must be about you. You have to know and understand that no matter what you have been through, in the final analysis, your purpose and destiny cannot be defined by it. Your purpose is far greater than what you have been through. Your light can shine bright in large part because of the darkness that is also there. You can't change the past, but you do have the authority to decide what today brings and what your future can look like.

Be well, my sister, and know you can be healed.

YOUR TRUTH

How did this chapter speak to you?

_____

_____

_____

_____

_____

_____

_____

_____

_____

_____

_____

_____

_____

_____

_____

_____

_____

YOUR TRUTH

What is your truth?

_____

_____

_____

_____

_____

_____

_____

_____

_____

_____

_____

_____

_____

_____

_____

_____

YOUR TRUTH

Plan of action to deal with your truth:

_____

_____

_____

_____

_____

_____

_____

_____

_____

_____

_____

_____

_____

_____

_____

_____

CHAPTER

7

Truth to the

Betrayed

Sister

be·tray′al

(bĭ-trā′)

noun To inform upon or deliver into the hands of an enemy in violation of a trust or allegiance; to be false or disloyal; to divulge in a breach of confidence.

"Whatever someone did to you in the past has no power over the present. Only you give it power."
OPRAH WINFREY

My sister, you are not alone if you have been betrayed. It is one of the most painful human experiences in life. I'm willing to bet that every woman in America has been betrayed at some point on her journey. The first time someone you deeply trust betrays you—stabs you in the back and in the front—is brokenness like no other. Your trust is completely shattered, and it rocks you at your very core. What is most painful is that only someone very close to you can betray you in such a profound way and make you hurt the way you do because it's unexpected. Think about it: we expect our enemies to say and do all manner of things to us, not the people we love and trust.

Betrayal comes in many different forms. It can occur in childhood within a family or as you are growing up. It serves to undermine our reality. Our innocence is taken away, and in some cases, we can no longer believe in people because the betrayal was so devastating.

One of the hardest lessons of betrayal came to our family when friends of our nineteen-year-old nephew, Jared, betrayed him. As a result of the betrayal, his so-called friends conspired and murdered him. Jared went with them to the prom, got one of them a job, dated another's sister. Because of their jealously toward him, they betrayed him and took his life. In the end, Jared was lured to his death by a close friend who flagged his car down to allow the shooter to sneak up behind him to kill him. He trusted the wrong people. It was the ultimate betrayal. Honestly, I think he realized who they were before his death as he pulled away from them; however, it was too late.

I think we ignore our spirit telling us who these people really are. They likely have a history of betraying people along the way. It is important to know that if they betrayed others in their lives, they will do it to you. It is a difficult and painful lesson to learn. Oftentimes, the red flags are there, and we just ignore them.

Perhaps your parents betrayed you when you were a child, or maybe it was a teacher or another adult. It could have been a girlfriend whom you loved like a sister, or it could have been your sister. Spouses betray other spouses every day. Clergy people or folks we hold in high regard betray us. Many families are torn apart because of betrayal. Maybe your betrayer is a lover or close friend. Sometimes our bodies betray us, and we have to deal with a chronic illness. Maybe you told someone a secret, and the person you told exposed it. As an aside, remember this soul-saving saying: *If you can't keep your own secret, don't expect anyone else to keep it.* A secret means you don't tell it. I don't care who you are dealing with—once you tell it, it is gone. People rarely keep a secret because they always have someone they feel they can trust to tell your secret to. Keep your mouth closed. Unless telling the secret can help a situation or a person, there is no need to tell it. Even then, you should seek permission because the secret does not belong to you. Trust is crucial, and it should be honored.

The greatest advice I can give you after being betrayed is to do your best to process the situation quickly, and then move on as soon as you can. Believe what you see in he or she and accept the integrity, or lack thereof, of the person who betrayed you. It is important that you begin to heal so the emotional scars don't damage your ability to have solid and meaningful future relationships. I want you to learn from the pain, but do not allow the hurt to govern all of your decisions about others in the future.

Years ago, someone who was like a sister to me hurt me. I loved her with all my heart. She betrayed me, and it broke my heart. For a long time, I was unable to allow myself to get close to another sister. As the years passed, I allowed another young woman into my life and began to mentor her. I once again let my guard down, and once again I was betrayed. She allowed me to open up to her, and when I did so, she walked out of my life. I guess she didn't get what she came to get, or maybe she did. She used me and made a complete fool out of me. Her own father tried to warn me, but I would not listen because I wanted to save her, and I refused to believe she was capable of betraying me. Nevertheless, I found myself feeling betrayed yet again.

What was so ridiculous is that it didn't need to happen. I didn't do anything intentional or purposeful to hurt them. Not anything! I was good friend. I was there when they needed me. In the final analysis, one of them deliberately wanted to hurt me, and the other had a personal weakness: she wasn't close to her own mother, so she never learned what loyalty and true love was about.

Dealing with repeated episodes of betrayal changes you as a person, and it also changes your friendships with others. These women who betrayed me took something special from me. It was my ability to love without doubting. In both cases, my spirit told me they were capable of betrayal, but I thought our close friendship was stronger than any force of the evil of betrayal. Yes, I referred to it as evil. It is evil.

The positive result that came from being betrayed is I learned what true friendship is and what it isn't. I learned to trust myself. I became more certain of what I needed and expected from others. I don't believe in people as much as I did before I was betrayed. I guard my heart closely. For me, I felt used and manipulated because the very people I went the extra mile to be there for were the ones who betrayed me. I treated them better than I treated my own family.

I purposefully didn't discuss in great detail the betrayal of a spouse or a man. To do so in any meaningful way would require the renaming of my entire book, as it would open a door for me that would require telling you about the horrors of picking the wrong guys. For me, being betrayed started as I observed my mother being betrayed. In other words, I grew up watching it. You would have thought that I would have learned from watching her experiences and what men did to her. Well, I didn't. Unfortunately, I repeated many of her mistakes. Not all, but certainly some of them. I guess I had to learn for myself the hard way.

I should have been wearing a sign that read, "Saving-a-man sister right here." It obviously was written somewhere because I always ended up with the wrong ones. I thought I had the power to take any man and bring out the best in him. Even the low-down ones who you couldn't trust as far as you could throw them. I thought I could save them. I saw goodness in them when they couldn't see it in themselves. Perhaps there was no good in them, but I desperately wanted to believe it.

In my younger days, I went into these relationships with men and created my own illusion of what each was and what the relationship was supposed to be. My hurt came from having to face the reality that it wasn't real. He wasn't real. The brother would go on to betray me, even when I knew he had done so in other relationships. But no, it surely wouldn't happen to me. Deep down inside, I knew what I had in him. The real pain came from the loss of the illusion of what I wanted and what I pretended to have, not from the betrayal of someone I knew was no good. That is all I'm going to write about the betrayal of men. Like a wise woman at my church once said during a meeting while we were discussing male/female relationships, "You knew what you got when you got him." An honest yet simple truth.

As you are dealing with the betrayal, allow yourself time to heal. Don't relive the betrayal over and over in your mind. After you have processed it, perhaps confronted the person, you have to let it go. You will be angry and hurt; that is understandable. Don't allow your anger to make you do something you will regret in the future. It may be better for you to write down your feelings so that somehow the pain can be drawn away from your heart. Writing often helps to sort it out. Writing helps me.

Believe what you know to be the facts and the truth. Understand that your trust has been violated. It is a loss, and you need time to grieve the loss of the reality that no longer is present. You need time to grieve the loss of a relationship. Expect to be sad, but the sadness will pass with time. You will be healed from this with time. Separate yourself from the person for a while. If you go back into a relationship with him or her, be clear on the terms and the expectations. Guard your heart. Eventually, to move forward, you will have to forgive what was done. Forgiveness is the key. Forgiveness is about freedom. It gives you freedom to move on with your life and to learn to trust others again. Don't allow anyone to take this away from you.

When my sister-friend betrayed me, it took me years to get over it. I missed being with her. I missed sharing my life with her and going shopping and laughing and crying together. It was heartbreaking not to continue to have her in my life, but I had to cut the ties because I could never trust her again. Once the breach in trust occurs for me, it is next to impossible to get it back. I have allowed people back into my life who betrayed me; I just will never allow them to occupy the same place of trust they had before. I could never let her back because the pain was too deep. I'm not angry with her anymore. I have good memories of the times we shared, and I really do wish her well. She taught me a valuable lesson about life and about forgiveness. She was the only person in the universe who could have taught me the lesson I learned about betrayal and how to forgive. I am truly a better woman for having learned the lesson. I rely more on myself, and I love God more because of it. Some lessons can be extremely painful to learn. It is clear to me that lessons on betrayal cannot be learned outside of experiencing them firsthand. These are lessons our mothers could never have taught us. Some things in life you have to learn for yourself.

YOUR TRUTH

How did this chapter speak to you?

_____

_____

_____

_____

_____

_____

_____

_____

_____

_____

_____

_____

_____

_____

_____

_____

_____

_____

YOUR TRUTH

What is your truth?

_____

_____

_____

_____

_____

_____

_____

_____

_____

_____

_____

_____

_____

_____

_____

YOUR TRUTH

Plan of action to deal with your truth:

_____

_____

_____

_____

_____

_____

_____

_____

_____

_____

_____

_____

_____

_____

_____

_____

_____

_____

CHAPTER

Truth to the

Sister

broke
(brōk)
adjective Lacking funds; having completely run out of money.

"You can fall, but you can rise also."
ANGELIQUE KIDJO

It's a sad yet profound truth that women in America are likely to be poorer than men. Over half the people living in poverty today are women. According to the Center for American Progress, Black and Latina women face particularly high rates of poverty. Poverty makes a woman vulnerable.

It is my hope that every woman reading this book will somehow make her way to this chapter of advice. Until we all understand that we are connected in the universe of humanity, and when one segment is hurting, it affects all of us in some way, we will never solve the problems that we face today in this country.

We should be our sister's keeper. We will never begin to rise above the all-too-common images of shattered communities with abandoned houses and burned-out buildings and protests in the streets over income inequality, until we understand all levels of our community deserve to have a chance at a better life.

The solution to this tremendous and complicated problem is that all of us need to start to care again and stop blaming the victims. We fail to make our public officials accountable to all their constituents. Poor people fail to realize they have power in the ballot. But it is hard to be motivated to vote or do anything when you are living in hopelessness.

Some argue that poor people need to pull themselves up by their bootstraps and make it for themselves. How can you pull yourselves up by your bootstraps when you lack boots in the first place? Boots represent opportunity, and opportunity left a large segment of our community a long time ago. Not to mention, the children who, through no fault of their own, must live in poverty with little hope and no plan for a way of escape.

Children living in poverty did nothing wrong. They didn't ask to come here, yet they are asked to go to bed at night hungry, walk into low-performing schools, head home to a community where they fear for their lives, with no tools to help them study, no computers, and little adult supervision to help and guide them. They wake every morning, hungry and to a world where nothing ever changes. The cycle continues with each passing year. Many students are acting out in elementary school. Some become criminals by the time they are in middle and high school. Small offenses, but crimes nevertheless. To deal with them, they are sent to special ed classes, and before you know it, they end up in juvenile facilities. From the juvenile jails they graduate to the institution of an adult prison. This is the cycle and future many of our young people face. And we wonder why they do the things they do? They have no hope. They stopped dreaming a long time ago. They have no expectations of anything positive for their future. They believe this is all they deserve and will ever get.

We then have the audacity to ask our young people not to have an attitude, not to be angry, not to be resentful, not to be profoundly discouraged, and want them to listen to their teachers and not get in trouble. The very act of disobedience is often an outcry of their pain and disappointment.

They are the true victims of a society that has turned their backs on them as we prepare to build prison beds based on their inability to read, guaranteeing a pipeline that leads to prison. When opportunity and hope are taken away, you take away a community.

What can be most devastating about poverty is the sheer lack of hope. Those of us who made it out of poverty or those who were raised in middle-class households all want the same things from life that people who live in poverty want: a chance at a better life. We want to walk in our purpose toward a destiny that allows us to live in dignity. Everyone deserves an opportunity. We just want a chance to make life better for our children. Poverty takes away any opportunity to create a long-term sustainable life and to pass on something better to our children. We can't continue to turn a blind eye to the deprivation of others.

Poverty takes on many faces. Yes, it can mean being homeless, but it can take on the face of what is now classified as the "working poor," defined as a person whose income falls below a given poverty line. This is the woman who goes to work every day, but because of her low wage, she doesn't have enough money to pay her bills.

In other words, being broke today could mean getting up every morning and going to a job that either pays minimum wage or barely a livable wage. It means working at that job for eight hours, having no benefits. Or, if benefits are offered, the sister cannot afford to get them. Although these mothers may have children in public school, they still are required to pay for aftercare. If they can't afford aftercare, the children are left by themselves. It would be easy to develop a plan that has an after-school program that kids attend for free, staffed by professionals who can assist with homework, tutor students, and provide mentoring and even a hot meal before they head home.

If a working-class woman has a baby or toddlers, she has to pay for childcare. After she pays for childcare, she has to buy food, pay for rent or a mortgage, a car or public transportation costs, utilities, and gas in addition to other debt that may have accumulated. She may have to get a part-time job just to make ends meet. With one job and a part-time job, she still may not have enough money to have a quality life.

Being broke is living from paycheck to paycheck, robbing Peter to pay Paul. God forbid an emergency occurs and she has to find the money to cover unexpected situations. Even with learning to shop at thrift stores and doing the best she can, life is difficult when you don't have the resources to live. She attends church and is asked to contribute there. She prays and stays faithful as well as grateful for whatever it is God blesses her with. There is nothing left. She wishes she could save, but there is no money for saving. She works to pay bills. The only money that comes in once a year is when she gets her federal and state refund checks. However, that money is usually spent before she gets it. Her bills get so behind that she uses the refund money to play catch-up. When car repairs are needed, there is no extra money to take care of it, so she makes partial payments on other bills to cover the costs because she has to have a car to get work.

She keeps moving and keeps trying, and she does the best she can, but she is broke and brokenhearted because she doesn't know how to make a change occur in her life.

The doors of opportunity were closed on women who are the working poor a long time ago. There is a great income divide in this country. The policies of the lawmakers are enacted to support and sustain the rich. They make no apology for it. These lawmakers have little fear because poor people don't see the value of voting. It's hard to comprehend any value for putting people into public office who talk a good game when they're trying to get elected yet do nothing after they are elected. They come into our churches during election time, and we don't see them again until the next election cycle. Politicians may go into public office with good intentions, but they are seduced by their egos and the fact that the problems are arduous and the machine of government has no will to want to help the disadvantaged.

I'm not suggesting the government can solve all our problems. Because of the enormity of what we face, it will take efforts from all aspects of the community to begin to solve poverty's ills. We can't merely throw money at a problem and believe it can be solved. However, as it relates to the role of government, I believe that if we can give tax breaks to corporations to relocate businesses to particular areas to stimulate job growth, the government should be able to create programs that invest in our people who ultimately sustain our communities. It does nothing for a company to locate in a community if the people are not educated, trained, and supported with affordable housing.

Let me emphasize that I am not naive enough to believe that there is one magic bullet to solve our problems, but it is certainly in the best interest of the corporate and business community to participate with the government, religious institutions, nonprofits, and the people themselves to develop solutions that close the tremendous income disparities.

My family, for many years, lived as members of the working poor. We came out of poverty because of opportunity. The greatest opportunity we took advantage of is education in a system that was exceptional and accessible. When I was young, my mother instilled in me that the key to opportunity was in education. Grants and scholarships were made available to go to college, and we were given a chance to make our lives better. I strongly recommend to any woman wanting to get out of poverty to pursue an education, whether it be college, a training program, or starting a business. You will never escape your situation making minimum wage. You must find it somewhere within you to want something better for your life. You sacrifice and deserve better than to live from paycheck to paycheck.

Poor women are not asking for handouts, but rather a hand that provides opportunity for them to earn a good living. They don't need another job training program; they need real jobs. They need jobs that pay salaries that will allow them to have a decent living. They want jobs that will allow them to move from poverty to middle class. All a woman who is facing a life of financial bondage wants is a chance for the American dream—a chance to be free.

Although I am blessed to call myself middle class, I will never rest as long as others, including my family members, have to struggle for a chance at life. As I have stated, the solution to the issue of opportunity does not solely rest upon the shoulders of any one entity, but rather our entire nation.

I believe there is still hope even when everything around you looks hopeless. There is a way out for you and your kids. You have to be willing to make the sacrifice and start over. You may need to relocate to a city where jobs are plentiful. You can't keep doing the same thing year after year expecting a different result. No one will come and rescue you. You're going to have to do the best you can until the voices of injustice rise up and say we must come together as a nation, and those who need help the most can get it.

You should look into going back to school to be trained in a particular area. The health-care field and the hospitality fields are areas where workers will always be needed. Any career in technology is always a good idea. The training can be completed, depending on the area, in as little as eight months to eighteen months. No matter how long it takes, the time will pass by either way. You may even consider going back to college. No matter how old you are, it is never too late. You can go to real estate school and get a license to sell real estate.

Have you ever thought about starting your own business? As an entrepreneur myself, I must be honest that it is hard work, but good work. Good work in that I get to co-mingle my purpose in life with my vocation. I control my time and my vision. Starting a business is no easy task. You need to become trained on the inner workings of business. This brings me back to education. I'm not suggesting you need an MBA before starting a business, but I do recommend a few classes on how to run a business. Research the business before you jump into it. Make certain your talents and gifts are suitable to be the owner of a business.

There are many nonprofits, including mine, that offer workshops on starting a business. It might be a good idea to attend a few of these seminars so you can determine if being a business owner is something you want to do. The only word of caution I give you is to please understand that when you own and operate your own business, you work twenty times harder for yourself than you ever worked for anyone else. The benefit is you control your destiny; you have an opportunity to create wealth and to pass something on to your children. Do your research, and see if starting a business is for you. The other possibility is that you can start a business on the side while you maintain employment and try to grow your business slowly and deliberately until you are able to make the transition to working for yourself full time. If you're not a risk-taker, starting a business may not be for you. You cannot fear failure. Failure comes with the experiences of trying something new.

Because you've been stuck with no way out, you must ask yourself about purpose and passion. What do you like to do? If you could do anything in the world, what would it be? Why are you not doing it? What can you do to put a plan in place to make it happen? Is it realistic? Do you need someone else to believe in you? Do your research and search for businesses that are profitable. Whether you decide to become a hairstylist or start a cup cake business; you get to control your destiny.

Is it possible for you to take on a second part-time job? You can work on the weekends or in the evenings, and the extra money can be used to pay off old debt and allow you to build savings and additional income. You can make cupcakes, bracelets, or flower arrangements. Whatever it is, you need multiple streams of income so you can fight your way out of your financial situation.

You have to do something! You have to come up with a plan of action to change the direction of your life. You work hard now, and it is likely making someone else rich. Even if you don't have the knowledge of how to move forward, as I previously stated, there are a number of nonprofit organizations that help people who want to be trained. If you can't do it by yourself, get with other sisters in the same situation and those who want more out of their lives.

If you don't have the strength to do it for yourself, at least think about your children. Children born in poverty are more likely to stay in poverty than are children not born in poverty.

Your children deserve a chance at a better life. Our children today are hopeless because all they see is struggle. They don't dream anymore because there is no opportunity. They get out of high school only to get a minimum wage job, which keeps them in the cycle of lacking everything they could hope for. Too many of our children end up going to jail or dead. Far too many of our girls go on to work, and shortly thereafter, the babies come. There is a little help from the government for the child, but just enough help to keep her and the child in bondage. It is a cycle of despair passed on from one generation to the next.

When you're poor, and when you're hungry, and that is all you see every day, there is little room for dreaming. Often, children who dream and have visions are ridiculed because only a few get out. And when many of us get out, we never go back to our communities to help with a way of escape and to lead others to a place of economic freedom. Our young people watch success displayed on television through the lives of celebrities and reality stars. Sure, the girls put on costumes of long nails and hair weaves to try and capture a piece of what looks like the American dream. She may not have the house or the career or the money, but she can purchase the hair and the outfit and pretend for a little while that she has made it out. No one ever sits her down and explains that life is more than getting dressed up in a costume and looking foolish while walking through the mall.

I understand poverty. I really understand what it feels like. I made a promise to myself a long time ago that I would never be broke again when I found myself not having a roof over my head. I was determined to never have to ask anyone for anything. Being broke means you are disrespected. Poor people have to struggle for everything in this life. People don't expect much from you. People living in poverty are treated as though they have chosen this life. Outsiders don't understand that people living in poverty would give anything to live a better life.

Being poor gives an appreciation for what is important in life. It makes you grateful for whatever you have. However, there comes a time when you have to decide that living off of the scraps of life is something you will no longer do. You have to see it in a vision. You have to believe in your heart and in your soul that you were created to live a better life on this earth. It's not easy, and you cannot merely speak it into existence. You have to keep trying and trying and trying. You have to be willing to work hard. You have to want your life to change. You must be determined to get out.

You could very well be educated and find yourself without a job. Perhaps you fell on hard times because of sickness or divorce, or for whatever reason you are struggling with your finances. You could be dealing with the fact that no one will give you a chance. Being poor is not always about being uneducated; it is about not having an opportunity. You just need an opportunity.

Finally, get off of your knees, as I am certain you've been praying to God for a long time for a breakthrough. It's now time for action. Stop begging and start moving. It's time. No matter how difficult life may be for you, there is hope. No one can take away your hope. I believe that God is still in control and has made a way for you to live an abundant life. No one is going to come and rescue you; you have to be willing to save yourself.

YOUR TRUTH

How did this chapter speak to you?

_____

_____

_____

_____

_____

_____

_____

_____

_____

_____

_____

_____

_____

_____

_____

_____

YOUR TRUTH

What is your truth?

_____

_____

_____

_____

_____

_____

_____

_____

_____

_____

_____

_____

_____

_____

_____

YOUR TRUTH

Plan of action to deal with your truth:

_____

_____

_____

_____

_____

_____

_____

_____

_____

_____

_____

_____

_____

_____

_____

_____

_____

Truth to the

Sister

con·trol

/kənˈtrōl/

verb Having a need to control other people's behavior.

"If you don't understand yourself, you don't understand anybody else."
NIKKI GIOVANNI

My dear controlling sister, you are likely to be the unhappiest of all the sisters featured in this book. You have to be unhappy if you believe you can control the behavior of others. Honestly, on some level, we all might want people to do what we want them to do, especially if it makes our lives easier, but we understand we can't control the actions of other people. To be deemed a controlling sister, you are the one who has yet to realize you cannot control the actions of grown people. You want things your way and believe in many instances that your way is the only and best way of doing whatever it is you want done.

It's difficult to be around you when you can't have your way. Anyone who is trying to control other people usually has a nice side to them when they're getting their way. However, deep down inside, you will never be content because in life things cannot always go your way. According to you, someone else is always doing something wrong. They are the ones with the problem. You easily and with little regard have no problem justifying your condemnation of them because you are judgmental.

Although you may not be a controlling sister yourself, we all know one or two. Some women have controlling mothers, sisters, close family members, or even friends with controlling personalities. It is important to understand a woman with a controlling personality or controlling spirit is a sister with deeper issues, such as codependency, low self-esteem, narcissism, or just sheer stubbornness. I believe that a controlling woman can also be a selfish person and does not take into account the desires of the adults around her. Controlling women can be self-centered and may be immature. They wear all of us out, and if you don't watch them, they will prevent you from having the life you are supposed to lead. They will manipulate you into giving in to their desires. If you are a people pleaser, you will find yourself in bondage, as they will seek to control you in many ways.

Now, by way of disclosure, I must admit I've always wanted things done a certain way. As long as the outcome was to my liking, it didn't much matter how it arrived at the end result. I have been accused of being controlling. I never saw myself as controlling, but I am willing to concede it if others felt as though I was attempting to control them. I can't argue with another person's feelings. As I think back on it, I must agree that I was controlling. I pray I have been delivered from it.

As I have matured through the years, I care less and less about what people are doing around me. It may be hard to explain, but there is something freeing about not caring. I only spend time concerning myself about life issues that are important to me, issues and causes I want to fight for, empowering others, and being a better person for myself. I refuse to get caught up in trying to tell people what to do anymore. People will be and do what they want to do anyway. I have too much living to do to try to control the lives of others. This is a liberating concept and one that I happily embrace.

It wasn't until I was trapped in a situation with a controlling person that I recognized some of the same behavior in me. I still like things with a high level of excellence, but I have finally grown to the point whereby it doesn't always have to be done my way. If I want it done a certain way, I will do it myself. Otherwise, I will accept what I am given. Because of my bad experience with controlling people, I also have emotionally separated myself from many of them. I dislike how they make me feel. They always want and need something. It is simply exhausting dealing with them. I also had to free myself from my controlling ways. I want peace and happiness, and you can't have complete peace when you are trying to do the impossible: trying to control the behavior of others.

Since I am on the other side of my controlling ways, I am empowered to discuss being entangled with a controlling sister. I want you to awaken so you can either be free from it or understand how to deal with a person who has this problem. It isn't a problem you can solve. You can only learn to deal with her or let her go. Perhaps you can see yourself in the words and encounters I have shared. If you are a controlling woman, you may wish to seek counseling or make the decision to abandon your controlling ways.

It may be hard to spot controlling people because they do a great job of covering up who they really are. Not all controlling people come across arrogant, but many of them do. They also appear to be self-assured, when deep down inside they have a deep-seated sense of inadequacy and insecurity. They may feel as though they are incapable of being loved. This may be the result of feelings from childhood.

From what I have learned along life's journey and from personal experiences dealing with controlling women, they create grand images of themselves to please or deceive others, and before long they begin to believe the lies themselves. I first encountered one of these women at my church. She had me fooled for years until we fell out. I had built her up so much that she began to believe her own press. She was controlling everything around her by always being available to help out. She crossed the line when she tried to control me, and I had control issues myself at the time. It was a mess.

I recognized that I allowed this person to control me for years with her many acts of kindness and her never-ending availability, which caused me to ignore every sign I saw in her as a controlling person as I just looked past it. It wasn't until I didn't do what she wanted me to do on an issue that I saw her true colors and realized what had been going on for years. Now, I am free of her, and she is free of me. I don't know about her, but I know I'm free indeed.

The controlling sister I find totally exhausting is the one who is the manipulative woman. I spent a great deal of time dealing with this kind of sister, as she was my best friend for years. In fact, she was more like a sister than a friend. She was a master of saying what people wanted to hear and what it would take to get others to do what she wanted them to do. Her manipulations were subtle and disarming. A controlling sister like this will have you on a string, and you won't even realize it. I certainly didn't know how much control she had over my life until she was out of my life.

She was always there for me, and I was always there for her. She always seemed so strong just when I was at my weakest. She rarely fell apart, and, in fact, I can count the times I even watched her cry. I see now it was because she couldn't identify with my pain or my struggle. She never embraced her own pain and merely lived a life where she covered it up. She couldn't feel it. She remained steady and strong because she lacked true empathy. Like the other sister I encountered from my church, everything went well in our relationship until I didn't do what she wanted me to do. As hard as it is for me to admit, I now understand she was jealous of me all along. She stayed close to me to control me so that I wouldn't get ahead of her. When it looked like I was taking flight, she did all she could to bring me down.

This relationship scarred me deeply for many years because I was deceived into believing I had a real sisterhood with her. I loved her deeply as a friend, and it was not pleasant to accept that it was never reciprocated. She was incapable of expressing genuine love and friendship. She is a controlling woman who carries deep-seated insecurity. I have no regrets about my relationship with her because we had some great times together. There is something special about having a best friend. I just get a little sad to think that none of the friendship part was ever real. I still can't be angry with her because my love for her was real, and I guess I understand her. I forgave her years ago, and although we will never be friends again, I absolutely believe she is a controlling sister who will never be for my good.

Maybe you are like me; I often attract these kinds of women to my life. I have someone now who pretends to like me, and yet I see so much of my other past friend in her. She has a degree of power and position that she is attempting to use over me. What she doesn't know is that I don't care. I truly don't care about her power. I feel sorry for her and her inability to embrace her authentic self.

The best advice I can give you is to be aware of controlling women. However, don't allow your past experiences with controlling women to prevent you from entering into wonderful connecting relationships with other women. I promise you that not all women are focusing their time and attention on trying to destroy you. There are many more sisters in the world who are real and honest and loving. There are sisters who can be and are good friends to other sisters. There are women who make good and loyal friends. They honor and appreciate the sisterhood. We just have to be brave enough to be in tune with the signs of controlling women and learn to either deal with them or walk away from the relationships before we invest too much into them.

Finally, to my controlling sister, free yourself from the need to control others. Get in touch with your pain. Your controlling ways are about you, and you will never find inner peace until you deal with your issues. You are worthy of living a life free from believing you have power over others. Once you let go of your controlling ways, you will finally be free to live the life you have been created to live. You will finally be able to rest in just being you.

YOUR TRUTH

How did this chapter speak to you?

_____

_____

_____

_____

_____

_____

_____

_____

_____

_____

_____

_____

_____

_____

_____

_____

YOUR TRUTH

What is your truth?

_____
_____
_____
_____
_____
_____
_____
_____
_____
_____
_____
_____
_____
_____
_____
_____

YOUR TRUTH

Plan of action to deal with your truth:

_____

_____

_____

_____

_____

_____

_____

_____

_____

_____

_____

_____

_____

_____

_____

_____

_____

Truth to the

Caregiver

Sister

care·giv·er

/ˈkerˌɡivər/

noun A family member or paid helper
who regularly looks after a child or a
sick, elderly, or disabled person.

*"I have found that among its other benefits, giving
liberates the soul of the giver."*
MAYA ANGELOU

I want to begin by saying that no one will completely understand the sacrifice you are making if they haven't had to be a caregiver to someone. Now that you have added caregiver to your list of the many roles you wear as a woman, I wanted to include you in the list of women to whom I felt compelled to give a word of comfort and advice. Caregiving is both a reward and a sacrifice. There will be joyful days and difficult days. I understand it because I have been in the position of caring for older parents and for my granddaughter. If you are like me, I have a caregiving spirit, but even with a willingness to care for others, I found a number of challenges that I didn't anticipate and some rewarding and difficult days during the process.

I don't know if it is the times we are living in, but the more I talk to people, the more I realize many women are in the position of caregiver. We all know providing care for a family member in need is something we have been doing in our communities for years. Many of us grew up in intergenerational households with grandparents participating in rearing the grandchildren. I think it's good. I grew up in the house with my grandparents, and I believe I'm a better woman because of it.

According to the experts, life expectancies are increasing,

and we all know the cost of caring for loved ones is on the rise; therefore, more and more of us will participate in the caregiving process. In addition, grandparents are taking a significant lead in helping co-parent or assist with our grandchildren. As grandparents, there is no greater joy than caring for our grandchildren, providing we're in good health and have the time to commit. It can be a life-changing, rewarding experience.

My advice is focused on those sisters who may be taking care of an aging parent or in- law or perhaps even a disabled spouse. I don't know if you are one of the mothers who is caring for a son or daughter with a physical or mental illness, or guiding your child through the world of autism. But regardless of your particular circumstances, you're facing a challenging role. If you're like most family caregivers, you aren't trained for the responsibilities you now face. No one will tell you your job is easy. It's probably the hardest job in the world. You probably never anticipated you would be in the situation of having to be a caregiver. You may be caring for someone nearby, and you travel to him or her daily to provide care, or you travel a great distance periodically to see about your loved one. In either instance, it is difficult.

I understand with all the other things you are required to do in your life, you desperately want to make certain that your family member is provided with the best of care. The good news is that they have someone like you who cares very much about them. You are the one in the family who demonstrates care. There are times when others in the family go on with their lives because they know you will be the one to step up and take care of the loved one. It isn't fair, but it is true.

There will come a point in this journey when you will get tired of having to be the "she-ro," the person who has to juggle a lot of balls in the air and dance while you're doing it.

The way it works, in the beginning you attempt to provide most care yourself. You soon realize the stress of trying to do it all and trying to do it by yourself can put you into a depression and can quickly become overwhelming. I want you to know you can be a good caregiver without having to sacrifice yourself in the process.

If you are in the role of caring for a loved one with an illness, try to learn as much as you can about the sickness and what he or she needs from you or any caregiver. Understanding what you are dealing with is a critical component to maintaining your power over the situation. I can tell you right now, even without knowing the particulars of the situation, you need help. You need to get someone to come in a few days a week for you to be able to step away from the situation and maintain balance in your own life.

If you talk to a few people, you will find some faced with similar situations. I want you to know you're not alone. You need support from people who are going through what you are.

One of the biggest issues I faced when I was assisting my husband in caring for his parents was I felt as though I needed to do everything for them. In actuality, they needed to maintain their independence to keep their dignity and integrity as they were aging and dealing with health issues.

While I was caring for them, I developed feelings of resentment because I felt my life had been interrupted and no one understood. I was on the bench, going to seminary, caring for my husband's parents, and traveling back and forth to Louisiana to check on my own mother. I had to be realistic about my limitations. It was important for me to communicate with my husband and to set clear limits on my time. It was not easy— no one wants to be judged—but I recognized that if I was going to maintain my sanity and my marriage, I had to be honest.

Once I accepted my feelings and was honest with myself, I felt much better about what I was doing. Caregiving can trigger a whole lot of emotions. At times I found myself angry, fearful that I wouldn't be able to meet all the responsibilities I had, as well as guilty for feeling the way I was feeling. There were days when I actually felt hopeless because I saw having to serve as a caregiver as something that was chipping away at my plans for the future. It was truly an array of emotions I felt until I was able to accept and come to grips with my role and my limitations. Once I embraced my feelings and developed a strategy, caregiving became a joy and an honor to fulfill.

Caregiving became a great aspect of my calling to serve others. I love family, and what better way to engage and be surrounded by family than to have them in your home and care for them? It was many days and tears later before I was able to get to that point of thinking. The bottom line is that it is important for you to acknowledge and accept what you're feeling, both good and bad. Whatever you do, try not to beat yourself up over your doubts and misgivings. I had to accept my feelings. It didn't mean I didn't love my in-laws, but simply, I was a human being who was doing the best I could.

Don't allow anyone to judge you. Unless they are equally stepping up to the plate, they don't get to judge you nor tell you what to do. They need to step up or shut up! Besides, you're just one person; you can't do everything on your own, nor should you. If you're caregiving from a distant location, you absolutely need help. This is when you should call on friends, siblings, and other family members, as well as health professionals. No matter what happens in this process, you need support. You must continue to maintain a life of your own because no one should sacrifice who they are as a person to care for another person.

You may be like me: I hate asking anyone for help, let

alone other family members. It is my last resort because I don't like people throwing favors in my face. When I ask for help, I feel uncomfortable. I also feel like I am imposing on them. There are times when I become resentful if I have been there for certain people, and when I finally need their help, they refuse to step up for me. I am usually never the same when that happens. Therefore, I try to avoid asking for help. However, with caregiving, if you don't take anything else away from my advice, please understand that you cannot give care to another person by yourself. It just can't be done.

Finally, I want to tell you that you need to look after yourself. You must maintain balance in your life. You need to see about your needs. Make certain that you take care of your health. Attend your doctor visits and check-ups. You can't care for anyone if you are not first taking good care of yourself. Don't underestimate the power of taking time off to relax on a daily basis. This will help with stress.

Plan small escapes. Leave the situation and do something that makes you smile. In fact, make sure you laugh at least once a day. Laughter is medicine for your soul. If you like watching a particular television show, watch it. If you like talking on the phone with a friend, or reading a book, or going on a nice walk, do those things. Whatever it is that requires you to do nothing but enjoy and feel good, do it. Exercise is a great stress reliever and allows you to forget about your situation for thirty to forty-five minutes. I like to write, so I get up every morning and write. Make certain you eat right and get enough sleep. You must find time to get your rest. Do nothing; think about nothing, and just rest. Also, if you are married, please do your best to maintain a healthy intimate relationship with your spouse. It is important that you maintain your marriage if you are caring for others. If you don't have a spouse, you should continue to date. If you don't date, at least get out with friends once in a while for a movie or dinner.

Through it all, I was able to survive caregiving because I was connected in the spirit to my God. I prayed daily. I mean a real prayer where I talked to the Lord through the day. It gave me strength. I sought from God the meaning and the lessons I was supposed to be learning. I realized that caregiving was a vital aspect of the journey I was on, but there were times when I didn't want to go through the difficulties although I knew in my heart that it was a part of the master plan for my life. I remained honest with God about what I was feeling and sought the peace that only God could give me in dealing with the situation.

If you are depressed, go get some help. Please go and see a professional. I didn't need to talk to someone, but I want you to know there is absolutely nothing wrong with seeking professional assistance in dealing with any anxiety you may be feeling. Don't allow yourself to get depressed.

As I reflect back on my caregiving days, I smile. I learned so much about love and sacrifice. It really became an honor for me to take care of my husband's parents. When they made their transitions, I knew in my heart I played a small part in making their last days their best days. I witnessed something in my husband that I never knew was there as I watched him care for them on a full-time basis. He demonstrated love to them that served to inspire me for a lifetime. I only hope that my children and grandchildren will care for me in the way that we care. Remember how I started this chapter. I said that caregiving is both rewarding and difficult. It is a journey of love and a journey of sacrifice. For those who give to others, your life will be rewarded in ways you could never imagine. After all, it is all about love.

YOUR TRUTH

How did this chapter speak to you?

_____

_____

_____

_____

_____

_____

_____

_____

_____

_____

_____

_____

_____

_____

_____

_____

YOUR TRUTH

What is your truth?

_____

_____

_____

_____

_____

_____

_____

_____

_____

_____

_____

_____

_____

_____

_____

_____

_____

YOUR TRUTH

Plan of action to deal with your truth:

_____

_____

_____

_____

_____

_____

_____

_____

_____

_____

_____

_____

_____

_____

_____

_____

_____

_____

11

Truth to the

Complaining

Sister

com·plain

/kəmˈplān/

verb Express dissatisfaction or annoyance about a state of affairs or an event.

*"What you're supposed to do when you don't like
a thing is change it. If you can't change it, change the way
you think about it. Don't complain."*
MAYA ANGELOU

Disclosure: Complaining for illustrative purposes only!

Stop already! You should be tired of hearing yourself always having something to complain about. If you're not, we certainly are tired of always having to hear your never-ending complaints about anything and everything you find dissatisfying. Big or small, you've mastered an ability to find fault in almost everything you encounter. Honestly, you don't realize how toxic endless complaining can be. Not only do you complain, but you are extremely negative. Personally, it's hard for me to deal with negative people. The energy that complaining people send out into the universe leads me to the dark side every time I have to deal with it. It's a heavy burden to carry when you have to deal with a person who constantly complains. I find myself having to remind them about all the things they have to be thankful for. I fall into the trap of trying to solve whatever they're complaining about so I don't have to hear it. I want to be supportive, but ultimately it causes me to withdraw from them because the hole is so deep within them that I find myself exhausted while in their presence.

I will attempt not to generalize as, admittedly, much of

my advice comes from my own conquered demons and my observations of others, but people who complain constantly are usually unhappy. You're unsatisfied with life and how things have turned out for you. Because you're not getting what you desperately need or want in life, you complain. I'm certain there are times you feel some degree of joy, but, overall, you aren't happy with your life.

Don't get me wrong; everyone is allowed to vent from time to time. I certainly complain when I feel like it. This is one of the areas God had to really work with me on. After getting in touch with my feelings, I realized I was complaining because I was not happy. You're the only one who can make yourself happy. It's not the job of the people around you to make you happy and to solve all your problems.

My issue is not with a person who has to complain occasionally to get something changed or rectified. A complaint that is raised to correct an issue or right a wrong is justifiable. However, constant griping is too much to take. It's perfectly fine to verbalize a problem in the hopes of bringing about a change. For example, my husband hoards things. I routinely complain to him that he needs to throw stuff away in the hopes that he will clean up one day. My nine-year-old granddaughter has taken on her grandfather's ways and keeps her bedroom messy. I complain to her to train her to be neater. If the complaint is done with a goal, it seems reasonable that complaints are warranted in those situations.

I don't even have a problem if, every now and then (the operative words are *now and then*) you need to get something off your chest by putting someone in check. Anyone who knows me will tell you that I'm notorious for having to give people a piece of my mind when I have witnessed intolerable behavior. I'm guilty. I am not malicious, but people will say and do anything today. They'll push the envelope and try to take advantage of other people. Because I hate playing games, someone has to be the adult in the situation and get it straight. I'm not saying my behavior is always right, but I'm attempting to correct a situation. Moreover, I only speak up when it directly involves me. If it is not my business, I stay out of it. But, I will never witness an injustice and not call it out.

We're living in a world that is out of order. People are users and take advantage of every situation around them. I have learned and adopted what my grandmother taught me as a soul-saving saying: *It's not what you say as much as how you say it.* In my younger days, I would let my emotions build up to the point that I would explode. Now, as I've matured, I can sit back longer, or I can just walk away before I feel the need to speak up. I still say what I have to say, but only if it matters to me. I found it's a waste of time trying to get an adult's behavior in check. It's likely they're not willing to change. For my peace of mind, I learned that not everyone is worth getting a piece of your mind anyway as they're not likely to appreciate it or even get what the correction is truly about.

Some of you have become comfortable complainers. Complaining has become second nature to you. You'll vent to anyone who'll listen. You may not realize it, but your constant complaining may have become a source of validation and support. You carry around so much pain that this has become your way of connecting with others. It's likely a way of making you feel less alone or even not as guilty for many of the frustrations you're feeling.

I recently had jury duty. After checking in for the morning, you're required to sit in a big room together. We were just sitting and sitting. When I first arrived, everyone was standoffish and to themselves. As the hours passed, people began to talk to one another. Everyone had a story about where they should be and why they didn't have the time to be sitting in uncomfortable chairs waiting for hours serving on jury duty.

Complaining became the rallying cry of the morning. We've all heard the saying, misery loves company. The complaining became a way for the people to connect in that jury holding room. As the hours passed, the conversations moved from complaining about why they shouldn't be there to talking about issues in the community, current events, kids, etc. It was interesting to observe.

If you're the sister who can never be satisfied with anything, you may feel I'm speaking directly to you. Perhaps you're the one who complains all the time to your family because, from your point of view, your husband and your children can't ever do anything right. God forbid you bring your complaining spirit to your job. You're the co-worker whom everyone hates to deal with because all you do is complain. You complain about the job (a job you should be grateful to have), your insufficient pay, and the inefficiencies of your co-workers. The list goes on and on. You're a master of being able to find anything to gripe about. You wear everyone out with your constant criticisms, all the while never being able to see your own faults. I guess you believe you can do no wrong. If your deficiencies are ever raised, you become defensive. You lash out at others, making snide comments to deflect their criticism.

I remember when I was on the bench, some would complain that the judges weren't being paid enough. They compared the salaries of attorneys at law firms with what we were making, and there was a great disparity. They complained about it all the time. I wanted to scream. First of all, we made the decision to be a judge. I wanted to say so badly to them that if they didn't like it, then they should leave the position as judge. There were hundreds of people lined up to sit in our position. It is a place of honor and privilege. I understood that one doesn't go into public service to become wealthy. It shouldn't have been about the money. Certainly, people should pay public servants an acceptable and reasonable salary, but you can't voluntarily go into public service and later complain that you're not paid enough.

Ask any teacher, and they'll tell you that they do what they do for the love of the students because they're clearly not paid enough. If teachers are not teaching because they love the kids, they will be the ones who are always complaining. Judges earn every dollar they make and more; it isn't an easy job to do, but a six-figure income still is not a lot to complain about. Just ask any regular person on the street, and they'll let you know how to thank God for the ability to make such a good living. Anyway, that was my complaint. I've wanted to say this for a long time. Just be grateful for what you have!

You may be the girlfriend we love, but you constantly complain about everything from your health, your family, and your career. We want to tell you to shut up and do something with your life if you don't like it, but we love you too much, and our mothers taught us never to tell another adult to shut up. But, girl, we just want you to know that you're likely running people away because you never have anything uplifting and positive to say. Have you forgotten that we all have our own problems, and we're tired of having to hear about yours all the time? Please, give it a rest and try to be considerate of others. Everything can't just be about you and your issues.

If you're the sister whom we see at church, we can always count on you to have to tell us how much you're struggling. Year after year, season after season, you're always dealing with something. It'll either be your children or something going on—it's always something. No matter how much you go to church, no matter how many times you go up to the altar to pray, we know that Sunday after Sunday, you'll walk through the doors, praise God, pray, and cry and still leave complaining. You never change; you just never change. You need to be praying for God to heal you from your negative and complaining ways.

I haven't forgotten about the hypochondriac, the sister who is abnormally anxious about her health. You're in bondage with your own mind. You're the woman who needs to stay off the Internet because you keep researching and self-diagnosing every ache and pain. We have to hear every detail about your doctor's visit, the medicine you're taking, or the medical procedure you're about to have done. You wear your "sicknesses" as a badge of honor. Honey child, you spend too much time focusing on and thinking about your health. You're fearful, and if you don't watch out, you're going to use that deadly fear to develop some kind of disease. Here's a soul-saving saying: *Whatever you fear will likely come to you.* Life is passing you by because all you think about is getting sick. You say you don't do this, but I'm writing to tell you that you do. We're tired of having to reassure you that you are fine and that everything is going to be all right. We support you, but you may need to go and talk to someone in the mental health field to find out where your fear is coming from. Constant fear can never be a good thing in someone's life. I know you are unhappy, but you really need to talk to someone.

In some instances, complaining has become a way of life

for you. No matter how well life is going, you still manage to find something wrong. You may very well deserve to have a better life. After all, you have suffered or worked to get it. You may find yourself disappointed about how situations turned out. You may not be where you think you should be. I was always attempting to achieve some goal or milestone. As soon as I completed one goal, I would move to the next. I never stopped to enjoy that I did what I set out to do. When I didn't achieve as soon as I wanted to, I became dissatisfied and found myself complaining.

You're going to need to search deep within yourself to figure out what the problem is and why you feel you're not getting what you deserve. Believe it or not, you likely lack the ability to love yourself. Therefore, you complain. You're unhappy with your life. If you are like I was, you may be hoping to find happiness with each accomplishment. You keep relying on something outside of you to bring you happiness. In some cases, you may feel as though it is the responsibility of other adults to fill you with love. But I realized it was my responsibility to love me.

Your soul, that little girl inside of you, desperately needs to be cared for, understood, and, most importantly, loved. You can no longer look outside of yourself to get it. There may come a time in your life when it seems that doors are closing on all your desires and dreams. Bad things will start to happen. You may be in a season that has nothing but struggle in it. Have you considered that the doors in your life may be closing to get your attention? This may be the time that forces you to do some inner work. After years of crying and praying and even being angry with God, you may need to learn the lesson that you must love yourself to experience happiness and fulfillment.

Loving yourself means believing you're worthy of being loved. From childhood, you may have not received all that you needed. You needed approval, caring, and attention from the adults around you, but they never really gave it to you. In some cases, you were hurt as a child, and you carry around this hurt as an adult. This pain and hurt has manifested itself into your wanting and needing someone (a spouse, partner, children) to give you what you didn't get. You feel you need others to help heal that pain.

The greatest lesson you need to learn is that if you don't find a way to give it to yourself, you will remain emotionally tied to the needs of that little wounded girl. It will become a vicious cycle of always feeling rejected and unloved. Your achievements may, in some instances, represent the fact you emotionally abandoned yourself, and you are merely using your goals, aspirations, and achievements for validation about your worthiness.

It's good to want to achieve goals in life. What are your reasons for doing what you do? Are you called to these achievements, or do you use them to fill the need to tell the world that you matter? You have to know you matter because relying on something outside of you will often end up breaking your heart. It will never have feelings or give you what you need. You'll look up and never believe you're in the right place because there is always more that you're supposed to have. When you can't sustain the feeling you're hoping for, you may get angry. Aren't you tired of feeling alone? Aren't you tired of people not understanding who you really are? These are all signals that it's time for you to love yourself. There comes a point on this journey when you must take the time and stop to find the meaning of your happiness. As painful as it may be to do the work of going back in your mind to the place of the loneliness and pain of your childhood, it is the necessary component to freeing yourself. You deserve to live a life of peace and contentment.

If you want to change and stop complaining, you have to be willing to do what I did: start the process of loving yourself. Begin by admitting that you're unhappy. Admit the reasons for the pain. Dig deep into your hurt and pour it out to yourself over and over again, until you get the pain out of you. Even if you get a new career, find a husband, get a new car, buy a new house, lose weight—whatever you have fooled yourself into believing is the source of your unhappiness—the bottom line is that you don't feel loved.

Hear me on this: as an adult, it is not the responsibility of anyone, not a man, not another woman, and not your children, to make you feel loved. At this point, your parents can't even give it to you because you can't relive your childhood. You can, however, find it for yourself. It will be a process. It will not be easy, but I suspect you're tired of living the way you've been living. I sure was.

For some of you overachievers, you continue to climb that endless ladder of opportunity because you desperately want to matter to the world. "You are enough" if you don't do another thing. If you don't get another promotion, get another degree, or earn another title, you are enough. It is not about the achievement; it's the fact that deep down inside, you're trying to prove something to the world. Maybe you keep fighting the feeling that you are not worthy. You don't want to be the little girl looking at the world through a screen door, never really ever fitting in. Whenever you become disappointed or things don't go your way, feelings of insecurity and insignificance surface. It's a cycle that just continues. You turn around, and you complain about everything. You need to understand and accept that everything you need to fix in your life to make things right lies deep within your own consciousness.

It's time to do some emotional and spiritual work and begin to develop a loving and caring inner adult self. You need to learn to give yourself the attention you need. Complaining has been your way of dealing with it. After admitting to yourself that you need love, you may need to speak to a counselor and get some therapy. Please resist the urge to tell all the people around you what your deep-seated issues are. Your workplace is off limits to your personal therapy sessions. Your spouse may not enjoy hearing your issues either. If speaking with a therapist is not an option, begin to read self-help books on loving yourself. It takes deep reflection and a willingness to search for your truth. Keeping a journal may help you get in touch with your feelings. Praying can be helpful, but it must be honest and real.

There are times you may feel like you blame God for how your life has turned out. Why didn't God prevent the abuse while you were a child? Why didn't God give you better parents? Why couldn't you live a better life growing up? Why was life such a struggle? Why is life a struggle now? If God is all-powerful, why didn't God fix it? These are real questions. I highly recommend you search within yourself for the answers and ask God the questions. God can handle it and loves us no matter how many questions we ask. I realize we have all been told to never question God. I disagree. These questions will likely bring you closer to God if you listen for His responses.

It's when you don't ask the questions that you become disconnected and separated from God. The reality no one wants to speak about is that with so many things going wrong, it may be hard to be in a relationship with a God who doesn't seem to want to help get you where you want to be. You need help and may feel God isn't listening. It's a discovery only you can make. I reconciled my questions to God by choosing to believe that no matter what life brings, God is for my good, and if I can believe and have faith, there are lessons I have to learn and grow from. I know that ultimately things will turn out for my good.

You deserve love. To find the happiness you're looking for, it all starts with your ability to love yourself. After searching for a long time, it feels good just to be whole. If it happened for me, it can happen for you. You just have to want it more than anything else. My prayer for you is that you will take the necessary time to really get to know the real woman God created you to be. Once you get in touch with yourself, you will not complain as much or at all. Remember, you are worthy!

Did you realize all of this is tied to your complaining? Once you accept yourself for who you really are, you will be free. You will understand that you have a great deal to be thankful for, in spite of what you think you do not have. You will want to live a life free of complaining.

YOUR TRUTH

How did this chapter speak to you?

_____

_____

_____

_____

_____

_____

_____

_____

_____

_____

_____

_____

_____

_____

_____

_____

YOUR TRUTH

What is your truth?

_____

_____

_____

_____

_____

_____

_____

_____

_____

_____

_____

_____

_____

_____

_____

_____

YOUR TRUTH

Plan of action to deal with your truth:

_____

_____

_____

_____

_____

_____

_____

_____

_____

_____

_____

_____

_____

_____

_____

_____

_____

CHAPTER
11

Truth to the

 Competitive

Sister

com·pet·i·tive
(kəm-pĕt′ĭ-tĭv)
adjective Of, involving, or determined
by competition: competitive games,
involving or determined by rivalry,
relating to or characterized by an
urge to compete.

> *"It is not necessary to put someone else down
> in order for you to rise."*
> JUDGE PENNY BROWN REYNOLDS

I'm the first to admit I hate being stereotyped in any way, shape, or form. However, I can say without a great deal of reservation that I'm sick and tired of how we treat one another as women. It's shameful, and it's one of the reasons we find ourselves in the state we're in today. When it comes to the treatment of women by some other women, it appears the widely held image of women not getting along with other women may be true. It doesn't make a whole lot of sense because often, women are not comfortable being competitive, yet we seem to have a reputation for being catty and tough with other women. Sometimes we go beyond catty and become cutthroat. It doesn't bring out the best in some women, and it can be absolutely stressful. What's worse is we often run to a man to help mediate a situation between two women. I wish I could shake some women into understanding what they are really doing when they treat other women the way they do.

I acknowledge that the generalization that women are tough on other women is unfortunate and unfair, but from my perspective, it's often true on many levels. I believe that overall, the majority of women treat other women with love and respect. However, a segment of the sisterhood is difficult to deal with and does their best to make life hard for other women. I realize there will be women who will argue that I do a disservice to women by raising these uncomfortable issues. We hide many issues in society and make excuses for everything because we hate discussing uncomfortable matters. I opened this book by sharing that I love women, and I love being a woman. It is because I love us so much that it is necessary to tell the truth about how we handle one another. I am just tired of it. It is so unnecessary. I realize it comes from a place of brokenness, but when are we going to come together? Where is the love? Where is the support?

Make no mistake about it—there are individual sisters who represent the best of womanhood in every respect. These women are not threatened by other women. These women are supportive and encouraging. These women know their place in life and are open and inviting about sharing information. It is a place that lets us believe that we can do anything. They seek to understand and uplift other women. These women are at their best when helping sisters become their best. We need more sisters to make an effort to be supportive and encouraging of other sisters.

Why must be we be difficult in our treatment of each other? One of my soul-saving sayings is *God has given an abundance of resources, and because of that abundance, there is enough to go around for everyone who wants it.* Competitive, ruthless women don't completely understand that concept. I want the competitive sister to understand there is enough in the universe for me to do well and for you do as well or even better. What I have in life has no bearing on what you receive or achieve. It is a principle I live by. Free yourself by operating in your own gifts and talents. Stop looking over your shoulders to see what someone else has. Rejoice in someone else's success.

Competition does not always bring out the best in women. Many women believe that they must compete with other women, when the truth is we are stronger when we connect and work together. Your gifts are not my gifts, and your gifts cannot cancel out my gifts—nor mine yours. There is truly enough of everything we could want or need in the world for everyone. There is truly enough for everyone.

Some women act the way they do because they are afraid someone will "find out who they really are." You don't own what you have, and you are living as though someone can come and take it away. It may be because others around you have a college degree, more years of experience, or better communication skills. Whatever your insecurity is, get over it. It's causing you to do and say things that are unbecoming of you and unprofessional in some cases.

It's a sad truth that we all know women who seek to find fault in other women, particularly attractive, strong, self-confident women, because they are threatened and have a poor self-image of themselves. Instead of looking inside themselves to deal with their issues, they manifest a spirit of jealousy, envy, mistrust, and fear on other women. The hostile competition masks deep feelings of insecurity. It breaks my heart when I have to deal with one of these women in business. They seem to be drawn to me only to get enough information about me to determine my many faults so they can walk away feeling good about themselves. They feel better somehow by knowing I have flaws. They leave, but only after doing anything they can to attempt to hold me back. It's a power they don't own, and everything they attempt to take from me inevitably comes to me. No one has power over another person unless it is given to them. You take away their power, and you will be able to see how tiny these kinds of women are.

Too many women are playing a role of what they think they should be. They merely emulate other women. There's nothing original about them. They take someone's hairstyle, makeup, or mannerisms. They may do something as drastic as driving the same make of car. They have no brand of their own. You think of them, and they may remind you of someone, but they have no identity of their own. In some cases, they are identified by what they do for a living. They use their position and power to validate themselves and make their way up the ladder of success by making certain they are the only one in the room.

There is absolutely nothing wrong with competition. Men have mastered it. This is one of the reasons women make less money than do men. Men learned at early ages the value of competition. While children, boys were competing in sports, and we were inside the house playing with our dolls, having tea parties, and learning the importance of friendship and teamwork. Boys were made to feel confident and encouraged to compete. Women are often ill-equipped to deal with true competition.

For many of us, competition between females becomes personal. It is unsettling and disconcerting to have to compete. Although I see it as merely an opportunity to utilize my gifts and talents, those who were not raised to compete in a healthy way make it their priority to see that the other person fails. Feeling and hoping failure will occur to someone else is never healthy. What you are suggesting is that for you to rise, someone else has to fall. It is a stressful and unhappy way of thinking. You focus too much on others instead of fulfilling your true potential. In competition, it shouldn't be about anyone falling down. Someone should not have to be marginalized or completely eliminated for you to be successful. As twisted as it sounds, it's happening every day. Many women refuse to believe they have the strength and know-how to compete without hurting someone else.

I strongly advise you to search deep within yourself to determine the kind of woman you want to be. Change if you need to change, but don't be the sister who has to hurt another sister to feel good. We love to build people up in order to tear them down. It will be important for you to begin to feel confident about who you have become. If you're not satisfied with your life, change it. The better you feel about yourself, the less threatened you will feel by other women.

Determine how you can work with another woman rather than against her. Don't be like a woman I recently met. She did her best to get close to me. She tried hard to pretend she wanted to be friends. I later learned she was doing everything she could behind my back to hurt me. I wasn't surprised by her actions because I've learned to spot these lost souls. She constantly complimented me every chance she got. She asked me a lot of questions about what was going on in my life and rarely wanted to talk about her life. She was scoping me out. Because I'm transparent, she began to feel that she was better than me because of the circumstances of my birth. She actually had the nerve to tell me she was sad for me. I had to reassure her that I had a wonderful life, and that the story has a happy ending. As time passed, she realized I wasn't as damaged by the dramatic events of my childhood as she thought I was, and she eventually disappeared. She came to get what she wanted, and she left. She realized she couldn't compete with me, so she took her ball and played with someone else. I still don't understand what she wanted. What were we competing for? It was clear she was not comfortable with herself. I would have given her anything she asked for if I could, but she didn't have the ability to trust that I was not competing with her for anything.

I am a firm believer that we are blessed merely so we can be a blessing to others. Your success should be used to help other people. You are not there just for you to walk around with the title. You have something to share. Giving back or inspiring others provides a completeness that can only be found by serving others. The door of opportunity was opened for you, and you have an obligation to open it for others. Don't be afraid. What God has for you, no one can take from you. Open up your heart and care about others.

Finally, competition does not have to be harmful and hurtful. Allow it to motivate you to be the best person you can be. Don't allow yourself to be stressed by competition. Don't think of what others are doing; just do the best you can do. There is only one you. No one can do what you do. They may perform a task, but they can't do it in the exact way that you do. You can be confident that you are uniquely situated to be right where you are. If you want more, go out and get it for yourself. You don't have to hurt anyone else in the process. Don't allow yourself to be forced to play by the rules of an insecure person. Sister girl, just be you. You will do well when you do you. The deoxyribonucleic acid, your DNA, makes you unique. You have distinctive characteristics that make you who you are. Embrace your authentic self. You will not be stressed, and you will realize that you do not have to put anyone down for your light to shine.

To those "mean girls" who grew up to be "mean women": Your childish, insecure, passive-aggressive behavior has been found out. It is unnecessary and unbecoming. There is nothing to fear. There is room at the table of opportunity for all of us. Pull up a chair and have a seat.

YOUR TRUTH

How did this chapter speak to you?

_____

_____

_____

_____

_____

_____

_____

_____

_____

_____

_____

_____

_____

_____

_____

_____

_____

YOUR TRUTH

What is your truth?

_____

_____

_____

_____

_____

_____

_____

_____

_____

_____

_____

_____

_____

_____

_____

YOUR TRUTH

Plan of action to deal with your truth:

_____

_____

_____

_____

_____

_____

_____

_____

_____

_____

_____

_____

_____

_____

_____

_____

_____

13

Truth to the

Depressed

Sister

de·pres·sion

[diˈpreSHən]

noun Severe despondency and dejection, typically felt over a period of time and accompanied by feelings of hopelessness and inadequacy.

"Don't wait around for other people to be happy for you.
Any happiness you get you've got to make it for yourself."
ALICE WALKER

It's time to remove the mask. We hate discussing depression or any mental health issues. I am not an expert in this area, so my advice is simply for you to understand that you do not have to live with depression. Yes, it is a disease. Don't allow others to make you feel like you should be able to snap out of it and just move on. It's more complicated than that. Living a life with depression is not easy. As hard as you may try, it's hard to get out of it on your own.

I want those suffering from depression to know they are not alone. Help is available. I want to remove the shame associated with depression by lifting the veil of secrecy that prevents women from seeking the help they need. For those who are close to anyone who is depressed, please don't minimize what they're going through. Although you may think there is any easy fix, whoever is dealing with depression can't just read a book or pray their way out of depression. What they need from you is a nonjudgmental listening ear. Care about them, and try to educate yourself on the disease.

Through the years, I've encountered both friends and family members who suffer from depression. I'm like that girlfriend who tells you what no one else will, something we all need. I want to let you know you don't have to pretend anymore. You don't have to lie and put on a happy face when deep down inside you are in pain. That's what real girlfriends do for each other. We get you to see the truth, but we do it in love because we care.

If you're someone who occasionally feels the blues, you may not be depressed. Bad feelings are completely normal, and they may come and go. Sometimes they may last for a couple of days. When it's cloudy and dreary, and the sun doesn't shine, people get the blues. Most of us have, at some point on our journey, short periods where we feel sad.

Clinical depression is a mood disorder that interferes with your life for an extended period of time. Your body feels heavy, and it takes so much out of you to do little things. Like so many statistics, women are diagnosed with depression more often than men are. What is heartbreaking is that most often, women fail to seek treatment.

These women live with a tremendous darkness and heaviness. They feel as though nothing can be done to help them. If we're going to be honest about it, there's a stigma about mental health disorders in our society. Therefore, I realize it may not be easy to admit that you have a problem.

There is a way to a better life for you. Women have mastered how to pretend they are doing well. We dress up on the outside, we continue to care for our children, and we go into our workplace, all while attempting to mask the depression. The people around you may suspect it because you may be irritable most of the time, or you lack energy, or you may even have difficulty concentrating. The folks who live with you may notice you have trouble sleeping, you are avoiding activities, and you stop doing the things that previously brought you joy and pleasure. You have a spirit of deep unhappiness and pain. They can only see what they observe; they may not know you have feelings of worthlessness, self-hate, and guilt. They likely don't know you may feel hopeless or helpless, and you have repeated thoughts of death and suicide.

You have managed to keep many of your symptoms a secret. For example, if you have a significant change in appetite that has led to rapid weight gain or loss, you are skilled at attributing it to an unrelated issue. Nevertheless, you have many of the symptoms, yet believe you are experiencing them alone.

You are depressed. There are countless causes for your depression. For one, I know it runs in families. Your depression could have been triggered by something stressful or an unhappy event in your life. The death of a loved one, getting divorced, losing your job, retiring from a career and feeling that your life no longer matters—all of these—can certainly cause a woman to be depressed. It may be a combination of many things. I know when you isolate yourself, it can compound these depressed feelings.

The bottom line is that no matter the reason, there is help for you. Eventually, your depression will affect your work and your family life. If it hasn't happened already, your physical health will start to decline. It can cause high blood pressure, pains, headaches, and all kinds of physical issues. I want you to live and not die. Depression destroys. You deserve to live. This doesn't mean you merely survive; you deserve to get up every morning to face a life of meaning.

You might be saying there is absolutely nothing wrong with being sad. Life is a series of ups and downs. Although you may not call it depression, you know in your heart that something is wrong. I want you to know that you don't have to keep it a secret. You're not crazy; you're actually in pain. It's important for you to know you are not alone.

There are women like Terrie M. Williams, who bravely

wrote a book entitled *Black Pain: It Just Looks Like We're Not Hurting*, which deals with the issue of depression. I highly recommend you read this book. I know Terrie personally, and she is an incredibly gifted woman. When I read her story, I was stunned. I never would have thought she battled with depression. She is a licensed clinical social worker. However, I know her from The Terrie Williams Agency, as she is a public relations advisor to celebrities. She is strong and accomplished. Her book opened my eyes to the issue of depression for many others. She writes: "My book is not a self-help manual, because there is no "self-help" for depression—if you're suffering from something you can pull yourself out of by willpower or your bootstraps, it's not depression."

Although I have experienced the blues from time to time, now I understand that occasionally feeling sad is not the same as being depressed. I always found a way to come out of it. Depression is not a quick fix where you can come out of it in an instant. Mental health should no longer be a hush-hush issue. It's time to remove the shame associated with it. It's time to get real. It's not about labels, but about ending a cycle of pain. Freeing you to a life free from the deep-seated hurt called depression.

There is a road to recovery. Like anything, it will require you to take action. You can't wish it away. You can't hope it away. I realize that when you are depressed, asking you to take action is not an easy thing to ask you to do. But, I never said it would be easy. I believe it requires you to focus on setting a goal. It doesn't have to be anything on a large scale. If you go out and walk or pick up the telephone and call a friend, this could be your first step. You should share with someone you can trust. If you tell someone about what you are feeling, you're not weak, and you're not a burden. You just need support to get started.

I am certain there is some aspect of your life that brings you joy. Try to fight through the heaviness and spend time doing things that make you smile, even if briefly. If you do it enough, it might just give you the courage to move forward. You have to believe you deserve a better life. If your depression is caused because of another person, try not to blame yourself. No one is perfect, and you don't have to do everything right. We all make mistakes, but you are important in this world, and you need to stop putting yourself down.

It may be hard to believe it, but what you are feeling is temporary. Life does get better with time. If you could just hold on and get the help you need, there is life on the other side of the darkness you feel.

Begin to care for yourself. If you've let yourself go, get out and get your hair done. You have to do something that stops the "sameness" of the situation. Avoiding these things will only pull you down further and further. You are jeopardizing your health, and for what? I hated exercising. There came a point in my life when I decided I was important enough to spend forty-five minutes, three to four days a week taking care of my body. I don't know if you know it or not, but exercise is an antidepressant.

One of the important pieces of advice I can give you is to seek help from a professional licensed therapist. They are trained to deal with depression. They will listen and care for you. Medication, often combined with therapy, is also available and helps you find the light at the end of the tunnel.

If no one on this earth has ever expressed to you that they care, I want you to know I do care. I care that you are in pain. This advice was the hardest to write because I didn't want to say the wrong thing. I wanted to speak from my heart.

I have never been depressed. I have had the blues, but not depression. I prayed so that I would be able to speak to your issue based on what I have experienced from being a support to my family members and my church members who have shared this kind of pain. I don't have the magic potion to fix you. The only thing I know to do is to make you aware of your options, give you a few suggestions, and encourage you to talk about your feelings to someone who cares. You need someone who will listen and not judge you. From what I have read, one conquers depression one day at a time and one step at a time. I hope reading this leaves you feeling better and knowing that you have already made the first step.

YOUR TRUTH

How did this chapter speak to you?

_____

_____

_____

_____

_____

_____

_____

_____

_____

_____

_____

_____

_____

_____

_____

_____

_____

_____

YOUR TRUTH

What is your truth?

_____

_____

_____

_____

_____

_____

_____

_____

_____

_____

_____

_____

_____

_____

_____

_____

YOUR TRUTH

Plan of action to deal with your truth:

_____

_____

_____

_____

_____

_____

_____

_____

_____

_____

_____

_____

_____

_____

CHAPTER

14

Truth to the

Sister

di·vorce
/dəˈvôrs/
verb To legally dissolve one's marriage with (someone).

*"Whatever is bringing you down, get rid of it.
Because you'll find that when you're free your
true self comes out."*
TINA TURNER

Getting divorced is one of the most difficult things a woman could do in this world. There is no such thing as an easy divorce. I certainly have had my share. It is almost always an emotionally trying experience. I don't care how common it has become (one out of every two marriages will end in divorce); divorce, for all women, is difficult and draining. It represents the ending of your marriage. In many instances, women feel personally responsible for what is deemed a major failure in life.

I want to use this opportunity to speak to three different sisters in the divorce phase: those who are contemplating divorce, those who are in the middle of it, and those who are on the other side. There are things I wish someone had told me before I went through the process. Certainly, the no-fault divorce has helped with the drama of the process, but it is never painless.

Those Who Are Contemplating Divorce

You may be contemplating divorce and find yourself in a lonely place. After all, who wants to get a divorce? You didn't get married believing that you would have to end your marriage. I've already said how hard it is. It's likely that by the time you feel you're ready to take the leap, the marriage has been gone for long time.

We marry for keeps. We marry because of love. Our dream was to find a life partner whom we could spend our lives with. We had such hopes and dreams in the beginning, but over the course of time, our dream became a nightmare. You may be going over and over again in your mind what else can be done to save the marriage. What you must understand as you contemplate whether to end the marriage is whether both of you are asking the same questions. Does he care that the marriage is on the rocks? Does he care that you may be walking away? A marriage takes two people committed to the hard work of being married. You can't want the marriage to work while your partner could care less. This is the time to walk away from your fantasy and deal with the reality of who this person really is to you.

You will never feel valued if you are not respected and appreciated. My soul-saving saying is, *You can't expect respect if you don't give it.* Some women believe this issue is one-sided. You can't cuss him out routinely, demean him, or in some cases, emasculate him and not expect him to respond negatively. Men, like women, just want to be loved and respected. What you have to remember is respect is a two-way street.

If you've been the only one giving, and you've been getting nothing in return, problems will always arise. Have you tried communicating and letting him know you're unhappy? Remember, you don't want to play the blaming game, but you should express your feelings about the marriage in specific terms. Is he willing to sit down and talk? Is he willing to speak with a third party in a counseling session?

If you want your marriage to last, I recommend you fight

for it. But, he has to want it, too. This is something you can't want by yourself. Sure you can stay, but if you're contemplating divorce, it is likely that you're not happy. In fact, you may be miserable. You want to live in peace and share your days in a marriage that is not perfect, but one you both are willing to work at every day. You just want a chance at happiness. You deserve it, and you need to search in your heart what is right for you.

Remember, you can't control how others treat you, but you can control how you treat others and respond to them. During this time, you have shown him what you will and what you will not tolerate. You have given this person permission to treat you the way you're being treated. I'm not putting the responsibility on you, but the truth is the truth. Your husband cannot do to you what you don't allow him to do. Your partner knows what he can get away with.

Before you walk away, ask yourself if you've done everything you can do. Have you given all you can give? Try to determine when and why you think things took a turn for the worse. Search deep within and focus not on the negative aspects of the marriage, but determine what good is left.

Abuse must be a deal-breaker. People may not agree with me on this, but I know in my heart that no one has the right to abuse another person. You are not your husband's property—you are a life partner. If you find yourself in an abusive marriage, you need to get out of it. If he hit you once, he will hit you again.

If he is verbally abusive, the abuse will kill your spirit. The abuser is in deep pain. You can't love him out of it. You get away from the abuse before it ends up killing you. You will either be dead, or the verbal abuse can wear you down so much with stress that I believe is equal to any punch. The bruises may heal over time, but verbal abuse stays in your head and is replayed over and over again. It stays in your soul, and it breaks your heart. Your self-esteem is taken away, and you lose your self-worth. If you are not careful, it is passed down to your children. Sister, if you are in an abusive situation, somehow get a plan of escape together to leave as fast as you can. It will not change. His lies and manipulation may vary from time to time as he tells you how sorry he is and blames you for what he is doing to you or your children. Abuse is a deal-breaker. You are worth much more. Get out!

If you are ready to proceed, it may be cheaper to attempt to handle the divorce yourself. I suggest this option only if he agrees not to hire a lawyer, you both consent to a no-fault divorce, you have no children, you have been married only a short period of time, and you have little to no property to divide. However, if any of these criteria does not apply, hire a lawyer. It doesn't matter what your soon-to-be ex says to you. You need someone who is experienced in this area of the law and who will fight for your rights.

I want to turn the tables a bit and speak to the sister whose spouse is contemplating divorce, or you've been served with papers, and you don't want him to leave. You may have been a faithful wife, and now you've been blindsided by this news. Any kind of rejection is never easy.

Perhaps he's come to you and said he's not happy in the marriage and wants a divorce. With men, there's always something behind the words you hear. They may not go into detail, but there's something deeper. Men are not naturally verbal anyway, but you better believe me, by the time he's said it to you, he's been thinking about it for a while.

There are countless reasons men seek divorce. I have counseled many marriages in the past, and the reasons men give for wanting to leave range from the man feeling that his wife has let herself go and doesn't take care of herself, she's put on weight, or she has stopped dressing sexy. Some men have said that over time they felt like they were married to their mother and not a woman they could have fun with. Many men hated being nagged and/or disrespected. They never felt like the king of their castle. As a man, they wanted to care for their family but they rarely were given the opportunity to do it. Obviously, when children are involved, whether from a previous marriage or the current one, it puts a strain on the relationship. Whether it was disagreements over how to raise the children or blended family drama, the issues became too much to take.

I never had one instance where the husband confessed to having another woman on the side. They spoke in terms of feeling neglected and underappreciated. I don't know if another woman is in the background of your situation, and that's why he wants out. But, I always believe that if the wife is honest with herself, her spirit will likely tell her if someone else may have entered the picture. Many times if you have to ask the question, you already know the answer. Maybe he realizes he doesn't want to be married, and it's not about another woman. There could be a hundred reasons why your partner may be contemplating divorce. The bottom line is that he is obviously unhappy.

If you love him, and you believe his contemplation is an outcry to save the marriage, by all means use this opportunity as a second chance. Try counseling. Get to the bottom of the disconnection or the reason he wants to leave you. Make certain this doesn't become a one-sided exploration. Remember what I said earlier: marriage takes two. Fault is not one dimensional.

What happens when you're the one who has been served with the papers? In fact, you don't want a divorce, and he's leaving you. Again, I can't say it enough, rejection isn't easy. It can be downright painful, particularly when you felt abandoned as a child, and you're now dealing with old wounds coupled with this fresh hurt. If you have received the papers, that means he spent time thinking about it, researching an attorney, meeting with the attorney, giving the attorney a retainer, reviewing the paper work, signing the paper work, and having the documents signed—I think you're starting to get the picture. By the time you're served, he's made up his mind. You can be as hurt as you want to be, but he's ready to let you and the marriage go to start his life in another direction.

Naturally, you're going to be upset. In fact, that's an understatement. Rejection hurts. Take time to process what is going on. If you're able to take a few days away from work, I highly recommend you do so. Having to put on a happy face at work while your life is falling apart only adds to the stress of it all. Be careful not to lock yourself away. You don't want this to lead to depression. Don't use this as a way of isolating yourself from others. After you have begun to process it for yourself, get to someone you can trust, like a close friend or relative. Do not talk to your co-workers or your supervisors about this. I don't care how close you are to them. You will be vulnerable and may give them details they don't need to hear. Keep your personal and work lives separate.

For God's sake, stay off social media. All I see on Facebook is people airing their dirty laundry. Whatever you put on the Internet will always be there. Besides, it's not the place to air your grievances. This is a private matter, and it's dealing with your life. Manage it with care and dignity. No matter how bad you feel, don't write about it online. The quicker you can come to terms with this, the better. You will grieve like any loss, but life will go on. The quicker you accept this rejection and the situation, the easier it will be for you to move on.

Try not to take it personally and allow it to strip away your womanhood. I know you may ask the question, how can you not take it personally, but it is about him and what he's dealing with. He may believe it is your fault, but that doesn't make it so. He made a decision and was selfish in doing so. If you received the papers without any warning, he showed you what he thinks of you. He is rejecting what didn't work for him, but you can't allow this to take away the essence of who you are.

This may be a good time to do something for you. After you retain the services of a good lawyer, get everything you are due, and make certain to care for your children's emotional well-being, do something that resets your life's course. Write a book, start exercising, or go on a trip. I don't recommend getting involved in another relationship. Too soon. I'm talking about doing something fun and exciting that will help you keep your mind off this devastating news. You can't allow his decision to stop your life. Life is about picking up the pieces and moving on. This will not be the last pain you deal with, but you will become stronger each time. This is a great opportunity to do some soul searching about what you want out of your life. You will become stronger. You will survive. This is temporary, and your future holds a lifetime of wonderful things yet to come.

Sisters Who Are In the Middle of It

While you find yourself in the middle of the divorce, you will be dealing with issues you never expected. By now you should have good legal representation and may be living separately. I say *may* because some spouses have decided to live under one roof until the divorce is settled. This is a difficult situation to say the least. The lawyer deals with everything from property issues, spousal support, child support, and child custody and visitation. It can become exhausting and stressful. You are no longer dealing with that handsome man who walked down the aisle with you, made love to you, sat in church with you, and may be the father of your children. You are dealing with a man who was raised to compete. Males learned it in childhood, while we hate competing. They are trained to want to win. We want fairness. This is why you retain expert legal counsel. You allow your lawyer to fight for your rights. You deserve to be treated fairly.

My big concern with you is that you don't allow yourself to give in to demands that will affect your life in the future. Don't get so worn down in the process that you throw in the towel to get the divorce done. Don't allow yourself to be so beaten down you forget you will likely be the primary caregiver for your children, and you need to be able to provide for them. The bottom line is to allow your lawyer to work on your behalf. Don't get pulled in to allowing your spouse to tear you down while you are ending the marriage. If it's over, it's over. If you felt you could deal with him, you would still be married. He no longer sees you as his wife, and your spouse is only looking out for what's best for him.

Be prepared for the people around you, including friends and relatives, to change with you, and in some instances, they will pick a side. Many of your married girlfriends will no longer want to hang out with you because you will be single, and they don't want you around their husbands. Yes, that's crazy and ridiculous, but it happens. I just don't want you to be caught off guard and not be ready for how you may be treated.

I don't know if you and your spouse attend the same church, but after the divorce, I doubt if both of you will continue to worship together. The person who remains is the one who had more invested in the church. You may be the one who sings in the choir or teaches Sunday school. The decision to stay or leave will evolve. Your church can be a wonderful source of support. However, if he is in leadership at the church and is active, you may feel that you are not comfortable seeing him every Sunday. I'm not suggesting you leave your church, but for your peace of mind, you may have to find another place to worship so you can start your life over. Pray to God about it, allow time to show you how it feels, and make the decision in time. The decision is yours to make, and don't allow yourself to be bullied by the church folk who are not short on opinions and judgment. Any decision you make with regard to your spiritual life with God is yours to make. Being free and liberated means you get to decide how and where you will commune with God.

Try not to let people shame you, particularly those little pretending women who volunteer at your kid's school. The ones who act like they have perfect marriages and perfect husbands. They may seem to have it all together, but there is no such thing as a perfect marriage. Don't let them put a scarlet letter on your chest and throw you out of the clique because you're going through a divorce. That's why you shouldn't be telling everyone your business. If they should ask, you just let them know you guys are no longer together. It's no one's business about the details of why you are going through your divorce. Please don't feel compelled to fill in the blanks.

Take time to be there for the children. Don't speak negatively about your soon-to-be ex-husband. Do your best to make certain the children don't blame themselves. Although you and I know they had nothing to do with it, children often feel guilt or blame themselves. Don't you carry guilt over it. Life is not always fair. You do the best you can. In the long run, it's better that they be in a house with happiness and joy and not one where they see parents who either hate each other or who rarely, if ever, demonstrate love. You hate that they have to go through this, but it is what it is. Just remember to allow them to express their feelings, allow them to spend time with their father, and don't speak ill of him in their presence. They definitely don't need to hear the details of the divorce process. Just continue to give them good memories and let them be kids. If they ask you a question, always be honest with them. Love them and nurture them and be their mother. Your daughters are not your confidants or girlfriends, and your sons should not replace your man. They need a mother who is strong and provides a safe environment for them to grown and thrive. Remember, it's not just about you when you have children.

Don't wait until the divorce is finalized before developing a life plan. Start putting pieces in place for this next season of yourself.

Those Who Are on the Other Side of Divorce

After the divorce is over, go on with your life. Starting over can make you nervous, but it can be exciting. You will be vulnerable, so be careful jumping into new relationships. Life after divorce is about rebuilding and redefining yourself.

You need to pick yourself up, but understand you are dealing with the death of a marriage. Allow yourself a period to mourn the loss. Loss is loss, no matter the circumstances. Your emotions are those of grief. Take the time to heal while evaluating the relationship's mistakes.

Learn to work through your feelings. Do some reading about how to get through it. Share your feelings with a trusted person or professional. It takes time to get over the loss of a marriage. You have to work through a number of emotions. The best advice I can give from my personal experience is to keep looking forward to the future. Use the past only for the purpose of gaining lessons needing to be learned. I never go back and allow the pain from the past to occupy my reality. It does no good. I had to learn to live in the now and find a place of contentment.

As you move on to your new beginning, whatever you do, don't carry the baggage from the old marriage into your brand-new life. Do not allow this divorce to define you. Reflect on who you are. Identify your issues. You can't deal with something until you know what it is. Try to understand who you really are and accept who you are. Create a reality that works for you. You were on a journey that required you to share. You may have felt that marriage provided you with a safety net, and now the net is gone. Force yourself to make the adjustment and face your new reality—your new normal.

Cut ties. Let him go. Let that particular dream go. If you have kids, you must deal with him, but immediately after the divorce, he can't be your friend. In years to come, you will be cordial for the sake of the kids, but you and he will not be vacationing or spending time on the phone talking. You need a fresh start. Take a break from interacting with the person. You maintain your power when you take the lead in cutting the cords. You must reclaim your life and your power. It is important to become aware of how you want to shape your future. Do you want to continue to live in the same area? Do you want to live in the same state? It's time to go back to school or start a business. Make this next season of your life a season about you.

Whatever you do, stay positive and focused. No one gets to define your life for you. The marriage is over, but your life is not. Look around and examine all the good things around you and determine how to make them better. Create a plan. See yourself every day as the person who you wanted to grow up to be. Become that person by not just dreaming about her, but by taking the necessary steps to becoming her. Take flight, and don't be afraid.

YOUR TRUTH

How did this chapter speak to you?

_____

_____

_____

_____

_____

_____

_____

_____

_____

_____

_____

_____

_____

_____

_____

_____

_____

YOUR TRUTH

What is your truth?

_____

_____

_____

_____

_____

_____

_____

_____

_____

_____

_____

_____

_____

_____

_____

_____

_____

YOUR TRUTH

Plan of action to deal with your truth:

_____

_____

_____

_____

_____

_____

_____

_____

_____

_____

_____

_____

_____

_____

_____

_____

CHAPTER

15

Truth to the

Sister

en·tre·pre·neur
/ˌäntrəprəˈnər/
noun A person who organizes and
operates a business or businesses,
taking on greater than normal financial risks in order to do so.

"Success doesn't come to you. You go to it."
Marva Collins

Everywhere I turn, I hear from women that they dream of being an entrepreneur. It became such an outcry that I started a business consulting firm to assistant people who wanted to jump into the world of owning a small business. As a business owner myself, I want you to know that the independence that comes from owning your own business gives you a freedom only a few people can hope for. The true gratification comes when you create a business that is in alignment with your life's purpose and passion.

Passion, without question, is the fuel for the commitment needed to start and grow a business, but passion isn't enough to make your business a success. It becomes clear after you start the process that it takes a great deal of energy and dedication to make your dream a reality.

I will repeat this over and over: starting a business and growing it is not easy. It takes a great deal of work including long hours, problem-solving abilities, capital, good people working with you, and a lot of good luck. You can talk to hundreds of entrepreneurs, and everyone has their own advice. You have to do what works best for you. Do your homework and, above all, stay focused and keep a good attitude. For me, attitude trumps experience any day.

A key reminder is not to expect the journey to be a straight path. Isn't that true with life in general? There will be many twists and turns. You can develop a business plan and find yourself, based on the market and the need, going in different directions. Once you define your value and stay true to your mission, you will become flexible enough to make the necessary adjustments and moves. Many of the changes that evolve in business will be adaptable and usually will work out for your good. Being rigid in life and in business makes matters difficult. You have to learn to roll with the punches. Successful people are those who see an opportunity at every turn, even if the turn is not what was planned or expected.

Remember, although you get to do things your way, you still need a set of principles and standards to live by. Decisions are made more easily when you have developed a set of values before you even get started. Be honest and work with integrity. Treat people right and be respectful. Always keep your word, and do what you say you will do. If something happens that you can't fix on your own, reach out to the person and make him or her aware of any necessary changes. Always be willing to admit when you are wrong and to apologize. Be on time for meetings, and care more about your company than anyone else does. These are a few of my business standards. They are not hard to meet because they are in line with who I am and my practice in life.

It is important to be willing to take the first step. Enough cannot be said about doing what you love doing. It will be hard to become successful if you are stuck in a business you hate. When you love what you do, it's likely you would be willing to do it for free. However, the point of the business is that you make money and, hopefully, lots of it.

Everyone has gifts and talents. Whatever your gifts are, the world will make room for them. There can be no failure if you are operating in your gifts. Enjoying what you do and walking in your passion are the prerequisites for operating a successful business. Fall madly in love with your calling. Even if people don't believe in your ideas and your concepts, you need to be positive and optimistic. You can't afford to get stuck in disappointment. It is a waste of time anyway. You have to believe in you and what your abilities are.

Confidence is required. You should not make a move until you have done your homework and research about the business you are interested in starting. Don't seek lessons just from those who have been successful; the greatest lessons may come from those who tried and couldn't make it work. They are able to share the pitfalls and can get you prepared for the unknown. I'm always interested in hearing both sides of the story. You will face many problems as a business owner, and you have to develop the ability to solve problems. You don't have to learn everything on the job. You can get the inside information by interacting with people who will candidly tell you the truth and not try to sugarcoat it.

There is a soul-saving saying that I firmly believe: *How you start off is how you will finish.* This saying applies to everything in life. In fact, I use it over and over again in other chapters. If you start out unorganized with little commitment, you will likely end up plagued with all the consequences of being unorganized. Getting a business started is difficult because you are going into uncharted territory. It isn't impossible because people are doing it every day. It's filled with extreme ups and downs. You just have to be educated and prepared. Also, you have to make sure you have an entrepreneurial spirit. There is a mindset you must have to own a business. You have to be willing to go the distance because results take time. Be persistent. It is a race of endurance and patience.

You also need to be a risk taker. You need to be a

dreamer—a big dreamer. You need to understand you will work far harder in your business than you ever did on any job. I could go on and on.

I learned so many lessons along the way, as I have been an entrepreneur for a decade. When I look back even to my childhood, I have always had an adventurous spirit. I yearn to fulfill my gifts. I hate feeling boxed in and limited. I don't believe in ceilings. I must be able to fly in everything I do. The good part is that if I didn't have my head in the clouds with my dreams, I never would have made the leaps I've made. Many people warned me not to do this or that, but there was something within me yearning to be free. I knew it would be hard, but I didn't realize how hard. Overall, I have no regrets because it did give me the freedom I was searching for. Most people who own businesses will likely tell you that they have few regrets, if any, after several years.

Let's begin at the beginning. Remember, all of my advice is my truth. It comes as a result of my experiences along my journey. I am a different kind of person. I go into anything that I do believing that it can happen. My ability to see success is why I feel free. The freedom comes from being able to wake up every day and see a thread of what I was created to do running through some aspect of my work. There's nothing like it.

Operating in your passion gives you the drive and the commitment to keep going when the going gets tough. It keeps you smiling when you're working nonstop. It keeps you connected to God because you recognize the gift you have been given, while so many people are stuck in jobs and careers they hate. Operating in your passion is the first step. The financial blessings that come are the added bonus for your labor. If your focus is on fulfilling your destiny, the money will follow. You never have to chase it or even worry about it.

One of my weaknesses is my inability to select the right people to work with me. It had been my problem for years. I usually have to go through a number of people to get it right. I wanted so badly to see the good and the potential in the people whom I hired or worked with that I often overlooked the obvious problems staring me in the face. I kept feeling like I had the ability to bring out the best in them. In business, you don't have time to hire people you spend half of your time mentoring. These relationships were all-consuming and often a weight around my neck. These people seemed to find me and wanted to work with me. They were sucking all my energy because they always had a non-business-related issue I had to hear about.

I am doing better in that department. I have become more selective. I have come to realize that it was the only area in my life where I didn't listen to my intuition. Every time I go against that little voice inside me, I tend to not make the best decisions. People today are often hard to figure out. They lie on resumes and pretend to be something they are not. Because I love giving people a chance, an opportunity to grow, it can be challenging trying to find the best people to work with me.

This is why my next bit of advice is so important. Remember, as with everything in life, surround yourself with the people who believe in you and your vision as much as you believe it. Negativity will get you nowhere. People often project on you their fears and doubts. To take a risk, you have to be willing to lose something. Otherwise, you're not taking a risk. The greater the potential loss, the greater the risk. You need a support system that gives clear advice. Now I only surround myself with people who have the energy. My team has to believe in my vision as much as I do. It is not just about hiring people who are experienced and knowledgeable, it is about surrounding yourself with individuals who focus on how to make your ideas and dreams happen. Who wants to work with people who begin their analysis with why something will not work? On the other hand, you need people around you who don't just tell you what you want to hear. They are thoughtful, critical thinkers. They should want you to succeed. If they are not on Team Penny, I don't want them in my space.

When I came up with the vision for the *SisterTalk* conference, I spoke with a number of people, seeking their assistance. I went to people who loved me dearly, and I was confident they had my back. I had confidence in them because they had been working with me on other projects associated with the foundation. I shared with them that God had given me a vision to have a conference, and I decided it would be in a few months. Everyone I talked to had the same reaction. They thought it was a great idea but felt that I didn't have enough time to pull it off. They told me of other events that were going on during the same time. I understood many of their points, but because the vision was mine, I had already processed much of what they shared. God told me it would be a success.

It didn't take me long to figure out that although they felt it was a great idea, and they wanted to help me, they didn't want to invest the time to make it come to fruition. I was not deterred. My husband kept saying he felt it was a great idea, and I should proceed. After a dozen or so people told me that they couldn't or wouldn't be able to help, I brought it up to a young lady I had mentored for years. She told me she would be there for me and, together, we could make it happen. After my conversation with her, I brought the idea to some of the women of my church, and they took the ball and ran with it. It was important that I surrounded myself with people who immersed themselves in my vision. The others eventually assisted, but only after they saw the reality of the conference brought to life.

In hindsight, I respect all the people who cautioned me because I believe in my heart they didn't want me to fail. They were honest about what they couldn't do. It was a great lesson that I learned in business. Keep only positive people around you when you are giving birth to a dream. You are too fragile in your decision-making to have to hear the voices of naysayers, especially when trying to execute something greater than yourself. At the end of the day, your name and reputation is on the line anyway, so you need to do what is best for you.

I realized that although they were supportive of me, they couldn't see what I could see. They were being practical and sharing their limitations. I am glad they eventually came on board, however, since I don't know what I would have done on the day of the event without them. Little do they know that they were almost persuasive, and I came close to not moving forward. But, there was something inside me, that little girl who enjoyed flying, and I listened to her.

I proceeded because I was operating with a vision and a purpose. Somehow, the disappointing events prepared me to be motivated enough to take the big leap. I had been mistreated by women who looked like me. We were supposed to be sisters, not because I knew them, nor were we friends, but because we were women, and that was supposed to mean something. It was heartbreaking on many levels. I realized that I had to do something. *SisterTalk* was born out of several injustices against me by women who felt threatened by me. I underestimated the power of some women wanting to be the "only one." They did everything in their influence to block my efforts.

I had to reclaim my power and teach other women that there was a better way. Hence, the creation of the *SisterTalk* conference. From those painful experiences came what will be an integral part of my legacy. It is amazing the way God works. But for those women who did me wrong, I never would have created the conference that continues to draw thousands of women from all over the country. I am still amazed by the whole thing.

Once you take one leap, taking risks become easier. All those people through the years who told me what I could not do served as a crucial part of the master plan in my life. The naysayers helped me know how much I really wanted what I was striving for. I don't like people underestimating my abilities. I see it as a challenge. I always manage to rise above their doubt because I know that when you have faith, there can be no doubt. I believe in me, and no matter what anyone tries to do to block me, I always find a way.

I tell this story for one reason and one reason only—I want you to know there will be times on your journey when you will have to walk alone with your vision. For me, I always felt the presence of God. It doesn't mean it will always turn out the way you want it to, but if it is in any way tied to your destiny, it will likely lead you to where you should be. It may not lead you to where you planned to be, but where you are supposed to be.

Deciding to go into business means you have to have a good understanding of who you are. You need to know yourself. Know your strengths and your weaknesses. You must have the necessary confidence to fail, but understand something not working is not the end of the world. As I previously stated, it provides a wealth of lessons for the next phase of what you have to do. Anyone can ride the wave of success. You have to be willing to fall and get back up over and over again. The person who can do this in business is a person who knows who they are. You can't take it personally, and you have to believe in who you are and what you have to offer.

To have an entrepreneurial spirit and to walk in destiny, you have to be willing to take a leap. It never occurred to me that failure would happen. I was naïve in that way. I should have considered it because most ventures don't make it the first time you try. Frankly, I realized I had only one life to live. I was compelled to try and start my first business. As long as I could on my terms, I knew it would work out. How wonderful it is to chart the direction of your life.

It is important that you not be afraid to ask for help. As women, we have a hard time asking for assistance. I know that I do. But, there comes a time when you realize you can't do it all. Men seem to have no problem asking. I don't know if we think it will make us appear weak, or if we have something to prove. No matter the reason, don't be afraid to ask for assistance. You don't have to know all the answers. This may be something new for you. Try to connect with people who have an expertise in the areas where you are lacking skills. Knowledge is critical, and you will need a great deal of it to be successful. Collaboration is good, and don't be afraid to solicit feedback.

Be your brand. Build on your brand and don't be afraid to reinvent yourself when necessary. Another soul-saving saying I live by is *Excellence must become your standard and not the goal.* Your brand will precede you and be there when you are not around. Ask yourself, "What is my brand?" When people think of you and the services or products you provide, what do they think of? Do you run late for meetings? Are you never prepared? Do you break promises or always make excuses? Are you well-groomed, and your appearance is always professional? What is your attitude? How do you communicate with others? What are you known for? What are your skills and gifts? What do you do that no one else but you can do? What separates you from others? How do you leave a lasting memory in the minds of other people? Do you project success? You build a brand by answering these questions and living out the answers daily.

Your public image matters. For example, I will not allow anyone to style my hair if his or her hair is not always looking good. A hair stylist is in the beauty business. What does it say about their craft if they don't care for their own hair, but expect money for their services? The same is true for a lawyer. I want a lawyer to look like the image of what a lawyer looks like. I don't want you to show up in court in a glittery, after-five dress. Instantly, I form an image in my mind that speaks of unprofessionalism and that the person doesn't respect the legal profession. We all have seen people whose branding does not match what they do.

Please pay attention to the way you present yourself. No matter what business you are in, package yourself in such a way that people will want what you are selling. Make certain to have an online presence and a website that speaks your brand. Be careful about the personal information you put online. Once it is put on the Internet, it is permanent.

Obviously, I could write an entire book giving advice

about being in business. I want to finally tell you to have courage. You can't be an entrepreneur and be fearful. You must have faith in your abilities and your desires. Be willing to sacrifice. It takes a lot of sacrifice. You must also have a quality of life outside your business. The point of freedom is that you get to be free. Free to enjoy some of the money you make. Free of stress. Free to appreciate what you do. Free to make your own decisions. Free to go and come as you please. Free to take a holiday without having to ask permission. Free to spend time with your family. Free to care for yourself. Free to fulfill your dreams. Having said all this, being an entrepreneur represents freedom if you listen and learn.

YOUR TRUTH

How did this chapter speak to you?

_____

_____

_____

_____

_____

_____

_____

_____

_____

_____

_____

_____

_____

_____

_____

_____

_____

_____

YOUR TRUTH

What is your truth?

_____

_____

_____

_____

_____

_____

_____

_____

_____

_____

_____

_____

_____

_____

_____

YOUR TRUTH

Plan of action to deal with your truth:

_____

_____

_____

_____

_____

_____

_____

_____

_____

_____

_____

_____

_____

_____

_____

_____

_____

CHAPTER

15

Truth to the

Grieving

Sister

---

grief

/grēf/

noun An emotional suffering felt
when something or someone is taken
away; deep sorrow, especially that
caused by someone's death.

*"There are just some things in life you
have to go through."*
JUDGE PENNY BROWN REYNOLDS

First: My Experience

As natural as it may be, grief is an emotional suffering that I wish no woman had to endure. I thought I knew something about it from the many counseling sessions I led in my duties as a minister. Through the years, and even before going into ministry, I had been there for friends and other family members during their times of loss. It was not until my twenties when my grandmother, whom I called Granny, passed away that I was first confronted with the true deep pain of grief. She raised me with my mother and shaped the woman who I am today. It was a pain that is hard to describe.

Other losses followed. In my thirties, my best friend Verneda died of leukemia. She was my only best friend in the world. I loved her, and she loved me more. She predicted all my successes and took me out of my sleeping car and pointed me to a light that shines on me even to this day. Lord, do I miss her. She would be proud of how my life has turned out. She typed my papers in college and fed me when I was hungry. She was a spiritual sister whose dimples could lighten any grim situation I faced.

My mother's passing absolutely changed my entire life. She lived the better part of her life being told that because of her many illnesses she would die young. My mother taught all of us how to fight to live. Her quiet, unassuming demeanor became even more significant to me after her passing. Honestly, I didn't know her greatness until after she was gone. She made so many sacrifices for my sisters and me. She kept me. What else is there to say? I grieve her daily. I think of her daily. I am my mother.

I will never see grief the same after the untimely murder of my 19-year-old nephew Jared, my sister Monica's only child. I had to put my grief on hold to be there for my sister on a daily basis for nearly three years. I woke up every morning and understood that my assignment was to help get her through her pain. Her entire life was dedicated to Jared. He was irreplaceable. I am still amazed at how she deals with the loss of her child. She reminds me of Mrs. Wilhelmina Armour, my son Michael's grandmother, who lost two children and yet had the love and strength like no woman I have ever met. When a loved one is murdered, you feel cheated and angry, and grief is replaced by the need for justice. Jared's passing forced me to dig deep inside and give all that I had to give emotionally to my sister with whom I had been estranged for many years. Upon hearing the news over the telephone that Jared had died, it instantly wiped away any petty issues that separated us. I have no memory of what those issues were. His passing brought us back together. It was a high price, but it was the unintended good that came from such a devastating loss. We will never be separated again.

And yet two more losses. I grieved the loss of my "spiritual truth-teller professor," Dr. Michael Dash, who had been making his way home for almost two decades but didn't leave this earth until he demonstrated the power of living in the face of dying. He taught us all how to do it with grace and appreciation. He is the first person on the planet to say these words to me: "You are enough." Upon hearing those words, he put me on a course to my destiny. I became whole, and it was the missing piece in my life. He was my go-to person. He never judged me but always gave practical and insightful advice. He sought my advice and respected it. I can hear him speaking in my spirit as I write. Through his dying process, I gained new understanding of what it meant to grieve. I learned how to let go and celebrate that he had finally arrived at his destination.

And soon after I said goodbye to Dr. Dash, my friend Gaylin Bernard, who many years before took me to one of my high school proms as a favor to our mothers, passed away. Gaylin and his wife Dolly gave me a great gift in Gaylin's transitioning period. I learned about sacrifice and prayer. I sent weekly cards to both of them for over a year upon learning of Gaylin's fight with cancer. They thought I was blessing them, yet I was being blessed in the process. You see, I had to read the cards and pray daily for them. I ministered to his soul and his belief that healing was possible. He was healed, but not in the way I thought. He would always say he was in a win-win situation. If the cancer was cured, he would win. If he went home to be with the Lord, he would win. He had such peace about the entire situation. He took the fear of dying away from me. You could tell that he was here only long enough to complete his purpose. He deserved and earned the right to be with God eternally.

My final testimony has to do with my in-laws who both transitioned in their nineties. Mother Lillie Mae and Papa Edward Reynolds lived beautiful lives. They showed me the beauty and blessing that is given to some who have lived fruitful and favored lives and have outlived most of the people they grew up with. They both transitioned with family surrounding them. There was praying, singing, and lots of goodbyes. Both experiences were peaceful and beautiful. We should all hope to transition in this way. After spending time working all of their lives, taking care of their family, and serving their churches and communities, one of the greatest gifts God gave them was to be cared for by family and transition with love and peace, as well as dignity and honor. They earned their rest.

For my husband, his brother Harold, and especially my sister-in-law Deborah, their transitioning obviously meant something different. A parent transitioning is life changing. But for me, it was beautiful and peaceful. I felt honored to have had them in my life. Through them I realized that I had become a different person. My honor only continued by being given the opportunity to do the eulogy for my husband's mother. It was something that brings a warm feeling to my heart.

I had a different experience for each of the passings I have described, and I grieved each one of them in a different way. I went through all the stages of grief, but I handled them differently in each case. It had a lot to do with where I was in my faith walk and the circumstances of their departure.

All of us have our own stories of grief. We have all lost someone special in our lives. It certainly brings out difficult emotions, and it takes time to let go of the sadness. Everyone handles grief differently. There is no right or wrong way to grieve, but the best thing to do is allow it to occur. It is indeed a natural process. To pretend that it is not happening hurts you along the way. You just have to allow it to take place.

Grieving isn't only about the loss of someone dying. Any loss can cause grief. You can grieve the loss of a marriage or the break-up of a relationship. People grieve the loss of good health or a job and financial stability. I have seen people lose a dream and never get back on their feet because they didn't understand that they needed to allow themselves time to grieve the loss of the dream. People grieve the loss of their pets that have become an important part of their family. Women grieve the loss they feel after a miscarriage or upon facing a serious illness, the loss of what their previous life was, or the disillusion of a friendship. Loss is loss. It comes when something or someone you love is taken away.

Don't allow anyone to tell you how you should be grieving. This is a personal process that depends on a number of factors. Remember, I said at the outset that I grieved the loss of the people in my life in vastly different ways. As I look back on it, my grief for each of them had to do with my experiences and where I was in my life, my level of faith, my relationship with them, and how I grew to deal with grief. One aspect that was constant was that it took time. Remember, you are on a journey to be healed, and healing takes time. As I was writing this chapter, I have been crying my eyes out as the memories of the people whom I love are being brought back.

There will be days when you will feel better. It may be months or years later when you wake up and find yourself reliving the entire scene again. There is no specific timetable for grieving. It is a process you just have to let occur. You can't ignore it. You can't rush it. You can't pretend that it's not happening. The best approach you can take is face it and deal with it the best you can. If you need to go and talk to a counselor, please do not hesitate to do so. It doesn't mean you are weak. It means you are human.

Because grieving is such a personal process, we all do it differently. People cope with situations on different levels.

There are those with deep faith who firmly believe the hand of God is at play with the loss. Prayer certainly helps as you get to speak with God and know that you are not by yourself.

There are thousands of books on the stages of grief. While in seminary, I took a class, and we discussed the grief process. We learned that in 1969, Elisabeth Kubler-Ross, a psychiatrist, introduced the five stages of grief. You may very well know them by heart. After that lesson and discussion, I never forgot them. It is amazing that I have witnessed these stages in different orders and at different times in the lives of others and my own life. We all experience, in one order or another, denial, anger, bargaining, depression, and, finally, acceptance.

YOUR TRUTH

How did this chapter speak to you?

_____

_____

_____

_____

_____

_____

_____

_____

_____

_____

_____

_____

_____

_____

_____

_____

_____

_____

YOUR TRUTH

What is your truth?

_____

_____

_____

_____

_____

_____

_____

_____

_____

_____

_____

_____

_____

_____

_____

_____

YOUR TRUTH

Plan of action to deal with your truth:

_____

_____

_____

_____

_____

_____

_____

_____

_____

_____

_____

_____

_____

_____

Truth to the

Sister

home·less
/ˈhōmləs/

adjective An individual who lacks housing, including one whose primary residence during the night is a supervised public or private facility that provides temporary living accommodations; an individual who is a resident in transitional housing; or an individual who has as a primary residence a public or private place not designed for, or ordinarily used as, a regular sleeping accommodation for human beings.

*"Doing the best at this moment puts you
in the best place for the next moment."*
OPRAH WINFREY

It was well over twenty-five years ago when I found myself having to sleep in my car. I gave my rent money to a no-good husband to pay, and he didn't pay it. Months later I received a final notice, yet I hadn't realized the problem since he had kept all the other notices from me. Although I was homeless for weeks (I don't remember exactly how long it was because it seems like a lifetime ago), I somehow never forgot it. You never forget the feeling of not having a foundation, a place of your own to lay your head. It is a feeling of having no stability. I asked myself over and over again, how in the world could this have happened to me? How could I have been so stupid to rely on someone who deep down I knew was no good—to trust him to pay to make certain there was a roof over my head? How could this have happened?

The shame associated with the realization that you have been betrayed and your options have run out is indescribable. Sure, I could have gone back home to my mother. She always had a welcoming heart and told us we could always come back to her. However, I kept this secret from my mother. She wasn't well, and I didn't want to place any shame or obligation on her. Mama had such high hopes for my future. After all, she was the one who constantly told me that I would go on to do great things.

How could I tell her that I gave the rent money to someone who was supposed to do right by me only to discover I had no place to call my own? It was horrible. I just couldn't tell her how foolish I was and how I allowed this man to take my money, leaving me nowhere to go. I was in a different state, and I refused to go back home. It never occurred to me to go to a shelter. I was working, and I just slept in my car. I put my stuff in storage, and I walked into my job every day, pretending nothing was wrong. It all seemed reasonable at the time. It wasn't until a woman I happened to work with (who eventually became my best friend who died of leukemia) walked with me to the parking lot. She glanced in the back seat of my car, and my secret was revealed. Verneda looked at me and held me as I began to cry. She asked no questions. She asked me to go back into the building. She made one phone call, and the next thing I knew I was in the home of an angel of a woman pastor who loved me and allowed me to stay with her until I got back on my feet.

I now realize that I was not alone at that time. Everyone who finds herself homeless has a story. We have heard the stories from people like Tyler Perry and Viola Davis as they shared the candid stories about being homeless and/or poor. It isn't some Hollywood story. It is real. For some, it is hard to tell. I guess it's the shame of it all. Even once the story is told, the current success that emerges often blocks the view of others because all they can see is the success, and they find it difficult to embrace past struggles. Others believe it is simply "a story" we tell just to tell it. Behind the words are a great deal of pain and shame. For me, my shame was that I allowed a man to control my life and my finances in such a way that it put me in a vulnerable position. I had the right to trust a husband, but I should never have given my power away. By the way, when I had to leave the apartment, he left. I mean he left and moved on to the next woman he would lay up with and take advantage of. Thanks be to God that he did leave because that was the beginning of a promise I made to myself about handling and managing my own affairs. I would never again give away my power to any man. In the long run, it might have been the best thing that ever happened to me. Don't get me wrong; it was a hard and humiliating lesson, but a necessary one. I wanted so much to be loved that he could have told me to jump in a river, and I would have, knowing I could not swim. In hindsight, his ill treatment of me made me realize I deserved better. I came to know there is no such person as a Prince Charming. If I was ever going to make it in this world, I had to work hard, pray daily, and work harder again. No one was going to come along and save me. I promised myself to take care of my business, my life, my finances, my heart, and my dreams, and these are promises I have yet to break.

It is important to note, my dear sister, that you are not by yourself in your current situation. Women and children represent the fastest growing groups of homeless in America. Children who grow up in this situation often proceed through life not feeling safe or stable. They lived doubled up and dreaming of having their own private space. I know it is hard. I know.

Along the way, I realized a trust had been broken. Just like my friend never asked how I ended up sleeping in my car, why you ended up homeless is not important. What is important is that you realize that you are not defined by where you are. In other words, your circumstances do not get to define you as a woman. You are in a bad place right now. It is critical that you never accept your current circumstances as anything but temporary. This is not your permanent future. You must say it every day. When you open your eyes, thank God for another day to change how you are living. All you need is the right opportunity, and you will be back on your feet. However, you have to put it in your mind and spirit that your homelessness does not define you as a person.

I know the shame you feel. But you know something, stuff happens in life. I can look back and understand the lessons. In time, you will certainly be able to do the same. You are in a traumatic situation. No woman grows up believing that her future has her living outside, in her car, or in a shelter. That was not the plan. For some sisters, you feel numb and disconnected, while others are struggling with depression. I know you don't feel safe, but you will once you are back on your feet and in your own place. When you are homeless, your sense of security is gone, and you have to find the fight deep inside you to get it back. Do not become overwhelmed to the point that you do nothing. Gather yourself and make a plan. There are services and people you can talk to who will help you develop a plan to get yourself and/or your children back into housing.

I watch kids every day make a life for themselves while living in extended-stay hotels. It has become so common that the stigma is gone in some areas, and it has become a viable alternative for entire families to live in a hotel room.

A part of the reason you feel the way you do is because being homeless does not happen over time. You usually end up homeless because circumstances happen unexpectedly, and you are unprepared. Lack of adequate resources remains a problem for women and their children. We live in a society that gives tax breaks to corporations to relocate to an area to create jobs, but has made it harder and harder for women to receive financial assistance to provide for their children. It is a vicious cycle generated by hate and not love, by ignorance, prejudice, and fear. There are politicians who run on a platform of cutting food stamps for poor people, and they take pride in doing it. As I have previously stated, no one is here to speak up for the poor. The truth is that people who are homeless would give anything to work and have a roof over their heads. They just need an opportunity.

If you are prideful, put it aside and seek the help you need. Come out of the shock and denial of it all and get your mind together. You need one objective: to find the strength to get your life back in order. Once you get financial assistance, there are programs that will assist you in getting back on your feet. You will need a phone so that when you apply for jobs, employers will have a way of reaching you. You don't need to broadcast your situation to others, as many will not understand. If you go to a church for help, then speak to the staff or pastor. Other people are judgmental, and you don't need anyone judging you at this time.

From your phone you can look up resources that are available for women with children who are homeless or facing homelessness. The Salvation Army, Catholic Charities, and other nonprofits are there to help with rental assistance and housing help for women with children. I highly recommend the Salvation Army. They have social workers to help you. If you are being evicted, the Salvation Army has emergency provisions to get you temporary housing with resources for food. They will allow you to meet with a social worker and assist with employment. The Salvation Army is one of the most organized agencies that really offer women a place where they can get their lives back together. Many agencies make a lot of promises, yet the Salvation Army has the resources and the caring spirit to help you get on a road of recovery.

After you begin the work of getting housing and employment and taking care of your children, please remember to take care of yourself. You are not a failure because you are homeless. You are in a bad way temporarily, and that is it. You are not the first, and you will not be the last woman facing a hardship. You will have long-term self-sufficiency once you accept that your life is your responsibility. No one else is going to save you. You can get help from an agency like the Salvation Army, but you have to come to an understanding that you are worthy of living a better life. You don't have to settle for the scraps and living on the margins. There is life after homelessness. There is a better life you can give to your children. They deserve better, and it is your responsibility to give it to them. Whatever circumstances got you where you are, take ownership of it and learn from it. If you don't know how to manage money, take some classes so you can become independent. If a tragedy led to this situation, you need to get counseling to deal with it. If you lost your job and had no means of paying your bills, learn the lessons from this.

The important point is that you pick up the pieces of your life and move forward with a renewed mind that you can and will do better. Never forget this, and once you are back on your feet, promise yourself that you will never be homeless again. Remember, it's just a matter of time.

YOUR TRUTH

How did this chapter speak to you?

_____

_____

_____

_____

_____

_____

_____

_____

_____

_____

_____

_____

_____

_____

_____

_____

YOUR TRUTH

What is your truth?

_____

_____

_____

_____

_____

_____

_____

_____

_____

_____

_____

_____

_____

_____

_____

_____

YOUR TRUTH

Plan of action to deal with your truth:

_____

_____

_____

_____

_____

_____

_____

_____

_____

_____

_____

_____

_____

_____

_____

_____

_____

CHAPTER
18

Truth to the

Sister

in·car·cer·ate
/inˈkärsəˌrāt/
verb Imprison or confined.

"Someone was hurt before you, wronged before you, hungry before you, frightened before you, beaten before you, humiliated before you, raped before you...yet, someone survived. You can do anything you choose to do."
MAYA ANGELOU

Getting caught up in the criminal justice system is not good, and it isn't easy to deal with. From the perspective of a former judge, it broke my heart to see women who would end up having to go to prison since many were mothers, and their incarceration devastated their families. My concern was for their children. The number of women and girls going to prison continues to rise. Although it seems no one cares, there are those of us on the outside who really do care. We pray for you, and we hope that while you are there, you can reflect to discover the reasons that led to you being locked up. There are a hundred excuses a person can give about anything. You have to own your situation, so determine how to put your life back together when or if you are scheduled to get out.

I have never been incarcerated. Another one of my promises. I have been in the position of having to put people in jail. It was never easy to do, but there are consequences for our actions, and we must pay the price for our wrongdoings. As necessary as it was, I didn't have to like doing it. I don't know of any judge who enjoys having to take freedom from anyone. It is a job that is necessary, and when you are guilty, you must be punished.

There are a lot of reasons you may have ended up in jail or prison. Perhaps the underlying reason for what you did had to do with the bad influences of others, whether that of a man, another woman, or family members. Perhaps you struggled with alcohol or drugs. You may even have issues with mental illness or have been abused. No matter the underlying reason, you now find yourself locked up, and your freedom has been taken away.

If you did what you did, it is on you. Until you take responsibility for your actions, there can be no growth and no progress. We all know you didn't grow up dreaming of being a criminal. Now, I am not naïve to the idea that a small percentage of people in this world are just no good. In fact, they are evil. They think nothing of getting over on others or hurting other people. They deserve to be in prison. Then there are those people who are good people but make stupid mistakes. Truth be told, we are all one bad decision away from going to jail. It takes only one bad decision.

Because you know more about survival inside the prison than I do, I will not insult you by attempting to give you survival advice. It seems silly to do so. My advice is to speak to a place deep in your soul. I know your heart longs to be out and with your family, particularly if you are among those sisters who are innocent yet are behind bars. It must be difficult. My word to you through the pages of this book is to tell you not to allow your mind and your spirit to become locked up. I know you are in survival mode, and all women learn quickly to do what they have to do to make it. Just don't allow your mind to become institutionalized. Hopefully, you have good memories you revisit, and I recommend that you stay away from the bad ones, like I do. I don't let my mind bring them back to my remembrance.

Try to hold on to the woman you want to be. You will never be the same again. Let go of the old you and embrace a new woman who will develop after a hard and trying experience. I advise you to write your feelings down in a journal if you can. If you don't feel safe doing it, then at least meditate on the kind of woman you want to be. Be honest about your situation. Accept your weaknesses and your flaws. At this point, you have nothing but time on your hands, so you can do the necessary work to accept yourself and come to terms with your past. If counseling services are available, take advantage of them. If any good can come out of being locked up and perhaps away from your children, it's that you have an opportunity to get some things emotionally straight that have been haunting you for years.

Tell the truth to yourself about who you are. It is the truth that will ultimately set you free. No one knows or can tell you your truth for you. It may be painful, but at this point, what is the worst thing that can happen to you when you find yourself locked up?

Don't stop loving and caring. Don't allow where you are to take away your humanity. The ability to care about someone other than yourself is an integral part of being human. I know where you are and that you have to be strong, but no one can control your ability to love your kids or your family. If you have kids, you can continue to mother them the best way you can. Write them and engage them on a daily or weekly basis. Listen to their stories. Really listen. Tell them you are safe, and it is not a horrible place where you are. Kids worry about their mothers. Let them know it is not their fault and admit to your mistakes. Hold up on making promises because you are not in a position to promise anything about the future when you have to work hard to get your life together once you get out.

The process of freedom starts while you are still locked up. If not, you'll find yourself back in two to three years. There is not much love waiting for you on the outside. Once you have a felony attached to your name, it is almost impossible to get employment. You should be thinking about ways to start your own business. Get as much training and education as you can. You are going to need it to get a business started. Get treatment for whatever you need help with. Use what is available to make your life better.

Don't expect anyone to save you. You made your bed, and people expect you to lie in it. People lack compassion and empathy. They want to define you for the rest of your life by the big mistake you made. You have to search within you to find your worth before you get out. I know that I am asking a lot of you, but until you know who you are and what you are worth, you can never be free and reclaim your power.

There are people like Nelson Mandela who spent time in prison only to go on to realize their true destiny. When you wake up every day, there are countless reasons to not care and to say forget it. But there is one important reason to press on in spite of where you are. You do matter. I'll say it again: you do matter. You were created with a purpose in life. God can use you even where you are right now. Your main focus should be on knowing who you are and that you are worthy. Although difficult, it doesn't have to be dehumanizing if you walk in your womanhood and believe you have a future. Allow this time to build your character. If you weren't loved as a child, begin to love that little girl who is deep inside you. Don't allow anyone to hurt her, and begin to trust yourself again.

It's not over for you until you are in the grave. If you are breathing, you still have a chance for a life. Make a plan, and write it down over and over again. Deal with your pain daily and learn to conquer it. Equip yourself with the tools to start over. Develop a relationship with God that is not merely convenient because you are behind bars. Confront God with your feelings of betrayal, and find your way back to a God who has never left you and will never leave you. You are worthy of life, and He will not judge you by the wrongs that you have done. You must forgive yourself before others will ever forgive you. You must forgive others, as forgiveness is always about what is inside of us.

Being free is truly free when you let go and embrace your truth.

YOUR TRUTH

How did this chapter speak to you?

_____

_____

_____

_____

_____

_____

_____

_____

_____

_____

_____

_____

_____

_____

_____

_____

YOUR TRUTH

What is your truth?

_____

_____

_____

_____

_____

_____

_____

_____

_____

_____

_____

_____

_____

_____

_____

_____

_____

_____

YOUR TRUTH

Plan of action to deal with your truth:

_____

_____

_____

_____

_____

_____

_____

_____

_____

_____

_____

_____

_____

_____

_____

_____

_____

CHAPTER

19

Truth to the

Sister

mar·ried
/ˈmerēd/
adjective (of two people) united
in marriage.

Will you have this woman to be your wife;
to live together in holy covenant of marriage?
Will you love her, comfort her, honor and keep her,
in sickness and in health, and, forsaking all others,
be faithful to her so long as you both shall live?

My sister, you are one of the lucky ones. You're married. You have found the man of your dreams, and the two of you are building a life together. Did you end up with your soul mate? Are you happy in your marriage? Does he make you feel better about life? Is it everything you dreamed of? Can you imagine living your life without him?

Marriage can be wonderful when you marry the right person. But if you chose the wrong man, it can be the worst experience of your life. With nearly fifty percent of marriages ending in divorce, if you ever needed advice in a particular area, it is in how to have a good marriage. Too many women spend more time fantasizing about the wedding, their wedding dress, and what their friends will think about the wedding that they somehow forget to take the time to deliberate whether the man they are marrying is really Mr. Right. The ultimate question has to be whether or not this man is the one you want to spend the rest of your life with. Will he be there for you in sickness and in health?

Women experience pressure to marry, and many times marriages struggle because women married for the wrong reasons. Some women are persuaded to marry because of their biological clocks are ticking, and they want to make sure they can become mothers. Others are looking for financial security, while some merely want companionship and are tired of being alone. There are women who believe that a marriage will help complete them. There are some who fall in love and never think about what will happen when the "in love" phase dissipates, and the woman is left only with friendship and companionship. Some women marry for the sex and because they hate dating. The reasons for getting married are endless. It is important to get it right the first time because it is a great deal of trouble getting out of a marriage. The dissolution can paralyze a woman's life for a significant period of time. Adding children to the mix makes the situation even more difficult.

We spend more time picking out a house or a car, than we do in making sure we are marrying the right partner. We don't want to invest the necessary time in premarital counseling to work out any issues on the front end of the engagement. When couples attend marriage counseling, it is normally done immediately before the wedding ceremony. By then, there is tremendous pressure to move forward with the plans, even when concerns arise. Many times women ignore the red flags because they are so desperate to have the man. They end up settling because their friends and family have told them that they are too picky. They become grateful for the warm male body in their lives instead of having a minimum standard of requirements.

An important point to always remember is if you want your marriage to work, you must refrain from mentioning divorce or separation in discussions and arguments. Don't put the idea in the air. Decide that you will do everything in your power to stay married. As long as you are not mistreated, betrayed, or abused, and as long as you can communicate with your husband, you should be able to stay together. Your love for each other will have varying degrees as time goes on. In the beginning, you will be madly in love. For some, this feeling lasts for years. The love will become stronger with time for some, and for others the "in love" aspect will fade. You must grow together and be willing to move in the same direction. The two of you must face life's challenges together. Nothing should come between you. When you feel yourselves pulling apart, you need to address it immediately. Don't allow a great deal of time to pass if there is any resentment between the two of you. It will not get better unless you communicate. Remember to be in a relationship, both parties must be willing to relate.

Marriage requires a daily commitment. It means you have to wake up every morning with the intention of bringing positivity to the marriage. Make certain there is a solid friendship. Don't take your husband for granted, and don't allow him to take you for granted either.

Whatever you do, don't forget to take care of yourself. Remember who you are as a woman. The marriage should enhance your life, not oppress it. You must be considerate of his feelings, but you must always make certain that you take care of yourself first. You cannot be anything to anyone else until you make yourself a priority. This means that you take care of your body and health. Your appearance should matter. Getting married does not give you license to let yourself go.

Your husband wants the woman he dated and was attracted to. He loved his girlfriend and doesn't want to see her go away. The marriage gives him something deeper. You should want to keep everything exciting and fulfilling. What a privilege to be able to share a life with someone. You need to act as though it is an honor to be with each other. There should be love in the air.

You should expect no less from your husband. He should be the boyfriend you had before you got married. He should send you cards and bring you flowers. He should run your bath and give you a massage or play footsy while watching TV. He should compliment you without your having to ask him. He should and can be the man that you dreamed of. When you're sick, he should be by your side. The two of you must be there for each other at every turn in life.

To the Newly Married Sister

Remember this, "How you start off is how you will finish." Whatever you allow to occur in the beginning of the marriage is what will likely occur throughout. Be careful what you agree to and what you look away from in the beginning. Ask yourself, "Is this behavior I can live with?"

Men are often creatures of habit. Habits are hard to break. If he forms the habit of kissing you when he walks through the door in the evening, he will likely continue to do it throughout the marriage. It will become a routine. But if he walks out of the house without saying goodbye, you'll have many arguments down the road trying to get him to do so. He may see it as an issue of control. Both of you need to get your likes and dislikes on the table at the outset.

A marriage is absolutely a partnership. There are different philosophies about who should be in charge of the marriage. Whatever your belief, be certain to keep your "voice." Your voice represents your identity. Sure, you become a couple, but it is important to maintain your individualism.

Each of you has a role. I recommend that at the outset you lay out the specifics of those roles. The two of you get to decide what the roles are. Although most model their marriage after what they witnessed growing up, the two of you must define the roles for yourselves. Put it in writing and come to an understanding about what it means to be a wife and a husband. What is your job description as a wife? What does your husband expect from you? What do you expect from him? Many times we allow society to define the roles of a marriage. These roles may or may not be realistic depending on your circumstances.

If you expect him to put gas in your car, clean the house, cut the lawn, pay half of the bills, do his laundry, take you out to dinner, and attend church, you need to communicate these expectations at the outset. If he expects to have sex once or twice a week, or he wants you to prepare dinner every night, he needs to communicate these expectations to you, and you need to determine whether you are willing to comply. Actually, all of these issues should have been discussed prior to the marriage, but you will be surprised at how couples never get to the details of being married. All the details are usually placed in the wedding planning, not the marriage planning.

It may require the two of you negotiating on many levels. However, there should be some issues that I will refer to as "irreducible minimal requirements." You must have these from a marriage. There can be no compromise. These usually involve your values and your morals. If you don't want a man who smokes, a man who goes out clubbing, a man who maintains secret bank accounts, or a man who lies or sees other women, you need to make it clear that these are deal-breakers. I mean it.

If you know that you are a church-going woman and your faith is important to you, why would you marry a man who does not care about having a relationship with God? The answer is simple: you think you can change him. You've convinced yourself that because of all of his potential, you can bring him around. Women are often in love with the potential of the man and not how the man really is. We fool ourselves into thinking the love will change him. We think he will want to change to please us. We become blinded by our love. Wrong, wrong, wrong! Ultimately, there will be problems. It is hard to change an adult. They have to want to change. If you don't watch out, the man will resent you for not loving him for who he is. His male ego will not allow it. Everyone can stand improvement, but the point of being an adult is that adults get to decide how they want to live their lives.

It goes both ways. He may be trying to change you. Suppose your husband married you at a certain weight, and immediately after the wedding he asks you every day to lose twenty pounds. He even tells you that he likes thinner women. He never raised the issue of weight before you married him, but now he wants you to be smaller. Wouldn't you resent him? It would hurt you deeply, and the relationship would suffer. In many respects, you will feel betrayed.

We must be honest with ourselves and with our mates about expectations. If you know you are marrying a man who expects intimacy at the highest level, and you frankly don't like being intimate, you will likely develop problems. You must be honest up front and work through the issues.

On the Issue of Finances

In a traditional role, the man is the provider. However, in some situations, the woman is the primary breadwinner. This shift of roles can change the dynamics of a relationship. However, if you set forth all the expectations at the beginning of the marriage, it can serve to eliminate confusion down the road.

Depending on your age, many of us grew up expecting a man to make a financial contribution to the household. Until I met my husband, I had to provide for myself. It was always a struggle getting the men in my life to contribute financially. They got away with it because I allowed it. I was thinking that a truly independent woman could take care of herself. They had a responsibility to contribute, and I never held them accountable. My husband is a provider in every way. Although there were times in our marriage when I made more money than he did, he always brought every single dollar he earned home. He, like his father, was traditional in the role of being the breadwinner. I am grateful to God that we have never struggled in the area of financial disagreements. It ranks near the top as one of the problem areas in failed marriages.

This is why I am telling you now, "You can do bad by yourself." Why would you want to have someone in your life who brings nothing to the table? Most women want men to stand up and be men. In our minds, a man works and takes care of his family. In a partnership, spouses contribute to every aspect of the family. If a woman stays home and takes care of the children while the husband works outside the home, the wife is still contributing. However, a man must contribute. Period. End of story.

Respect is critical in a relationship, and if we are going be honest, as women, we cannot respect a man who does not step up to the plate financially. For any real good woman, the man doesn't have to give her diamonds and the stars and the moon, but we do expect the man in our life to pay some of the bills and to contribute to the household.

If a man finds himself without a job, he must still manage to contribute to the household in other ways. He must assume additional responsibilities until he is able to find a job. It is difficult for a woman to tolerate a man not working and just laying around the house. It can be temporarily accepted if the man is in school, working at a home business, or going out every day looking for a job. In these cases, the woman knows in her heart that he is trying. Men get points from us for trying. However, while a man is trying, we will not accept him having a bad attitude. You should be standing together supporting one another, not throwing in his face that he is not working. You have the right to expect an effort on his part to find a job. You may have to remind him and, most of all, encourage him. You can't put him down because of the unemployment situation. Remember, you are a team.

The days of a woman taking care of a man are over. I've heard of women who are so desperate to have a man in their lives that they do all the work, and the man doesn't have to do anything. I have only heard of them; I have never met one. How can a woman feel good about being used and taken advantage of by a man? This kind of relationship is one-sided. Marriages must be balanced with both parties giving as much as they both can.

Another problem that arises for couples is spending habits. I am of the belief that each person in the marriage must have his and her own money. There should be a joint house account, but each person should have his or her own personal account. I hear about women who hide bringing clothes and shoes into their house so their husbands don't criticize them about their shopping. It is important to have your own money that you get to control. If you are not good at managing money, then your spouse may be better suited to handle the household finances. But to maintain independence, you need your own money, and he needs his own money. Once you are spending your own money, you should not allow him to take on the role as your parent in telling you how to spend your own money. If it is happening, you're allowing it. This is an issue of control. It is your money to spend as you please.

My husband loves buying stuff on one of the home shopping networks. I don't think that everything he buys is practical, but it's his money to spend the way he pleases. I may make a comment to tease him from time to time, but again, I am not his mother who gets to dictate what he can and cannot do with his money. Your husband doesn't have the right to tell you what to do with your money. You need to let him know that, as an adult, it is important for you to make decisions and have the freedom to spend your money as you like. Tell him you enjoy being a grown-up. If you explain it enough and avoid making it into an argument, he will eventually get it. Stop sneaking around, and proudly bring your purchases into the house. Start acting like a grown-up and not his child.

On the Issue of Respect & Control

Another issue that arises and one that you need to be mindful of is the issue of caregiving. Unfortunately, many women assume the role of caregiver to their husbands. In reality, the two of you should be caring for each other. You must always be aware not to become your husband's mother. It's not your job to pick up after an adult. If his socks are on the floor, and occasionally he forgets to pick them up, give him a gentle reminder. However, you don't want to start sounding like his mother. No man wants to be married to his mother. They want a wife who is a lover and a friend. They do not want to feel like they are little boys. You risk having him feel this way when you're constantly whining about what he should or should not be doing around the house. Again, lay out the expectations in the beginning.

In our home, the last person to get out of the bed in the morning makes the bed. We agreed to this rule in the beginning. It works for us. Because I'm an early riser, I'm usually up first every morning. There are times when I like making the bed. I really don't have a problem doing it. We most often make the bed together if I am still at the house. However, we have an understanding about our responsibilities just in case I don't have time to make it, or I don't feel like doing it. In our home, I do all the cooking (when I feel like it), but my husband keeps the kitchen clean. We each do our own laundry. Now, some people may think our system is unconventional. I am neither his mother nor his maid. He is not my father nor does he have his foot on my neck. We are a team, and we work together as a team for the benefit of our lives together. We have never gotten in an argument about the bed being made every day because I told him in the beginning that this was important to me.

As important as it is for you to keep your voice in the marriage, it is equally as important for him to keep his individualism. A man wants to be a man. If he likes sports, playing basketball or other games, do everything you can to encourage what he enjoys. I engage my husband in discussions about sports. He doesn't have many male friends, so he talks to me. I am not excited about the subject matter, but I enjoy hearing him talk. He also engages me in discussions that are important to me. I know there are times when he couldn't care less, but he pretends to be interested, and that is good enough for me. He is not going to like everything I like. He does need to respect my likes. For the sake of your marriage, the two of you should find a way to manage the incorporation of your hobbies into the union. It will make your life better.

On the Issue of Trust

Trust is the most important piece in a marriage. No matter what you do, always be truthful. Honesty is the foundation of a marriage. No one likes a liar, and you definitely don't want to spend the rest of your life with a liar. Let go of secrets in the marriage, and keep an open dialogue even when you are afraid.

My comment does not mean that you have to reveal all of your secrets from your past. Your former relationships are irrelevant and add nothing to your present marriage. Never discuss your prior relationships with your husband. Don't allow him to talk about his. How can discussions about other men or women add to the fulfillment of your marriage? Does it bring anything good to your present situation? The answer is no, it does not. Always remember not to tell your husband what you went through or tolerated from another man. He might think he can do the same to you because you tolerated it in the past. Talk to no one. There is some information you need to take to your grave. We are in a society where we tell too much. We go on television and tell it, or we blog about it. We even go to church and freely confess all of our past deeds. There are particulars you just need to keep to yourself. It is most important to stay away from revealing all the details about other people and what you did before the marriage.

On the Issue of Arguing

Be careful when you argue. Words can hurt. Words are powerful. Sure, you may be able to apologize, but you cannot take words back. In fact, words have staying power. In the heat of anger, we don't stop to think about the ramifications of what we are saying. You must learn how to argue fairly. Deal only with the issue at hand. You cannot be historical in an argument. In other words, you cannot raise issues from the past. I don't care how immediate the issue was. Whether five years or five days prior, it isn't appropriate to bring up past issues when dealing with a particular matter that has no relevance to the past issues.

It is best to deal with an important issue when everyone is calm. Always be honest and truthful. It is not what you say as much as how you say it. Why would you decide to discuss a matter that is crucial to you when you're in the middle of arguing? Speak when you are in a good mood to talk. A good time to talk about topics may be after sex or any time of intimacy. You need to be feeling really good about one another to deal with a challenging or uncomfortable issue. You should know better than anyone else when you have those wonderful calm moments in the marriage. Be strategic in how you approach your mate about issues. Minimize arguments. Keep them as infrequent as you can. Confront your issues, but attempt to do it in a constructive manner.

On the Issue of Girlfriends in Your Relationship

I'm the first to admit that I love having girlfriends in my life. I have, however, learned my lesson when it comes to discussing the events of my marriage with my sister friends. You have to be careful about the kind of outside advice you receive. It can be difficult for a single sister to relate to the give-and-take that is necessary to make a marriage work. Both parties have to be willing to make sacrifices. There is much compromise in a happy marriage. Remember, your girlfriend has your best interests at heart, and she may see situations only from your perspective. Her advice is often biased. You have to trust that she really does have your best interests at heart.

So-called friends have betrayed me in the past. Many times, other women will attempt to undermine your relationship, and you may not realize it or believe it. They do this by raising questions that cause you to doubt and question situations. Be careful. Every sister who claims to be your friend may not be good for you. A sister friend should encourage you. She should attempt to find the best in the situation. She should be honest in giving her opinion but know when to back off. She must respect your decisions and be there for support if you make mistakes. She should never tell you, "I told you so."

Don't you ever allow a friend or a relative to speak badly about your husband if you have a man who is not abusing you or who is not in the wrong. Be careful what you share about your mate to your friends. Not everyone can handle negative details. Your friends or relatives may hold what you have shared against your husband. Long after you and your man have made up, they will still be holding a grudge.

Seek the wisdom of your mother, an older woman, or a woman of faith, someone who you know does not have a jealous spirit. Never tell every private moment you and your husband share. There are some details that should be between only you and your spouse. I learned a long time ago to stop running my mouth about my business.

I am not suggesting that all girlfriends don't mean you well; you just need to be mindful. Recently, I had a friend share with me that she was exhausted from her day at work. She stated that she was going home to cook something that her husband had requested to eat. I almost put my two cents into the conversation by telling her that she wasn't his cook and that she should go home and get in the bed. I was looking out for my friend. I love her so much I wasn't taking into consideration that she enjoyed cooking for him. I didn't say anything because I remembered telling myself it was not my business. If she liked doing it, then I liked it for her. It was more important that she continued to be honest with me about sharing her day. I did not want her to become defensive. Had I said something about the situation, she may have not felt comfortable telling me about her day in the future.

If you want a good friend, you have to be a good friend. Sometimes it is in your best interest to keep your mouth shut. After all, it is only your opinion, and there are many ways to handle situations.

On the Issue of Children in Your Marriage

Children bring a great deal to a marriage. The most important thing is to stand together. If children feel there is any division, they will attempt to use it for their benefit. Remember, they are kids. They don't realize that any division hurts the family unit. Children want what they want and when they want it. The only way to have a successful marriage with children is to stand together in decision-making. Both spouses must parent the children. Your greatest responsibility is to make certain you give your children good memories.

Spend time as a family and make your children your priority. They did not ask to come into the world, so we have to treat them as though we are happy they were born. Raising children is hard, but it is even harder if you are attempting to do it alone.

On Having a Good Life

Marriage can be wonderful, but you have to be willing to put in the time and the commitment to making it work. It is not always easy, but when you begin to finally get it right, it can be the best thing in the world. It takes time to make a marriage work. There must be mutual respect and honor for the marriage. It must be cared for and treasured. There will be valley moments. During these difficult times you will either be drawn together or torn apart. Marriage requires a sense of humor. You cannot take yourself seriously, and you must be willing to allow for mistakes.

God must be in the marriage. You become closer when you learn to pray together. Faith is the glue that holds a marriage together. Intimacy is critical and keeps the love fueled. Do activities together, and don't forget to go on dates. Communication is key. Life is to be lived. How wonderful life is for the woman who finds a man who wants to live life to its fullest.

YOUR TRUTH

How did this chapter speak to you?

_____

_____

_____

_____

_____

_____

_____

_____

_____

_____

_____

_____

_____

_____

_____

_____

_____

YOUR TRUTH

What is your truth?

_____

_____

_____

_____

_____

_____

_____

_____

_____

_____

_____

_____

_____

_____

_____

_____

YOUR TRUTH

Plan of action to deal with your truth:

_____

_____

_____

_____

_____

_____

_____

_____

_____

_____

_____

_____

_____

_____

_____

_____

CHAPTER

20

Truth to the

Sister

sin·gle
/ˈsiNGgəl/
adjective Only one; not one of several;
unmarried.

*"You are the designer of your destiny;
you are the author of your story."*
LISA NICHOLS

Much has been written in the national media regarding the "plight" of the black woman and her single status. A major network even did a story on the high proportion of black women, forty-two percent, who have never been married. They posed the question: "Why so many single, black females?" One national newspaper carried a story written by a male professor arguing that black single women are justifiably bitter because "black women are the most un-partnered group of people in America." I don't believe that black women are bitter. Do you?

The statistics are not favorable on many levels regarding the black family structure, particularly as it relates to the high percentage of black children born out of wedlock. The facts are the facts. I will not argue with them. I do, however, believe there are historical reasons that contribute to this phenomenon. It is a reality that black women outnumber men, and there are a great percentage of our men in prison. Furthermore, with this country's history and its welfare policies, the structure of the black family is a complex problem that cannot merely be painted with a broad brush. Single black women are not the source of the problem. It's a symptom of a larger issue. The shame or stigma previously associated with having a child out of wedlock has all but disappeared. From the child's perspective, I am happy they are not born into a life of shame for a situation that was not of their making. However, the situation has obviously gotten out of hand because people don't see the family unit in the traditional way, with two people raising children together.

Celebrities, whose glittery and glamorous lives are often emulated by their fans, have led a great number of women into believing that having a baby without a mate is acceptable. They have led a generation of young people to a destructive place of difficulty by glorifying having children with no spouse. The reality is that the majority of women don't have a nanny and have little family support to assist in the rearing of the children born to single-parent households. Life is not the way it used to be where we all lived within blocks of each other or in the same town or neighborhood. The cousins played together, and it was an all-for-one attitude about family. Now, women are struggling trying to raise their children while male-dominated state legislatures have watered down child support laws such that men are not meeting their financial responsibilities. As I have stated, it is a complicated issue, and the entire blame does not fall solely upon the single women. Frankly, I am sick of how black women are often wrapped up in stereotypes that have been perpetuated for years in the media. These stereotypes have been reestablished with the influx of the "nonreality" of so-called reality shows on television. With that said, there is a great deal of pressure on the single black woman today.

On Wanting to Be Married

It is not easy being single if you spend your entire life focusing on wanting to be married and regretting and questioning your inability to find a mate. The issue becomes more profound when you consider that your biological clock is ticking, and a woman's value is determined, in many instances, by her ability to bear children. This unfortunate premise has deep historical and religious roots.

I have reflected a great deal on this issue before discussing it as I recognize that it serves as a place of pain and disconnect for a number of single women. The fairy tale we learn as young girls misleads us all. We are taught that the ideal future involves finding Mr. Right or a knight in shining armor. The story continues by stressing that a complete life means having children and living happily ever after in our castles in the suburbs. We grow up and become adults, only to look around and see no Mr. Right. Some of us can't even find Mr. Wrong. Where are the men? Where are the good men? Where are they? You can't have the fairy tale without the prince, right?

There were plenty of men when all the single sisters were in high school and college. This is the reason that so many single sisters decided to put marriage on hold, opting instead to focus on other areas. These women thought they had time to get married. Some women used the time to find themselves and build a nest egg for the future. They were sure that the men would be waiting for them when they were done. Some sisters focused on taking trips with their girlfriends to see the world. (This is, by the way, an excellent option from my perspective.) Some likely focused on living life, getting educated with additional degrees, or building careers. When they are finally ready to live the fairy tale, one piece is missing—the man. The would-be husband is nowhere to be found.

To be fair to the brothers, I must acknowledge that good men are available. There are men who want a wife and a family and love God. However, there are many no-good brothers who want to have their cake and eat it too. They know the statistics better than the women know them. They know women outnumber them, so they pick and choose as they please. They are spoiled and sometimes disrespectful. They can be users and play on a woman's emotions. Some of them are filled with drama, and, frankly, some are downright crazy.

Believe it or not, there are groups of brothers who have sex with other men and yet play a role of being heterosexual to the world. They are merely looking for a leading lady in their fantasy life instead of having the courage to be who they really are. It's a shame they feel the need to live in the shadows, but we live in a world that does not allow people to be who they really are. These men owe it to themselves and to the women they are fooling to be who they are. If they are having side sex with a man, they are not heterosexual. To the single sister who is allowing him to engage in this, you are fooling yourself if you believe he will ever be completely devoted to you. It is a sham, and it will never be real. He needs to go on with his life and allow the sister to go on with her life.

As a sister who has never had a problem finding a man, I was raised in both a single-parent household with a mother who never married and also with grandparents who were married for over fifty years. I saw life from both sides. Marriage was obviously the goal in light of how I came into the world. I saw relationships as a way of making me feel whole. I would go in and out of them in search of the fairy tale. I was always searching for my Prince Charming only to discover that the fairy tales soon became nightmares because I kept selecting the wrong men. I have finally come to terms with the reasons behind my poor choices. Although these husbands were not right for me, everything was wrong inside me, which was why I kept selecting the wrong men in my life. Back then, I got from them just what I thought I deserved.

The greatest gift I can give to you is to let you know that

your worth as a woman cannot be determined by your ability to be married. Aside from the statistics, I don't believe every woman was created to be married. There is something magical about being single that is often not embraced in society because of the constant pressure to be married. Do not get me wrong; it is a wonderful experience to share your life with a man who enhances your ability to be your authentic self. There is no doubt about the power that comes from traveling your life's journey with a great partner. However, as a single woman, you are given the tremendous gift of being able to chart your own course of life without regard to the desires or wishes of anyone else. You can fly, and there is no one there to tell you how high you can go. Being single can be wonderful.

There does come a time when you have to decide how you want to proceed with your life and accept your reality or decide to change it. My mother would say, "There is somebody for everybody." I believe it. There is a man out there for you. I don't know if he is your Mr. Right, but he is definitely out there. You will need to change your mindset to find him, and I will get to that discussion shortly. I just want you to remember not to judge your worth or success based on your ability to get a husband. I have already established the difficulty in finding a man just based on the numbers. So how do you reconcile your desires with reality? What is a girl to do? You may enjoy being single, but your goal is to have a husband. When the clock is ticking, and you feel that time is running out, what are your options? How do you find the man of your dreams no matter what the reality looks like?

For the single sisters who are unsatisfied being single and who refuse to accept they can be just as fulfilled in their current status, I have a few words of guidance. There are good men available, no matter what the media would have you believe. Yes, women outnumber men. But remember what my mother said, "There is someone for everyone." Your person is out there for you.

The media often describes black men as deadbeats, no-good men who either go in and out of prison or live on the down low. I just painted a picture of some of the men who are in that category, but I believe the majority of our men are walking every day in their manhood. They are real men who are caring for their children and owning businesses and contributing to their communities. There are hardworking black men who treat their women like queens. They take care of their families. They are providers, and they love us unconditionally. There are black men who are not insecure, and they are family oriented with a great deal of love and caring in their hearts. They are successful and love God. There are single men who are looking for a great woman to build a life with. They approach me all the time in the grocery store, on planes, everywhere. I am not naïve enough not to know they may be looking for a side sister. I am just telling you that they are out there.

I love black men. In fact, my personal preference is a black man, but I believe that people get to love who they want to love. Race should not be an issue. You should look to find a man who shares your morals and values. Know before you find him what you want. You likely have a list of qualities and characteristics you must have. That list may very well be keeping you from finding your future husband. After all, it is likely that you will be more educated than he. I am not suggesting you compromise, but I am merely telling you that you can build a life on what matters most, not on a dream list of superficial qualities that don't matter in the long run.

If you have a man who shares the same morals and values

and aspirations in life, you can make a life with him no matter how many degrees he has or does not have. You are looking to build a life together, not just a kingdom of things. Look for a man with a heart, who will love you in the good times and the bad times.

If you have been unsuccessful finding a good black man, one alternative may be that you look outside of your race to find a life partner. I am not suggesting that you purposely seek someone outside of your race, but I think it might be a good idea to keep the option open. Love is love. When we all get to heaven, race will not matter. If you fall in love with a man outside of your race, let it happen. Don't allow yourself to be judged by others. Just love whom you want to love. I couldn't be a minister and not tell you that love trumps everything. Love is the cornerstone of my theology. Just find love.

The unfortunate truth is that marrying someone outside of your race adds another layer of issues to deal with because we continue to live in a country with unresolved racial issues. Your family may not like it. His family may not like it. Your children will likely have issues from ignorant people, as well as other women and men may not like it. It isn't easy for interracial couples. I am just sick of people being in the judging business. Live your life and stop worrying about what others think. Just understand you will have to work on your happiness and face challenges. The bottom line is you have one life to live, and you should not allow anyone to judge you or decide for you whom you can love. Be you and love whom you want to love. You can marry whom you want to marry. The issue is finding happiness and walking in your purpose. Just remember, if you marry someone of a different race, know that you will face challenges and be ready to work through the challenges before you get married. If you can process everything that comes with it, I say go for it.

Stop compromising your core values to get a man. You should seek someone who wants the same things out of life that you do. Make certain you select a man who wants to be married to you. You don't want someone who is struggling with marriage and commitment. If he loves you, but he has a hard time giving up his other women, baby, let him go. You want a partner who wants you to be you. He is not trying to change you or make you into the person he wants you to be.

For those of you who have a checklist and are delayed in finding that "perfect" man, I want you to know that it is rare to find a man who has all the qualities on your checklist. It might make more sense for you to make a shorter list of what you cannot live with. This is the list of deal-breakers. For example, I will not share my man with another woman. Some men today are expecting women to share. They will let you know at the beginning that they are seeing a number of women. You get excited about his revelation because his so-called honesty is refreshing, and you end up compromising and sitting around waiting for him to schedule you in for a date with the rest of his other women. You know deep down inside that you do not want to be in a line of women for one man. You do not have time for those kinds of games. Let that brother go and move on to the next one.

Other deal-breakers could include a man who smokes or refuses to go to church. You may not want a man with children or who does not have a job. Whatever it is you know you don't want on this side of finding him, you will never be able to accept on the other side of getting him. You will not be happy if you settle for anything that goes against your core values. It is best to establish your standards early so you don't get confused by what you do like about him or your desperate need to have a man. If the brother is fine and cute and can handle his business with you in all areas, you oftentimes are willing to overlook a great deal. You understand what I mean. Don't allow yourself to be captivated by the outside trimmings of the man. Look into his heart and his soul to determine if he is worthy of your love and your time.

You almost lose your mind when you run across a man whom you think has money or a great career. Be careful about embracing a showy man. It is attractive to find someone who looks nice, dresses nice, and has a nice car and house. Those things on the outside have little to do with wealth. All it means is he can purchase or pay on nice things. You have to look beyond what is on the outside and pull the curtain back to see how much baggage is behind all of his shiny new stuff. It may very well be real, but you can't take everything at face value with men. They are just as broken as we are. You need to make certain that your broken pieces fit with his broken pieces, or that you both are whole individuals who can build a future together.

Please let me clear on this: *your stuff is not better than anyone else's.* If the man is a problem, all that you are and all that you have will never change him. Sisters must stop believing they have something so extraordinary that will convince the brother to change. He will change his ways when he decides to do it. If you are worth it to him, you will not have to do a thing. He is falling in love with the woman you are. Don't you make the mistake of trying to be what you think he wants. He may be attracted to that pretend woman for a little while, but it is not sustainable because it isn't real. Be you and let the chips fall where they may. I knew a sister who became obsessed with the interests of every man she dated. If he liked rap music, she started playing it in her car. If he liked basketball, suddenly she wanted me to join her at all the games. It was the saddest thing to watch. At the end of the day, the men would always leave her because she was never operating in her authentic self.

For long-term success in a relationship, you cannot compromise on issues that deep down inside you know you cannot tolerate. There is no changing him. You are getting what you are getting. You can help usher in superficial changes that may improve his look or organizational skills, but the core of his being is something you cannot change. Stop being desperate and be honest with yourself. Don't waste your time with a "piece of a man" or a man you would have to spend a lifetime putting back together again and who still will not be happy. It is perfectly fine to help your man reach his potential, but make certain you help him after he is married to you. I made the mistake once of building him up and getting his life in order, and another woman became the beneficiary of all my hard work.

No person will have every quality you want. It makes good sense to not waste time dealing with a person who has issues that you could never adjust to. Don't settle for what you know you can't live with. If he cheats while you are dating, he will cheat when he gets married. His cheating has little to do you with you but rather his inability to be committed. Why would you settle for a man who cheats with other women? You can pretend that you don't know it, but if you have to ask the question, then you already know the answer. Let him go. He will never do right by you, and you deserve better.

If you find a man who is possessive, be careful. This is the kind of behavior that feels good in the beginning but can lead to a path of destruction. Wanting to know where you are and the constant calls and texts may appear that he is into you. However, this may be a sign of a controlling guy who sees you as an object. He could be the wolf in sheep's clothing who will put his hands on you down the road. Listen to your spirit about him. Get away from him as fast as you can. His initial affections that don't feel normal are signs of more bad behavior to come. Men who want to know everything about you, from where you are, whom you are with, what you are wearing, etc., simply want to control you. Girl, you better block his number and run away as fast as you can.

Likewise, if you are dating a man who hits you before he marries you, he will always beat you when you are his wife. Listen to me: he will never change, no matter how much he says he loves you. He is a master of saying he is sorry and he wants to do better because you are the best thing that has ever happened to him. You see his potential, and it is his potential that you love. Any insecurities you may have, a man like this will use them to keep you in bondage. Leave now. You will never be able to say that you were not told in the beginning. Leave.

Before finding your future husband, become the woman you want to be first. Become independent and self-sufficient. Do the things in life that please you. Get your education and get closer to God. Do what you dreamed of doing now. Serve others and do volunteer work. Become a good person and stop hating on other sisters. Stop complaining and always having negative things to say. Spend time taking care of yourself. Read and travel and open your mind to the world that is before you. Get out of debt and build wealth for yourself. Be the woman you want to be before you find the man you want to spend the rest of your life with.

On Being Your Best Self

When it comes to your health and body image, start making yourself a priority. Don't keep your hair styled just when you have somewhere to go or you have a date. Life is not a dress rehearsal. You need to look good every day. This should not be a part-time situation. Stop being lazy about taking care of yourself. You keep complaining that you can't find a man when you don't have yourself together. Men are attracted to what they see on the outside. Deal with the real issues surrounding your weight gain. You don't have to be a size 4, but you need to find that healthy weight that makes you feel good about how you look so that when someone gives you a compliment, you can accept it and move on.

If you want a husband, then look like someone's wife. It is a hard, cold truth, but there are women who never struggle getting a man. These women may not be the most beautiful or thinnest women, but they exude self-confidence, they are put together well, they know who they are, and they have their life together. This is what men are attracted to.

These sisters are not sitting around home complaining to their girlfriends that there are no good men. They are making themselves priorities. These are the sisters who go to the store to buy an outfit because they like the way it looks on them, not processing first in their minds whether their man or some other men might like it. They want to look good for themselves. Plain and simple.

Go in your closet and get rid of those old clothes that make you look old. Find your sex appeal and become feminine again. What kind of nightgowns do you sleep in? Find your way back to pampering yourself before you want a man to do it. Wake up every day and go out of your house looking like you are headed somewhere. Don't you ever go outside of your home not looking good. I am sorry, but some of you leave your house looking like a hot mess. You will go to the grocery store in sweat pants and a T-shirt. I look around and shake my head. I keep saying to myself, do these woman have any home training, or are they just lazy? Life is too short for you to live on the sidelines. Be who you wish you could be now. Money is not your issue because there are too many places to get nice clothes at a discounted price for you to be walking into somebody's mall or store in baggy pants and a big shirt. Or, excuse me, walking around in tights that show your legs with your big stomach hidden behind a flowing blouse that belongs on a girl ten years your junior.

You spend a lot of time working during the day. I worked for both state and county governments. I am a sister who shops at thrift stores as well as department stores. I know there are low-cost clothes to purchase that will not break your budget. There is no excuse for women to wear shabby outfits to work. Your job is not a club. There is professional attire, and there are play clothes. I would see women walk into the courthouse with capris on and flip-flops. I could not believe it. I have watched young women attorneys who put on any-thing, and they seem not to care about their professional appearance. But, here we go—no one ever told them. This also goes for doctors and other professionals. I was also shocked to see how some professionals dress in the workplace. You may not need to wear a suit to work in your respective profession, but a nice pair of slacks, a skirt or dress with a cute blazer, or a professional top and or sweater is acceptable. I don't know what the problem could be. Perhaps they are so caught up in their intellectualism that they believe they don't need to look nice on the outside. I wonder if they have given up.

Make no mistake about it; there will be women who criticize my advice to you, but I frankly don't care. They are haters anyway. I want to see you happy. Some women never had their mothers teach them how to care for themselves. You don't dress up only when you are going out or to a special occasion. Walk into your office or job and have the people around you ask where you are going today. I meet people from my church in the stores during the week, and I can barely recognize them. Why wouldn't you want to look your best every day?

Look good for you. Be honest about your weight and your health. The weight issue is a big problem for many sisters. Nobody sat us down and said that gaining weight with age would be this big of a problem. Family members would joke and make comments that our eating habits would eventually catch up to us. However, no one was honest about telling us we have to eat half as much food as we did when we were younger, and we have to let the sweets go. Yes, the sugar is not good for you. If you could ever let all the white stuff go out of your diet—stuff like white rice, sugar, and white bread or pasta, you would feel better and look better for years to come.

I have purchased every pair of Spanx on the market to look good on the outside for others. When I took them off and looked in the mirror, I didn't like what I was seeing. I finally had to decide for myself that I wanted to look good for me. My decision was not for my husband. Although I hate to exercise, I mattered enough to decide to take care of myself and exercise whether I liked it or not. I could no longer get up in the middle of the night and eat a bowl of cereal or ice cream. In fact, I cannot eat past seven p.m.

You and I know that being overweight has deeper implications. It is not about the food. Although I am a foodie and love to eat, I had other issues going on, and I used the food to make me feel better. In some instances, you may have health issues causing your weight gain, but the vast majority of women gaining weight are not dealing with the underlying reasons for the weight gain. Putting that aside, I am addressing the five pounds that became twenty pounds that became thirty pounds. For some, there is an entire wardrobe you can no longer fit into. Use that as your motivation to turn things around in the weight department. This has to become something you do for yourself.

If you are like I was, I ordered and tried every quick fix trick that you hear about to lose the weight. There is no miracle cure for weight loss. You have to burn more calories than you take in. You have to let the fried foods and chips and candy and ice cream go. You can't get up late at night, eat, and go back to bed. You cannot pray this weight off or simply fast for two weeks and expect to lose ten pounds. You may go up and down, but you need to make a lifestyle change.

Do what I did and start off slowly, with fifteen minutes of exercise. I moved to a half hour, and now one hour, over a period of six to eight weeks, three to four days a week. When I feel stressed, I exercise. It helps. Now it is second nature to me. You have to move or walk or exercise four to five times a week. This is the simple truth. If you say you don't have the time, you are fooling yourself. It is a lie. You must make the time. Get up out of the bed and start walking. Put in a walking DVD or walk around the neighborhood or go to the mall and walk. Stop eating as much. Eat more fruits and vegetables, and always eat breakfast. You are the only person who can decide for yourself that you deserve to be the woman you dreamed of becoming. You get to decide. No one wants to spend their life with someone who is still trying to find herself.

Find who you are first, and everything will come to you. When you are not at your best, it is a spirit that comes from your being. You can have a cute dress on, but if you are not comfortable in your current size, you will never be able to fix yourself enough to be satisfied. Ask God to help you and start out with baby steps. I pray while I am working out, and I thank God for my good health and the ability to take care of myself. Get started. You can't say you were never told.

Being your best self may mean you need to deal with the pain that is inside you. Girl, you may need some counseling. If you are depressed or unhappy a great deal of the time, you may need to go and talk to someone. There will be good days and bad days in life. However, if the majority of your days are bad, you need to make a change. You are allowing your life to be filled with drama and despair. You need to get to the bottom of why you are so unhappy. Why are things always happening to you? Why can't you find your peace? Is it a violation from childhood? Is it something from your past? Why do you have such low self-esteem? Are you lonely? Do you hate how life has turned out for you? Whatever your reason, you need to seek counseling. Whatever you do, don't allow anyone to dismiss your feelings. If you are sad, try to figure out why and do something to correct it.

Your best self includes your ability to continue to dream. Whatever you do, keep envisioning a better future. I do not want you to stop having aspirations. If you can still breathe, and you are reading this book, it is not too late. Do not allow your life to pass you by without fulfilling your destiny. You can no longer carry fear in your spirit. What are you afraid of? Stop worrying about what people think. They don't care about you anyway. Who cares what they think? They wish they could dream again.

Once you link up with God in your endeavors, there can be no failure. There can only be life lessons. Anything that is done to the glory of God will never fail. Your dreams matter, and you should spend all the days of your life making them come true. I wake up every morning—every morning—doing something toward the fulfillment of my many dreams. I am a dreamer. I am proud to say it to the world. Little children have dreams as they are growing up. Adults take those dreams from them. Their surroundings make them believe their dreams are not possible. My mother made me feel that I could dream and dream big. I believe with all my heart that all things are possible. I love how it feels to dream. I love when I put my plans on paper, and I love when it all starts coming together.

Being your best self may mean that you come to understand others and not take their hatefulness personally. There will always be forces and people who will come into your space to tell you that your dreams are impossible. I am flexible in my planning. I dream of big ideas, and I let details play out as I go along. In other words, I may knock on a door that is closed, but I look around to see who may be standing at the door next to me and why God has placed them there. I see everyone I meet as someone who may have been sent to assist with some aspect of my dreams. I take no conversation or encounter for granted. Even when I am told no, I am grateful. Even when someone is revealed to me as someone who does not like me or does not have my best interests at hand, I am grateful. I just see it all as a means to get where God is sending me.

I had people constantly telling me what I could and could not do. I presented them with an idea, and instead of finding reasons to help me make it happen, they listed a number of reasons why I should walk away from my dream or my idea or the vision God had given me. They bothered me for a second, just one second. One of them had to ask if I was still on the telephone line because I emotionally disconnected from him so fast he could feel it in his spirit. After these negative conversations, I would pull myself aside and have a talk with God. I'd ask for clarity and start over. I realized they couldn't see what I could see. I realized that they were living lives in fear and not possibilities. They were relegated to their day-to-day living and could not see the possibilities of what I was trying to do. I completely understand that I do not need their approval or assistance if they cannot see my vision.

I decided to limit my interaction with them and instead surround myself with people who can see what I see. In those cases, the men and women who were offering me advice were attempting to look out for my good. I believe it. They didn't realize my story and all I had been through. They didn't understand that I was not about to allow a few nos to discourage me. They didn't understand that I believe in myself too much to doubt what could be done. They just didn't understand who I am.

I recently had to cut someone out of my life. My son Michael said that I taught him the same thing, and he cautioned me not to do it. I shared with him that it takes a lot for me to let people into my space, and once they are in my life, if they don't do right by me, they have to go. I have no interest in dealing with them. I want to live my life with people who are on Team Penny. I will be on their team. I pride myself on being a good and loyal friend. I will go to the ends of the earth for the people whom I love, but I expect the same from the people who call themselves my friends.

If you are not on that level, then we are mere acquaintances. I expect my friends not to talk behind my back. I expect my friends not to be insecure when dealing with me. I expect my friends to be loyal. I can't have people around me who are competing with me. I didn't compete in law school, where the entire process is built on competition. I certainly am not going to live my life with people who want what I have. I want them to aspire to their greatness, but not resent mine. We are all originals, and no one can do me but me.

I strongly advise you to be clear about the people you allow to be on your life's journey with you. There are a lot of great women out there. They want to see you soar, and they will be your friends until the end. However, there are some low-down sisters who will cut your throat if you don't watch them. They specialize in becoming friends with you so they can always keep up with what you are doing. They talk about you, and secretly they resent your ability to dream. Be careful of them because they do a marvelous job of pretending to be friends. It is something you will have to learn as you go through life.

On the Issue of Other Women

I started the *SisterTalk Empowerment* conference as a result of being treated badly by women who looked like me in a professional context. I wanted to create an experience that showed women and an entire generation that there was a better way to deal with one another. I grew sick and tired of the backbiting and evil ways of some women out here. Who raised these women? They just hate for the purpose of hating. I actually have people on my Facebook page who don't like me, but they are on there so they can keep up with what I am doing. These are the sisters who seem to resent that you are living your best life. They make up things about you. They will do everything in their limited power to try to block you, and they will never help you.

If you are single, they resent you. They may be in miserable marriages, and they see your life as something they secretly dream about. They attempt to shame you for being single, and you fall for it. The only advice I can give you in dealing with these kinds of women is to limit your involvement with them as much as possible. If you have to work with them, then learn to play the game. Do your business and never let your guard down around them. While you are sleeping, they are plotting on how to bring you down. Learn to pray for them. They are a sad bunch—they are. They are so unhappy and are so insecure that it is painful to watch. They are merely playing a role.

On Being a Sister Hater

You can only love others when you love yourself. Love is so critical to a viable life. If you want to live a life that matters, start loving people. Stop being angry all the time and talking about other women behind their backs. Stop disliking other women when the women have done nothing to you. Why can't you support other women? Why must you always be in a relationship with another sister for you to get something out of it? Why can't you just be nice with nothing in return? Who was the last sister you helped? Why did you help her? Can you compliment another sister? Why do you think other women are out to get you?

Dig deep inside yourself to figure out what is causing you to be so hateful and underhanded with other women. Why are you trying to block them? Don't you understand that what God has for them is for them? You can't stop a move of God even if you tried. Don't you understand that you have been blessed so that you can bless others? If there is another sister you can't stand because you believe she has it all or because she is smarter, ask yourself why you hate her so much. I want you to know that you are the problem. It is about you and not the sister. She is merely living her life. We have to stop this madness of trying to do whatever we can to hurt another sister. Aren't you tired? I know this for sure, I am tired of watching you cut up and be deceitful. Find some self-esteem and stop hating on other women.

On the Issue of Your Finances

Girl, get your money and your mind right. Blackvoice-news.com reports, "Black women are the only group that has not recovered the jobs they lost in the recession." It goes on to say that the net worth among single black women is just $100. We already know that women of all races are paid less than men. One of my goals is to educate and empower women in the area of finances. You can read for yourself the many reasons behind the financial well-being of women. You just need to be educated on the idea that financial freedom gives you true independence. It opens the door for you to live a life of options.

You have to stop focusing as much on what you make and focus instead on what you keep. Women spend a lot of money. We make eighty percent of the spending decisions in our homes. We need to begin to develop a better relationship with money and how it can be used to create freedom for ourselves.

Too many women use shopping as a way of working through the emotional pain that is deep inside. If we are lonely, we can always go out and buy a pair of shoes. Shopping can make us feel good while we are doing it, until the credit card bill comes in the mail, and we become stressed.

I highly recommend that you think about securing multiple revenue streams. As a single sister, you are it. You don't have the benefit of a husband to share the finances in your life. If you work for a company, why not develop a passion and make it profitable for you? Start thinking about something you love doing, something you would do for free, and figure out a way you can make money from it. If you are apprehensive about going into a venture by yourself, try and connect with someone who is willing to partner with you to make it happen.

Learn to save. Save your money and get out of debt. Financial freedom changes your life. The objective should be to keep as much of your money as you can. Delay your gratification so that you can control your finances and not spend all the days of your life paying on credit cards or paying loans back. Put money aside for emergencies. Your rainy day fund must have enough to sustain you for at least six months. Start out with one month and let it grow. I have a savings account that can sustain me for two years if anything happens that I am unable to work. I never use the money for anything else. I have separate savings for household and automobile emergencies. I pay myself, and I invest in my future. You may think you have time, but the years will pass quickly. I am not suggesting that you deny yourself the things that you want in life. I am sharing that as you get older you will need money for your long-term needs as you are a single sister, and everything stops with you.

If you do find a man you want to marry, be sure to get the financial situation handled at the outset. I would not marry a man without finding out his credit score and his credit history. It will tell you a lot about his issues regarding accountability and his relationship with money. Can I say this again? "You can do bad by yourself."

It is time for you to grow up and develop a relationship

with money that involves you not just spending money but learning to use it to your advantage. I hate seeing sisters broke when they are working hard. Many times a broke sister will put up with certain men because of finances. If we are going to keep it real, you may even be sleeping with a brother, married or otherwise, because he is a good provider. He is nice to you. He buys you gifts and purses, and may even pay a few bills. When you are financially secure, you can buy your own things. Being financially independent gives you a number of options, and you rarely have to put up with what you don't want to have to put up with.

On Sleeping Around

I realize this is a touchy subject. You are single, and you want to save yourself for your husband, but there is no husband. You are a woman, and you have needs. You hear at church and in the mosque not to have sex outside of marriage, and you feel guilty every time you do. You are ashamed, and you don't know what to do. You want to know how can you be single, saved, and yet be satisfied. What should you do?

As a minister, my responsibility is to tell you not to have sex outside of marriage. As a grown woman, I believe it is between you and God. You have to find a place in your life where the decisions that you make do not bring shame to you. No person is perfect. We all do the best we can to do right. You just have to search within your heart for your truth. Do what works best for you in the context of your relationship with God. I will not condemn you, but I will love you through it. It is grueling for single women today. I understand, and I just tell you not to allow anyone to make you feel bad about you and oppress you in any way.

To the single sister sleeping around with married men, it is time to let that other woman's husband go. There are reasons you are promiscuous. You may not have time for a real relationship. You may be busy with your career, and you are not ready to be in a relationship. Like some men, you may fear commitment. Because you have been hurt in the past, you may not know how to be in a relationship. You may think that this is the best you can do, being someone's other woman. You may feel that you are not worthy.

Because of the shortage of single men, you are likely settling for a married man. You think it is exciting, and you enjoy that he makes you feel special. There are some of you who sleep with married men for revenge. You see yourself getting back at someone, but you are the only one being hurt in the long run. You may be sleeping around to get over the pain of another relationship. Whatever the reason, you need to be honest with why as a single woman you would lower yourself to be someone's side woman. You are going to get hurt. It will eat away at your self-esteem. It is not worth it. You have to care more about yourself than to lower yourself to a place where you can never grow or be the woman you have been called to be.

I am not being judgmental, but someone has to tell you the hard, cold truth. Your friends will never trust you around their husbands. You will find yourself alone and isolated. If you make a decision to sleep with a married man, you are deciding to give up a part of your life for him. Trust me, he is not worth it. For men, it is about the sex. For you it is about wanting someone to love you. He is always going to be Mr. Wrong. Even if he leaves his wife for you, how can you ever trust that he will not treat you the same? Know that you are worthy of better. You are someone to love, and you certainly don't need to fall in love with a man who is not your man in the first place.

It is important for you to know that I understand your desire to be loved. As women, we want to share our lives with others. You have so much to give and to share with others. I want you to decide that you are important enough to love yourself. You are special in this world. There are people who love and care about you. I want you to walk in the fullness of your womanhood by understanding that what you have to offer deserves a man to believe that you are worthy of being first in his life. Your willingness to accept anything less comes from a place of brokenness. Somewhere in your life, there was a breach. You can repair your past by believing that you are special and you are worthy of being loved in a way that brings dignity to your life. Embrace this truth and allow your-self to finally be free.

YOUR TRUTH

How did this chapter speak to you?

_____

_____

_____

_____

_____

_____

_____

_____

_____

_____

_____

_____

_____

_____

_____

_____

_____

_____

_____

YOUR TRUTH

What is your truth?

_____

_____

_____

_____

_____

_____

_____

_____

_____

_____

_____

_____

_____

_____

_____

YOUR TRUTH

Plan of action to deal with your truth:

_____

_____

_____

_____

_____

_____

_____

_____

_____

_____

_____

_____

_____

_____

_____

Section
II

GIRL PLEASE

LIFE LESSONS FOR TEEN GIRLS

BE YOURSELF

LOVE YOURSELF

ENCOURAGE YOURSELF

ACCEPT YOURSELF

EMPOWER YOURSELF

VALUE YOURSELF

KNOW YOURSELF

CONTROL YOURSELF

HUMBLE YOURSELF

BELIEVE IN YOURSELF

RESPECT YOURSELF

STAND UP FOR YOURSELF

SPEAK TRUTH TO YOURSELF

The Power of Dreaming

When I was growing up, my grandmother, mother, and aunts spent a great deal of time making sure that there were certain lessons learned to be prepared to walk into complete womanhood. I learned to cook, to clean, and to wash, iron, and fold clothes. I learned to sew, especially how to hem a dress and sew on a button. With no man around my mother's home, I learned how to cut grass and change a tire on a car. I learned how to dress properly and how to love fashion. I learned how to play outside with other kids and how to enjoy eating, dancing, and chilling.

I learned how to send thank-you notes when someone is kind. I learned how to say good morning when I greet someone and how to enter a room and speak first. I learned to never leave my house with a bonnet on my head or hair rollers, but rather to always be dressed, always! I learned to bathe in the morning and at night. I learned to never leave dishes in the sink. I learned to not be jealous of another woman. I learned how to open up my heart and love everyone. I learned how to love God and know that there was nothing greater in the world. I learned to pray before I ate and when I lay down to sleep. I learned not to talk behind some else's back. I learned how to treat people and how to not be mean. I learned that bullying is not right. I learned respect. I would never talk back and be smart with an older person. I learned not to put on too much makeup or show my stomach as a young lady.

I learned to wash my hair often and to always have my clothes ironed. I learned to get permission and understand that I was not grown. I learned a young lady crosses her legs and how to sit up and not slouch. I learned that going to church is a necessary part of life. I learned that lying feels bad when you get caught, so we shouldn't do it. I learned my education was a ticket to my dreams. I learned that friends come and friends go. I learned the importance of family. I was taught these lessons intentionally in some cases, but a great deal of them came from how the women in my life shared wisdom. I watched, and I listened. I learned from watching. I listened more than I spoke. After all, a child's place back then was not being involved in grown folks' conversations. We were seen and not heard when grown-ups were speaking.

Not only did I learn life skills, I learned hard lessons about relationships. From what I watched growing up, I learned lessons about men. I learned that men could hit women, and no one seemed to have the power to stop it. I knew from childhood that it was wrong, and, although it was unacceptable, because no one said it to me, the messages were confusing. I was an innocent bystander. The women around me never verbally communicated that it was unacceptable, quite the contrary, but because I witnessed it, the message became loud and clear to me: allow it because it is a part of life. While I was watching it, I vowed I would never let a man put his hands on me. What do you think happened when I grew up? You guessed it. The same thing happened to me. I selected men who put their hands on me.

It wasn't until years later when I finally "discovered" myself and my worth that I realized I deserved better. I was able to break the cycle of what I watched both my mother and grandmother go through. Even the neighbor next door had to endure beatings; so did many of my friends' moms. It was as common as breathing where I came from. I watched my aunt be hit as well. It was everywhere.

As much as I read, and I read a book a week, sometimes more, I never had a book of advice where the words sounded like me and spoke to my issues, where the advice was real, and I did not feel embarrassed to read it. Nothing spoke to the issues I was facing. Graduating from high school, my mother gave me a book entitled *Miss Manners: Guide to Excruciatingly Correct Behavior* by Judith Martin. The book sits on my shelf today with a copy of Alex Hailey's *Roots*. These were guides, but they were missing what I needed. People growing up back in my day kept a lot of secrets. They did not always speak about the obvious. I'm sure women sat around and talked the way we do today, but no one talked to the children about what they witnessed going on around them.

Let me go back and explain the "book" issue. Both my grandmother and mother gave me a book a week to read. We had bookmobiles that came to the neighborhood so children could check out books. It was better than the ice cream truck. It was thrilling when it rolled through. It was the best thing in the world to be able to check out a book. It was the greatest gift that I was given. Because of it, I love reading and the power of words. I knew I wanted to be an author, among a long list of other options, all because I read those books. Read as much as you can. It opens the doors to your mind. Don't just read on the Internet. Read stories, and read biographies. Reading broadens your horizons.

If I only had had a book about what was going on in my life—the abuse and struggle surrounding me—I can't imagine how it would have changed my life. If I only had had someone to let me know that I could control my life and that I had power. I often wonder where I would have ended up in life if I could have taken my power back sooner.

I laugh to myself when I write these words because with the help of God, my life turned out well after all. When I think about all of my blessings, I am grateful: being an author, controlling my destiny, having good health, earning three degrees, holding positions of authority and power, getting to preach the Word of God, visiting the White House, walking red carpets, receiving an Emmy Award nomination, living in Hollywood, putting on a robe and presiding in a seat of justice, traveling places around the country, meeting people from everywhere, speaking to thousands, raising a son I can be proud of and a granddaughter whose dreams are larger than mine ever could be, working to help poor people, having a church family that loves me, having my sisters who believe in me and support me, having a husband who is always by my side, getting to live debt free without financial worries, and honestly, the list could go on and on. Important note: I wake up every day listing my many blessings; I write them down. It is the way I continue to stay humble before God. No matter what is going on in our lives, there is always something to be thankful for. You just need to remind yourself of it on a daily basis. It really keeps you grounded.

In spite of all that I went through, God made it all happen. If it happened for a child who is the product of a rape, brought into this world through the worst of circumstances, God can and will open doors for you, and nothing is impossible. I never let anything I saw as a child stop me from dreaming. I never let the situation of my birth stop me from living life to the fullest.

I dreamed and dreamed, and in the end, it was the only thing that helped me survive and thrive. During the drama-filled episodes of watching my grandmother and mother being hit or listening to men talking to them badly, I would pretend that I was a grown woman living in New York City or Paris, where the days were sunny, and I walked around in pretty clothes and sat at a café having tea. I would take one of my mother's magazines and pretend I was one of the high-fashion models. I would envision my life as a successful woman living in a big house wearing wonderful clothes. I would pretend that I had the life of Diana Ross, my idol at the time. She was glamorous and wore beautiful gowns. She was everything. I would use a towel and tie it on my head to pretend it was her long hair. I would take a brush and use it as a microphone and sing on my front porch. I had concerts where the trees, grass, and animals in the yard were my attendees. My granny listened all the time. I sang and sang and sang.

In many ways, it was a wonderful time for me. Even though I had to witness those bad situations periodically, my granny and mother made a good life for us. Because my mother was so beautiful and smart, I would sit around and try to duplicate her handwriting. I spent a great deal of time daydreaming about life where men did not beat women, and life was not a constant hustle to pay bills and figure out how to make it.

My mother always worked at a good job, but all responsibilities fell on her. She was mother and father. She worked and was sick. She provided for us, and I felt like I had everything the middle-class kids had. I had dance lessons and singing and piano lessons. Our mother had to work a few jobs to make it happen, but she made a way for us, with the assistance of my grandparents. My mother put up with a lot for her children. I am the mother I am today because I had the best example of a woman who sacrificed everything for her four daughters.

My dreams carried me through my childhood. Honestly, my dreams allowed me to deal with my life as an adult. This is why I treasure dreaming so much. My dreams saved my life. I never lost my hope. My dreams made me brave and confident because I believed with all of my might that God would one day allow them to all come true. If I worked harder than anyone else, with God's help, I believed it would happen for me. I would say to my young self, "I know women were not created to be treated the way I saw them being treated." I knew men did not have the right to beat on them.

I knew that we are beautiful and smart, and we could run the world. I knew it from childhood, and I never let it go. I saw laughter and pride in the eyes of the women who raised me. I saw beauty and culture, and I saw compassion. However, I also saw tremendous pain. I felt their pain. I stopped being a child while I was still a child. I have been a grown-up for a long time. That never should have happened. There is an order to things. Exposing a child to adult pain has lifelong implications. It is why I can feel the pain of others, even today. I have a high degree of empathy for others, but it would have been nice to have a normal childhood where I did not have to witness the women I admired and worshiped being beaten. A place where I didn't have to worry about grown folks' business. The good part is that they protected me and never allowed anyone to hit me. I never received a spanking when I was a child because they took all the pain that was being given out during those days.

It is wrong for anyone to put his or her hands on anyone else. Do not allow it in your life, under any circumstances. My *Miss Manners* book never talked about this, but I want you know it from me. No one has the right to hit you or speak to you badly. No one has the right to put you down. No one has the right to bully you.

My granny saw visions. She was a saint of a woman. She was gentle and kind. She was the most giving person I have ever met in my life. I learned to give from her. She was a praying woman and embraced the gifts of the Spirit. I am so grateful for the wisdom that was passed on to me. I am strong and brave because of the lessons I was taught. I made a great number of mistakes along the way, but I learned more. Learning is key to forward movement. Learning helps you find truth.

You Are Not Invisible

This is real talk for a generation who has a great deal of false images presented to them as real. You are often seduced by fame. In some cases, you are obsessed by it. Mainstream and social media are integral aspects of life. What others think about you controls how you process information and dream. You care a great deal about the opinions of others such that it causes you to be unhappy and in some cases has led to suicide by your peers.

You have had to bury your friends and relatives at young ages. This is outside of the order of things. You should never have to bury someone who is a teenager. This changes your worldview and does something to you. You see life as temporary instead of understanding that consequences sometimes have permanent results. You are exposed to issues and situations before you are mature enough to handle them. In the long run, all you want from life is to be loved. If your family would give it to you and listen to you and try to understand you, you would not do half of what you do.

You need love more than you need clothes or shoes or anything that is purchased for you. You want to matter. You don't want to feel invisible. You want someone to care about you. It is a basic need. If your family will not do it, you will find it outside of your home. It is simple to understand. It is my hope that you can find a way to love yourself so that you do not give away your power to others. Other people, especially boys, can smell this need a mile away. You are controlled by others when you seek something they have. You have to grow to a point where you love yourself completely. I know it is not fair that you don't always get the love you need from your parents or your family. Life is not fair. However, you can even things out a bit by learning that you can love yourself. You can love that little girl inside you who needs the acceptance and begin to care about your future so you can make it right for yourself.

You want to matter in this world. You want to matter to someone. You do matter! You are not invisible. I am certain you matter to your family, but in some cases the adults in your life never learned how to parent, or they do not understand how to show you love. They are sometimes selfish. They may be playing a role, which explains why it feels like they love you while at the same time it feels that they don't care. They are doing what was likely done to them or what they observed. They are clueless to what may be happening inside you. You would give anything to be able to talk to them, but you believe they cannot handle it or that they don't care. You are afraid to be honest. I understand. Been there, done that. I get it. You have to do it for yourself. Love yourself. Matter to yourself. You are not invisible.

Learning As You Grow

Growing up, I did realize that I didn't know it all, but like most teenagers, I was attempting to find myself, and I wanted to make my own mistakes. One was to get pregnant when I was eighteen years old. Trust me; I did not try to get pregnant. I was on my way to college. Why would I have wanted to have that happen? Remember, in my dreams I would be living in New York City or Paris. How could it happen to me?

My story has a happy ending, but because of it, I missed out on a great deal that I should have experienced during the college years. I graduated from high school and had a scholarship for college. I found out I was pregnant after I graduated from high school. It was the talk of my little town. All the girls who did not like me had a field day getting the news out to as many people as they could. Remember, there was no social media back then. They could not tweet it or post it on Facebook. They managed, nevertheless, to get the word out faster than a speeding bullet.

I was in disbelief because I got pregnant the first time I had sex. How could that be? Sex hurt so badly and lasted only a few minutes; surely it was a mistake. I never did it again until after I had the baby because it hurt too much. I was preparing to go to college and could not believe it was happening. I walked out of the doctor's office, and I was afraid to tell my mother. When I finally had to tell my mother and my granny, I saw something in their faces that changed the way they saw me. They never looked at me the same. They were disappointed in me, and because of it, I spent the rest of my days determined to prove to them that I would make it in life. I vowed to myself that one day I would grow up to make them proud.

I am living the happy ending. I am right where I am supposed to be in life. It is clear to me. I am the total sum of all my experiences, both good and bad. My son graduated from college and is a successful professional doing well with his life. I have a smart and loving granddaughter. I have a stepson who is climbing the corporate ladder and likewise has a great life. My sisters are my dearest friends. I get to be creative and wake up every day waiting for the day to unfold. There I go again; listing everything I have to be thankful for. Forgive my repetitiveness. I just can't thank God enough.

After my bad marriages, I am finally in a twenty-plus-year marriage where I have never been hit or abused. We have a good life. I have the house that I dreamed of having. I continue to dream and do anything I want to do. I have freedom. I love my family, and I have everything that is important in this world to have a good life. I am able to give my granddaughter the world. I spend my life helping others and fighting for people who do not know how to fight for themselves and causes that are worth fighting for.

So much happened from being a teenager to where I am now. It was a long and hard road to reach my truth. I don't want you or any other young lady to ever have to go through the pain and heartache that I had to endure on my life's journey. I have dedicated my life to making certain that you know that you have options. I want you to keep dreaming and believing that you can do anything, no matter what is going on around you. You can love you and not have to depend on others to do so.

When I was a teenager, I made mistakes, just like you will. There is so much you need to learn about life. Some of you want to be grown up but don't know how. You may feel like an adult because you are treated like one or expected to act like one. Nevertheless, you are a child—a teenager. Adults love to tell you what to do. If I got to talk to my thirteen-year-old self, there is a great deal I believe she should know.

Every girl needs someone to believe in her dreams. You need someone to care about you and your future. For those young ladies who have a father and mother who are raising them, it is a blessing and something to be grateful for. If you don't have parents, there are adults who will love you and be there for you, regardless. If you have parents, but they are clueless, the same holds true for you. You need to find an adult female who can look out for you. You need an adult female you can talk to, not just someone your own age. A person your own age makes a good friend, but she is not in a position to give you the best advice. Wisdom comes from knowledge and experience. They don't have enough experience with life yet to give you long-term advice about life's issues.

You need someone with true wisdom who cares about you. Learn through the pages of this book, too. These lessons are written to help you to find truth and to grow into womanhood so you can avoid as much pain as possible. Challenges are unavoidable, but they help you become strong. These are real talks that no one ever had with me, but I wish they had. I want to make certain you know what to expect as you travel on this journey toward womanhood.

On Being Enough!

Has anyone ever told you that "you are enough"? It wasn't until I was over the age of fifty that I heard the words that changed the direction of the second half of my life. Three words came from a former male professor after I graduated from seminary. I had completed high school, college, and law school. I had already been an assistant state's attorney, a prosecutor, the governor's lawyer, a sitting trial court judge, and had earned a master's from seminary.

I was living my life. A telephone call one morning changed everything. My professor had battled a terminal disease for nearly twenty years, and there was no way anyone could have ever known based on how he lived his life. He and I talked all the time. We shared everything. He was direct and sometimes hard to read. He didn't allow for many excuses to be made around him. We respected each other. I respected him for his brilliance, and he respected me for being a judge and his former student. We talked about world affairs and our family challenges. We talked about God. He was greater than a father figure. I believe he was placed in my life to open the door to a freedom I could have only hoped for.

One morning I was going on and on with him over the telephone about how things were not going as I had planned in my life. I told him how three different black women in three different situations blocked and plotted to hurt me professionally. It appeared they had been successful. He was the only person I could be completely truthful with about how hurt I was. It wasn't so much what they did, it was the fact we were supposed to all be sisters. This was hurtful not only because of our race, but also because were we women. Their attempts to block me had nothing to do with me and everything to do with them feeling threatened. I kept talking about it. He waited and said nothing. Suddenly, I realized that I was doing all the talking, and when I got quiet, he finally said, almost in a whisper, "You are enough."

Before that moment that Dr. Michael Dash said those words to me, no other person on the planet had ever said that I was enough. He repeated it over and over again. It stopped me cold. I began to weep. I reached back to my childhood and grabbed hold of an emptiness that I thought could never be filled and cried my heart out. I wept for nearly forty-five minutes, and he never said anything other than "You are enough." I can hear his deep baritone voice in my head even now. My God, my God. What words! When I finally finished weeping, I didn't know if he was still on the phone. I asked, "Are you still there?" He replied, "Now that you know that you have nothing to prove to anyone, go on and live your life. No one has power over you now. You are enough."

I will never forget that day as long as live. I finally realized and believed I was enough. I became whole. What a gift he gave me. I so desperately needed to know that I could finally stop having to prove myself, that I deserved to be in this world, and that I would not be defined by a title or position in life. I could just be myself.

Dr. Dash passed away and made his way home. I was with him at the end. I miss him tremendously, but he departed having given me the greatest gift a human being could give another human being.

I want you to know that you are enough! You are enough because you were born and are on this planet as someone who is special. God loves you and created you just the way He wanted you to be. "You are enough" means that you do not have to prove yourself to anyone. It means you can accept yourself for who you are. You don't have to be perfect. You can love yourself. You can come to understand yourself. You can embrace your weaknesses and faults while still celebrating your strengths. You really are enough. You are enough! You are not defined by what you have or don't have. You are not who other people say you are. Whether your parents understand it or not, you are powerful. You are powerful because greatness is before you.

You are not a mistake. You are not a problem. You are not a bother or someone to be thrown to the side. You are loved. *You are loved.* Even when life doesn't go the way you plan, it has nothing to do with the girl you are. You were created with a destiny and a plan. Your job is to figure out what those are. You can do anything. You can be anything. But you are not defined by anything outside of you. You are enough. There is nothing that needs to be added or taken away. There is nothing that needs to be changed. You are enough just being you. Being who you are is the most powerful thing in the universe.

If you wish to improve something about yourself or change something, that is fine. Being enough is different. Being enough is coming to an understanding that at your core, in your soul, you know that you are enough in this world. No one can be you but you. You do not have to work at being you. No more pretending or wishing to have what others have. You realize that you are good enough all by yourself. You love you, and if no one else loves you, you love you. You are enough!

I recommend that you say this to yourself every day until you really believe it. I believe it when I heard it because I had been waiting all my life to hear it. I was finally at the point on my life's journey when I could believe it.

On Being Your Best Self

As a teen, you get to decide the kind of woman you will become. You can take on the ways of your mother or grandmother. You can learn attributes from your coach, teachers, or other relatives. You get to decide what kind of personality you want to live with for the rest of your life. Do you want to be a positive or negative person? What kind of personality do you desire? Your personality is different from how you react to things on the outside. A study published in an issue of *Social Psychological and Personality*, written by Christopher Nave, suggests that throughout our lives our personalities stay pretty much the same as they were in childhood. The study did suggest, "While personalities can change, it's not an easy undertaking."

I am not a psychologist, but I know if you are determined to do something, it can be done. I believe positive habits can transform your life. In other words, if there are things you didn't learn when you were younger, and you are hearing them for the first time through the pages of this book, you can embrace them, adopt them, and change what you do. I believe that change can occur.

You need to ask yourself, who am I? Look at yourself in the mirror and dig deep for a definition. Who are you? Not who the adults around you think you are. Not who your friends think you are. Who are you when no one is looking? Who are you when you are by yourself? Who is the real you? By getting to the point of knowing who you are, you can get yourself ready to reach your full potential, including making changes if you desire. Your possibilities are endless, but if you don't know that fact, it is meaningless. Your goal in life should be to become everything you are capable of becoming. It doesn't matter if you have not decided what you want to do, but you should seek to do your best to reach your full potential. You were born with gifts and talents. As long as you operate in them, you will always do your best. My motto is "Excellence is the standard and not the goal." Because none of us can be perfect, we have to strive for excellence.

As a teen, you may have a hundred reasons why you think you are not good enough. When everything around you is not going well, and when no one believes in you, it is easy to beat up on yourself and begin to believe you are what everyone is saying. No matter what anyone says or does, no one can take away your potential. Your potential belongs to you. It is deep within you, and your job is to always remember that it is there.

No matter what happens in your life, always be optimistic. I am extremely optimistic. I cannot stand being around negative people. In fact, I stay away from negative people. They will make you forget the potential you have. For you to stay positive, it will be necessary for you to write down every day what you are grateful for. Every day should be something different. You should always think positively, no matter how bad things might seem. Most of them are merely temporary anyway. People make the mistake of believing that they are permanent. People who reach their full potential always believe they can do it.

What are your goals? What kind of person do you want to be? What are your goals while you are in school? What are your goals after school? Do you seek to do well in school? Goals give you purpose, meaning, and direction. Always keep goals in your life. Write them down. It's hard to reach your full potential if you don't have your goals written down.

Surround yourself with positive role models. If your peers are going nowhere in life because they do not see their potential and have no goals, they will likely want to take you with them. Break free from the do-nothing kids who don't want anything. They have miserable lives, and they want you to be miserable with them. They are not really your friends. They are broken and need so much. You have to push forward to make a way for your journey.

If you are going to reach your potential, I want you to understand that you may sometimes fail. Life will not always go as you plan. You have to be flexible and not take it personally. Use every defeat in any area as a way of learning and growing. Just promise yourself to do better the next time.

Take responsibility for making yourself happy on the inside. Don't look to others for that need because no one can make you happy. Remember, we talked about not giving away your power. Dreaming and having a wonderful imagination are critical to happiness. Take your imagination and let it guide your goals and ambitions in life. After you have determined who you are and recognized all the potential inside you, you can begin to work on the outside.

Respect Is Everything

We live in a world today where respect is hard to come by. People are disrespectful to one another. Children are disrespectful to their parents and vice versa. People are disrespectful on television and social media. They are even disrespectful to the President of the United States. It is disgraceful, and they wonder why teens don't have respect. It is because the adults don't respect one another.

If you don't respect yourself, you can't respect others. You have to learn how to respect yourself. You have to know who you are in this world. You have to treat yourself with respect by treating your body with respect. For instance, I understand that tattoos provide you guys with self-expression, but you have to consider how you want the world to see you because you will be judged how you present yourself. You have one time to make a good first impression. If you have written across your neck "I love Pookey," and you grow up to be a doctor, a judge, or a teacher, how can I take you seriously? At the time you get the tattoo, it may make sense to you, but what are the permanent implications of marking up your body such that it interferes with seeing your true beauty? In some cases, the more some people feel ugly inside, the more they mark up their bodies where people can see so that you don't realize what is really going on inside them.

I think tattoos are for adults. Even when adults get them, however, I think they need to place them where they cannot be seen. To put one on your face or your neck limits your possibilities. You will be judged. If you dream of acting, it may limit roles you can play. Some employers will not hire people with visible tattoos. Therefore, think long and hard about getting one even when you are a grown woman. I am all for free expression, but I am also for being smart about strategy. I don't want you to do anything that can end up being a barrier for you in the future.

On the issue of respect, please wear clothes that are not revealing. What do you have to prove? Wanting to be noticed in that way is a lack of self-esteem. You don't have to show your body—wear short skirts or have your stomach showing—to be a woman. Class and beauty mean that you wear clothing that flatters your body. You don't need to wear revealing clothes. You can wear holes in jeans as a fashion statement, but must they show your thighs? If you have to constantly pull down your dress or skirt, it is too short. Stop trying to be like the reality stars and the people you hear on the radio. All that stuff is a costume for a role they are playing. On the opposite side, don't ever go out of the house like you just rolled out of bed. Don't leave your house wearing a hair bonnet or pajama bottoms. You should have your hair combed and put on proper clothing. Dress in a way that makes you proud to be lady. A lady doesn't need to prove to anyone she is beautiful. She knows her beauty first starts on the inside and is shown on the outside. Respect yourself enough not to have to show your body to feel good about yourself. You are wonderfully made, and it is unnecessary.

Respect requires that you are not loud in public, acting like an alley cat. You should not curse in public. You should not fist fight others. You are better than acting like that. Don't allow anyone to make you look and act like a fool in front of others or ever, for that matter. Think about what you are saying before you say it. You are a child, and although you need to stand up for yourself, do so in a respectful manner and get away from the person who is pulling you away from being a respectable young lady.

Respect requires that you show respect to the adults in

your life who are doing you no harm. You can't just talk back to your parents, teachers, etc. Now, if someone is physically hurting you, you don't owe that person anything. You have to tell someone and get away from him or her as soon as you can. However, you cannot walk into a classroom and get smart with your teachers. You must show them respect. You are not grown, and you are there to learn. The same holds true when your parents or guardians attempt to give you guidance or don't do what you request. You don't have the right to disrespect them. Once, a 12-year-old girl, while attending church, stepped out and started being disrespectful to me. I realized that the child had no respect for herself, and no adult in her life had taught her what respect means. It is humbling yourself and understanding that you have to exercise self-control and think before you act. Understand your place, and yield to people who have authority. It is about treating others the way you want to be treated. It is also about self-care and honor because you love yourself, and you are enough.

On Keeping Promises

If you say you are going to do something, keep your word. Growing up, I experienced many broken promises in my life. Because of it, I never promise to do something and not follow through. It is time to start making promises to yourself about how you will live your life. Promise yourself never to do drugs, or have sex before you are married, or be disrespectful, or bully others. Before you can make a promise and keep it to others, you have to keep them to yourself. Promise yourself you will do well in school. Promise yourself that you will work hard and make your education a priority. Promise yourself you will be a success in life and never go to jail. Promise yourself you will never drink and drive. Make promises and learn how to keep them. Once you master keeping your own promises, it will be easy to do it for others.

On Understanding Education Is Power

You desperately want to feel powerful. Somewhere along the way, though, you will start understanding that knowledge is more important than power. It is the key to changing how you live your life. An education changes everything. It makes life better and gives you a future. Not everyone will go to college, but if you can, I recommend it. College is not just about going to class; it is about introducing you to people and circumstances that provide you with a worldview that is essential for your personal and professional growth.

However, let's say you want to use a gift or talent God has given you that doesn't involve a college degree. Educate yourself about your craft. Go and get formal training to learn everything you can. Take as much of the luck out of your dreams as possible. If you are prepared and have knowledge of what you want to do, you retain your power. You have given away your power when you are ignorant. Knowledge is the formula for success. Learn to be prepared. I cannot overstate this enough. Being prepared is everything. Study when you don't want to study. Keep pushing. When you don't understand, get help and don't stop until you understand the answers.

Whatever path you take, you want a future, and you want to dream, so you must get an education. No one will ever be able to take your education from you. With everything that goes bad around you in life, your education is your way of escape. Fight for a good education. Make the teachers and the adults who oversee your life provide you with the best education you can get. You get a good education, become prepared, work hard, pray and trust God, and continue to dream big dreams, and you will be successful. You must never give up.

On Fear and Doubt

Fear is a powerful emotion. As far as I am concerned, it is the number one factor holding people back in life. You cannot go where you are supposed to go in life when you have fear. You must believe and tell yourself that you don't have to doubt. I don't care what your life looks like; keep holding on to your power. Let the fear go. It has some of you in bondage. Some of you fear that you are not loved or that your life will not turn out the way you dream of. You fear you will not be able to get into college or be able to pay for it. You fear that you will not have friends or anyone to love you. You fear no one will accept you for how God created you. Let go of the fear.

You have power within you. Once you let the fear go, anything is possible. When you live in fear, you make poor decisions. Your actions are based on a destructive force and not a positive one. Be brave enough to live your life without fear. It will change your outlook and how you dream. Don't worry about failure. Pick yourself up from it and keep moving. Stop fearing!

On Not Having Sex

You need to wait until you are married to have sex. If the boy really loves you and cares about you, he will not ask you to share that personal part of yourself. Some of you are being intimate with girls and not really understanding that it is not acceptable. Also, oral sex is sex. You are too young for any of this. You are merely doing it to matter to someone. A person would never ask you to do something of this nature as a teenager if he or she really cared for you. Your hormones may be raging, and you may think you want it. You may like the feeling. I don't want you to regret it. The consequences are too important. You will be an adult for a long time. Just calm down and know that if the other person who is pressuring you does not understand, there will be other people to love you—truly love you. You owe it yourself to keep what is most precious to yourself.

If you have been violated sexually, either as a child or as a teenager, it was wrong. It was so wrong. I am so sorry. There are times when this happens; you may believe that you deserve it. I want you to know that no one had the right to hurt you in that way. Sometimes after this happens, girls will continue to have sex with others because it is what they now consider love to be. *It is not love.*

You can right the wrong that was done by telling someone you trust, by talking to a counselor or other adult, and by taking your power back. The man does not get to take away your joy or your life. You cannot give him that kind of power over you. Every time you have sex while you are a child, it is not right. You deserve better, and you can decide to have better. You get one childhood, and you have to treasure it and make the best of it. Many times, it sets the foundation for your entire future.

On Dealing With Peer Pressure

You have nothing to prove to anyone. Be your own person and don't allow others to dictate to you or try to make you do things. You are a leader, so you don't have to follow them, do what they do, or be what they want you to be. You have the power to decide the direction of your teen years. Who are they to pressure you into doing what they want? Cut them off and let them go. Real friends don't put pressure on friends.

On Basic Beauty Tips

Too many young ladies don't know the first thing about taking care of themselves. First, you must bathe or shower every morning or every night. When you were a little girl, some parents felt that you didn't need one every day. Now, though, this will be the only way to keep you from smelling during the course of your day. Morning baths and showers rejuvenate and refresh you. Evening ones remove the day's grime. If you want to stay fresher, do both.

If you have hair under your arms, it is time to shave the hair off. You may wish to use products that can remove the hair without using a razor. Do not leave your house without putting deodorant on. Use lotion on your legs and arms. Brush your teeth, floss, and use mouthwash in the morning and at night. Wash your face and do not allow others to ever put their hands on your face. Don't you touch your face without first washing your hands. Make certain that your hair is always combed nicely and that it's clean.

Never wear wrinkled clothes. In fact, select a couple of outfits the night before that you may wish to wear to school, or pull out your uniforms and have them ready. You don't want to do anything in the morning that gets you frustrated. If you are able to wear perfume, spray a little on. Put a touch on your neck and your wrist, but don't use too much. You want to wear perfume, not have perfume wear you. Also, wear some kind of jewelry—anything that makes you unique and allows you to be yourself. If your parents allow it, painting your nails is always nice. However, once your nail polish starts to chip, take it off immediately.

You don't need makeup. At your age, you wear your beauty just being you. Make sure you moisturize your skin. You should keep your eyebrows brushed. Don't worry about having them waxed or plucked. I would keep them as thick as possible. Don't allow anyone to make them thin. Chapstick helps keep your lips soft. Lip gloss is always fun. It will keep your lips shiny. Just keep it as natural as possible.

You need to eat breakfast. It is the best way to get your mind working. Also, you need to drink at least eight glasses of water a day. Beauty starts on the inside. It doesn't matter what your outfits look like on the outside; they will not mean anything if you don't feel good on the inside. If you feel beautiful deep down inside, you will be beautiful on the outside. You will not need others to compliment you because you will know you look your best for yourself.

You Are Not What the World Says You Are

You are a young lady with dreams and aspirations (what you long for). I don't care how many names people call you. It does not matter what the news media says or your schools say about your test scores. You are a girl who has the ability to grow into womanhood with grace and dignity. You have power. You have a say-so about how your life turns out. How can you expect to turn your dreams into reality if you don't believe in yourself? You have options. Those options will allow you to fly without ever looking down. Remember to love yourself, accept yourself, empower yourself, value yourself, control yourself, humble yourself, believe in yourself, respect yourself, stand up for yourself, and speak truth to yourself. You get to decide. Now you know.

YOUR TRUTH

How did this chapter speak to you?

_____

_____

_____

_____

_____

_____

_____

_____

_____

_____

_____

_____

_____

_____

_____

_____

YOUR TRUTH

What is your truth?

_____

_____

_____

_____

_____

_____

_____

_____

_____

_____

_____

_____

_____

_____

_____

_____

YOUR TRUTH

Plan of action to deal with your truth:

_____

_____

_____

_____

_____

_____

_____

_____

_____

_____

_____

_____

_____

_____

_____

_____

Section

III

The

Sisters

Speak

sis·ter

(sĭs′tər)

noun

1. A female having the same parents as another or one parent in common with another.
2. A girl or woman who shares a common ancestry, allegiance, character, or purpose with another or others, specifically:
a. A kinswoman.
b. A woman fellow member, as of a sorority.
c. A fellow woman.
d. A close woman friend or companion.
e. A fellow African-American woman or girl.
f. A woman who advocates, fosters, or takes.

A sister can be seen as someone who is both ourselves and very much not ourselves—a special kind of double."
TONI MORRISON

Women connect with other women. We share together. We laugh together. We cry together. When we truly connect, there is nothing more powerful in this world. We are special in that we learn life lessons not only through the process of our own experiences but from listening to the testimonies of our sisters. Advice is given and advice is taken. We share a common bond and are connected in the spirit when a woman is brave enough to share her joys and pains.

It was important to me that this book places women and teen girls on a path that would allow them to embrace their own truth. "The Sisters Speak" is real talk from a gathering of women who have stories to tell. These contributors are women of courage. They believe in the sisterhood. They are not consumed by envy and jealously because they have been through a great deal in life and frankly, they will not waste their time with the destructive energy that those twins bring. They have faced struggles on various levels, but in the end they have managed to stand tall. They are different ages, from different backgrounds, with different careers. They are smart. They are reflective. They love God. Most importantly, all of them continue to dream. They share because they love you. It is their truth. It is wisdom. It is real talk.

Let it Begin

To the sister who is optimistic, but stuck:

Seek inspiration. We would recommend that you study the scriptures and pray. Start with the book of wisdom—Proverbs. Choose one passage to meditate on each day. Pray for exactly what you want. Ask God for vision, for guidance, and for purpose. Then, listen for the still, small voice that answers. It is impossible for God to ignore a sincere prayer.

Be patient with yourself and take small steps. Do one thing that advances you toward your goal each day. For example, if you want to write a book, don't attempt to write it all in a weekend. Systematically write one page a day. By the end of a year, your first draft will be complete.

—**JANICE AND DAVIDA MATHIS**

To the sister who cannot let go of her past:

Your purpose is constantly chasing you, and it will not stop until it puts you into a position where you can move forward and walk into it. Once we get to a place where we have a glimpse of what our purpose is, and we have made up our minds to walk into it, that is the part we rejoice over. That is the part that gets us most excited. The only problem with being transformed to the new you are the parts of the old you that still exist. What happens when there are contradictory parts of you that want you to go back to being the old you? I am not talking about the parts of you that you hated in the first place. I am talking about the parts of you that you liked. The things you used to do for pleasure and enjoyment. The way you used to be for pleasure and enjoyment. The way you used to be that if people find out right now, they will all start to look at you funny. Those past thoughts, habits, and urges present themselves to you on a regular basis, and you are in a fight for your own sanity.

For some there exists a battle between your old self and what you must become to fulfill your destiny. The greatest reason you haven't claimed the victory yet is because you cannot change what you can tolerate. Until you can no longer let go of the things that are keeping you from your destiny, they will persist in your life. If the same issue has been bothering you and stopping you from becoming great, it is because you like it, and you have identified with it.

It is time to face those issues head on. You identify with your weaknesses more than your power and love your distractions more than your potential. Your potential is crucial because what you are to become is predestined. Even more, once you become blessed, everything that is attached to you becomes blessed. When your purpose is released, lives get changed. Your distractions and your weaknesses have bound up your potential. You spend less time changing lives and more time distracted.

You spend less time blessing your friends and family and more time afraid. Are you willing to kill all the parts of you that keep you from unleashing your potential? Are you willing to be real with yourself about yourself and be freed from what has kept you from living your purpose? If yes, then claim the victory over the battle between your potential and your past.

Your potential is not for me to unlock; you have to want your future for yourself.

—CHELSI GLASCOE

Oftentimes, we dwell on our past. Whether things happened in our lives that put us in a good place or a bad place mentally, emotionally, spiritually, or financially; whether it made us happy or had us in bondage with no movement; whether we had a stable support system, or whether we were in a positive environment with family and friends, or whether we became whole or un-whole in our relationships or marriages, the past is always in our lives to remember.

For some, your world has crashed, and what was once comforting to you has all been taken away, and there's no outlet for the hurt, guilt, or shame. There comes a time when you must trust God and stop trusting man. Trust God in knowing there is always something greater for yourself and your future. Start visualizing yourself for who you are, not who or what you once were.

God doesn't make mistakes. I believe certain things happen not to punish or hurt us as human beings, but to simply plant thoughts in our minds and hearts so that we're able to learn not to take life's precious treasures for granted, as we can sometimes do. The past is just that; it is behind you. Start practicing by speaking into existence what can and will be in your present and future. This will help you make your days rewarding and positive. Sure, you'll never forget things of the past, but knowing God's promise to you, it will allow you to forgive yourself so that your future will be meaningful, and you can live life abundantly.

—**Keisha Brown**

Reliving the past keeps you stuck on pause, unable to initiate closure and/or detain a healthy and holistic lifestyle. Let's review basic driver's education. When you are learning to drive a vehicle, one of the first instructions is to check your side and rearview mirrors. You are then instructed to adjust each mirror so that you have an understanding of where you are in relation to traffic behind and around you. The rearview mirror helps the driver gage speed and distance. The driver is then told to only glance in the rearview mirror and not to stare at length, which could have fatal consequences. More than a glance in the rearview mirror impairs the driver's forward vision. The same example can be used in comparison to reflect on our lives and how we live our lives always looking at what's behind and barely giving time to that which is approaching. For some of us, the rearview mirror is not a reflective aid but a crippling crutch that we've become dependent on while trying to negotiate our existence in the present.

Mirrors provide a two-way reflection. What you see is what you get. When we don't like what we see, we have the choice to change the image. A rearview mirror is a tool used to keep the flow of traffic steady as we proceed forward. It is not a way that we should live life, with our eyes glued on what's behind us while never putting what's behind where it belongs—behind! Our lives are filled to capacity with memories of the past, which hold us captive. We look back with the hopes of changing the outcome of previous situations. The way to change the outcome of previous moments of indiscretion, violation, humiliation, arrogance, and ignorance is living forward and taking from the experience that which is meaningful to our future progress. Some of us have both consciously and subconsciously acquired the nasty habit of memorializing our past. That is, we place an altar at one of the tragic intersections of our soul and set up camp for the rest of our days, and every time life hurls a blow our way, we return to the altar of our past, continuously blaming ourselves for the hazardous conditions with which we are faced. Our past is to be commemorated, not memorialized or even idolized. Commemoration calls for remembrance and reflection. Memorializing particular blocks of time obstructs our path and keeps us living in the shadows of what could have been or what used to be. Say this affirmation: *I am not my past.*

Our past is a marker, not a precedent set to dictate how we will live the rest of our lives. In some instances, we have become dependent on our past. We are dependent on feelings of shame, guilt, and regret. Whenever we encounter someone, we always reach for the infamous *Woe Is Me* story. We begin to relive, regret, and regress. Moving beyond our past requires us to stop playing the same old tapes! Biblical scholar, writer, and ordained minister Rev. Dr. Renita J. Weems suggests that we always have two tapes playing in our psyche. She says, "The first tape has been playing since our formative years. Recorded on this tape is old-time religion; passed-down traditions, whether good or bad; first hurts, and first failures, etc." The second tape Dr. Weems suggests plays an updated version, which I call the "remix" of our lives. That is, the second tape plays music we've chosen. It plays our constructed ideas about self, faith, spirituality, sexuality, etc. While the first tape never ceases, eventually, the second tape should drown out the sound of messages that no longer serve our future. Living life addicted to a warped tape will keep us in one of two places: spiraling out of control or stuck on pause.

While we should not be enslaved to our past, we shouldn't run from it either. It's only by owning it that we are able to move beyond it. Our past is not our enemy! It is our thoughts about the past that are the culprit. Our past is not taboo nor is it forbidden fruit. The past assists us in unlocking life's mysteries with the hope that we will no longer live disconnected lives but accept who we are and what we've been given. The very experiences that almost killed us, both literally and figuratively speaking, hopefully help us realize the power of the Spirit that has been a mainstay in our lives even when it has not always been recognizable. Everyone who walks the earth has tried to live life looking through the rearview mirror at one time or another. We are not the first. We are all books filled with pages of incorrect grammar, fragments and run-on sentences, split verbs, and dangling modifiers. The most famous person we can imagine is familiar with disappointment, pain, regret, rage, and hurt. As a result, the famous person has struggled like you and I have with drowning out the sound of old tapes playing the same old songs such as low self-esteem, limited self-worth, and the need for guidance from outside sources. We should only drop by every now and then on our past experiences to pay our respects. Doing this is liberating! It affirms that while pain is inevitable, misery is indeed optional!

Our past actually knows its place! We are the ones who move it from its position of former to present so that we are confronted with it every waking minute. But what if we adjusted the rearview mirror a little more? Maybe our past is calling us to reconcile who we were with who we are becoming. Maybe our past is calling us to recognize that what happened to us does not dictate the rest of our lives. If we were to continue with the above suggestion, which is in the past lay the mysteries of life, then we could maybe find solace in our current state. I believe that the mysteries sit idly waiting for the spotlight of our souls to search them out. I believe they cannot be released or reduced to retrieval within the boundaries of our physicality nor under the auspices of our own intellectual infidelity. In trying to apply what we already know, in trying to get up, get out, and get something, we've been deceived by our own issues of incompleteness, abandonment, and estrangement. The duplicity of our desires consumes and clouds the only access road to our past—the Spirit. We have to reconcile with ourselves to become one with our inner being, which both compels and propels us to live the life we desire, dream of, and want.

Reconciliation suggests a prior wholeness. It eludes that two parties were once conciliatory. It is really hard to reconnect without an initial connection. So what am I saying? Living life through the rearview mirror prevents us from becoming whole. It keeps us from participating in true reconciliation. The Sikhs are a religious group that believes reconciliation is a process that begins first and foremost within. Letting others and ourselves off the hook frees the spirit to guide us back to the spirit source wherein the mysteries await. What mysteries you ask? I am speaking of the mysteries that provide us with the strength, determination, and fortitude to go through the fire of the past and not be burned. I am speaking of the mysteries that guide us through life's expected and unexpected dilemmas. The mysteries make us aware of the road signs: no U-turns, caution crossing, green light, yellow light, red light, and *stop!* These are the mysteries that enable us to forgive what appears unforgivable and to forgive who seems unforgivable. Such mysteries are waiting for us to release them that we might move beyond that which has held us back, stifled our success, wrought havoc on our emotions, and sabotaged our worth as women.

It's time to take the emergency brake off our lives. It's time to live a fully connected and whole life. There is a vision waiting to be lived with your name on it. There is a moment waiting to be experienced with your initials. In the words of "Ms. Lucy," a childhood rhyme, "Jump in the car. Put your foot on the gas. Jump back and let your destiny pass." We can never move forward as long as we hold on to that which is non-retrievable. While we can never physically relive those moments, we can release them so that we can heal, get up, get out, and get something.

—REV. MELVA SAMPSON

Read the book of John. It is all about God's love for us. There is nothing as inspiring as knowing you are fully and completely loved with all of your shortcomings, misgivings, and apprehensions. If God loves you and forgives you, then you can and should forgive yourself.

Create separation with your past. If it is an unhealthy relationship, leave it. If it is an unsatisfying job, go to school at night to learn a new skill set. Don't wallow in what-ifs. Make new friends. Find an inspiring church and get active in it.

Help someone who is less fortunate. Find a cause. Nothing is as satisfying as helping others. The better you feel about today, the less important yesterday becomes. Remember that every successful person first experienced failure.

—JANICE AND DAVIDA MATHIS

To the sister who cannot let go of her past, I say to you, your past is your testimony! Whether it is good, bad, or indifferent—it is yours. We all got "past." People you look up to and admire got past; people you abhor got past; people you do not know got past. Looking at me, you cannot see my journey, my past. You could never imagine the thrills/chills, fears/tears, of my past. There is so much I will always remember and cherish; there is equally as much that I choose to forget. To live a healthy, productive life means I cannot allow my past to be an affliction; rather, it is my platform to exclaim who I am in the present and who I will be in the future.

I say to my sister who cannot let go of her past: let it be your benefit and not your burden. The benefit of the past is that you can say, "I've lived it, learned it, loved it, hated it, been there, done that." That was then; this is now. Because of my past I know more; I know better; I know different. I can testify!

This is a simple truth—it doesn't matter if you are proud of your past or ashamed of it—it is *past. It is what it was.*

Can't erase it, can't replace it, and can't change it. But I sure as hell can learn from it! Someone said, "Life is the only discipline where you get the test before you get the lesson." Your past is a lesson learned; your future is a new test. Don't fail the test before you take it.

Holding on to what's past diminishes the present and retards the future. For example, those who dwell on holding tight to a past of fame or fortune that is long gone will likely lose sight of what could potentially be greater rewards. Don't deprive yourself of endless possibilities. Those who will not let go of the pain and heartache of a past filled with mistakes and hurtfulness find it difficult to envision a future of hope and retribution. Don't sentence yourself to a life of misery and regret. Don't poison the present and choke the future. One thing is for certain: you cannot have a do-over of your past. Let it go. Put it where it belongs—in a special place behind you.

Make it your personal resolve: "Based on my past, I rest assured my now is better than yesterday, and my tomorrow even greater."

If you've allowed your past to be a burden, release it; if necessary, share it with another sister for the purpose of ensuring she does not go through what you've experienced. Be the living testimony of a brighter day. Your release will lift your burden, and you will become a guiding light for someone else.

If your past was all that you ever dreamed of, and now it's a memory—savor the memory. Then put it in a special place and dream again. For as long as you are breathing God's air and doing His will, all is possible. Past is past; the present is God's gift; the future is the manifestation of that gift.

—SCARLET PRESSLEY-BROWN

As a child, I often heard my parents say, "You can't drive a car and stay in the road while looking in the rear view mirror!" To that end, I would tell my sister to keep her feet moving forward! It's easy for someone to tell you to move on in life without any suggestions of how that would be accomplished. I would tell my sister to continue to get up every day, continue to go to work, school, the gym, etc. The beauty of the sun setting daily is that's another opportunity to close the book on what transpired today, get up tomorrow, and try something new. With time, every passing day is also part of the past.

—SHIRLEY LANGLEY HENRY

We are all on a journey. A journey that God has designed. Along that journey there will be several "hiccups" on your path. It is vital that we do not allow those hiccups to delay us, distract us, discourage us, depress us, deter us, detain us, or destroy us. Those hiccups show up in the form of people, situations, or circumstances that are sometimes beyond our control. It is important that you remember God has designed your journey, and that *He* is in control if you let Him take the wheel. You must be sure to put your ear to the ground so that you can hear clearly His directions and instructions. The Lord has ordered your steps, so when you experience life on your journey, you must resolve in your heart and your mind that you will not get stuck in your past and that you must keep moving full speed ahead! If you believe God has His hand on your life, you will know that looking back will only delay the process and get you off track. Isaiah 43:18-19 says, "Do not remember the former things, nor consider the things of old. Behold, I will do a new thing. Now it shall spring forth: shall you not know it? I will even make a road in the wilderness and rivers in the desert."

For the "new things" to spring forth in your life, you must let go of the old things! I know that it is difficult to release and forget those things that have caused you so much pain and hurt, but my question to you is, "Why do you want to hold on to pain and hurt?" What rewards come out of holding on to the pains and hurts of yesterday? A friend of mine would often say, "God wants to turn your scars into stars and give you power in your zero hour!" It's your time, daughter, to shake it off! Stop looking in the rearview mirror of your life, honey! Move forward, press toward the mark, take the shackles off your feet, and let it go ... once and for all! Let your desire be to have that "new thing" spring forth so you can enjoy what God has in store for you beyond each door that He will open wide on your journey. Remember, if you trip or fall on that journey, don't look back! Get up, shake the dust off your feet, and keep it moving, baby!

—DEETTA M. WEST

To the sister who is contemplating starting her own business:

Find a Small Business Development Center. Many major universities have them. They are sponsored by the Small Business Administration of the U.S. Department of Commerce. They offer many free resources, including advice on business taxes. Get a separate tax ID number for your business income and expenses. Keep records of your financial transactions to ease headaches when tax time comes. The IRS is the only entity that can invade your bank account and shut down your business. Make tax preparation a priority. Read everything you can find about your industry. Talk to industry leaders. Attend conferences related to your business. Offer to volunteer if you can't afford to register. Write a business plan. Read economic trends to make sure there is demand for your product or service. Learn how to use a computer and the Internet. Seek out free resources, such as Goodwill Industries, that offer classes for new entrepreneurs. Save money. You cannot have a successful business without capital, and most funding sources are not willing to put up their money if you don't already have "skin in the game." Count your own money. Don't trust complete financial management to anyone. Review and understand your own bank statements and tax returns to avoid unpleasant surprises. Watch your overhead. Strive to have the business pay as it grows, rather than putting in all your retirement savings. There are two paths to a profitable firm: increased revenue and decreased expense. Don't neglect either. Become a savvy marketer. Learn the tricks of Internet marketing to grow your brand.

—Janice and Davida Mathis

Plan, prepare, and then proceed. In the planning stage, make sure you have enough money saved for the rainy days. It always rains! Prepare by getting the proper skills and/or education, and remember that office location is important. Also, identify professionals to assist you, such as an attorney, banker, accountant, financial advisor, etc. Know that successful business ownership is hard. If it were easy, everyone would own one. Expect long days and short nights. If this is your God-given gift, you can expect to reap the financial rewards as well! Finally, just go for it!

—**Shirley Langley Henry**

The first thing I would ask you is, what is your passion? What is it that you really love to do? Figure out how to create a business doing what you love or at least that is directly connected to the industry you are interested in. If it is something you are passionate about, it won't feel like a job. Sometimes your happiness is more than a check. Make sure you do your research on whatever industry you are looking to enter. Find companies/people who are doing the same thing you want to do and use them as a guide. Success doesn't happen overnight, so get ready to put in some work. As an entrepreneur, you are always working. There are lots of long hours, mistakes, and continuous learning. You must also be willing to switch your plan up if it is not going the way you want it to. That one new change may make the difference in your business. I had to learn that my business was *my* passion and not anybody else's. I couldn't get mad when people around me couldn't help when needed, or they weren't excited about certain opportunities. This was my dream not

theirs. When you love what you're doing, you put in the time and go the extra mile. Follow your passion!
—Christi Hector

**To a sister on what it means to be a real sister
to another woman:**

When it comes to being a real sister to another woman, it means growing with one another, never having jealously in your heart, and always having each other's back. Being a real sister means being happy for the good things that happen in her life, as well as hurting when she hurts as she finds herself going through bad days. A real sister prays for and with her sister friend. You cry with her and teach her all there is to know. A real sister tells another woman all the things that you wish someone had taught you. Above all, a real sister tells another sister the truth and speaks that truth only out of love, not anger.
—Keisha Brown

For some reason, we as women allow society to promote negative behavior among each other as the way we communicate. All women do not communicate by physically hitting or cursing each other; the majority of us support one another and want the other to succeed. If that sister is looking for a job, help her out, review her résumé, tell your contacts she's looking for a job. If your friend breaks up with her boyfriend, and you knew he wasn't any good for her, don't kick her while she's down and say, "I told you so;" comfort her instead. I really hate to see women, especially black women, hurt, condemn, disrespect, and fight each other. To me it says something about their character and lack of respect for themselves. To be a real sister to another woman, you must be able to praise her accomplishments without jealousy, tell her the truth when she doesn't want to hear it, give her a compliment, listen to her without judgment, admit you're wrong when she's right, and love and respect her. A sister is there when no one else is there.

—TYISKA DEMERY

If you're going to be a real sister to another woman, the most important component is trust. She has to be able to trust you with every word, deed, and secret she shares with you. Be there for her with an open heart and an open mind. Encourage her even when you don't feel like it. Don't be judgmental, and always be honest with her no matter how uncomfortable it may be to tell her the truth. Don't talk bad about her to others, and defend her when others are against her. My best friend and I have been friends for over forty years. Even in our early years, these standards were set, so this is why we have remained friends for so long. Many women don't know how to be a real sister because no one has been one for them.

—MONICA COLEMAN

My sister, when God blesses you to be a blessing to another woman, you should feel privileged. A real sister doesn't care if she is connected to another woman by blood. She is there when times are good and when times are bad. Being a real sister means no matter what you are going through, you have someone by your side who will pray with you and help you get through the tough times. A real sister takes the time to get to know a person, to connect with her. This is not by chance; God will let you know the connection because He is allowing you to connect. When this connection happens, you become sisters in Christ. Oh, what a blessing that is. A real sister prays for her sisters; she prays that they are blessed. Being a real sister also means being honest and true. There will be times when you will have to tell the truth, and it may hurt, but be truthful no matter the situation. A real sister will accept the truth with love because she knows you love her and that your intentions are good. Real sisters are a gift from God. They connect because God lives inside them. Therefore, nothing but love can be given from them. For real sisters, jealously doesn't exist. There is no place for it. They lift each other up in the name of Jesus on a daily basis. Real sisters don't have to be around each other to pray for one another. They don't have to talk every day, but they know they are there for each other.

My sister, when God blesses you to be a blessing to another woman, you should feel privileged. A real sister doesn't care if she is connected to another woman by blood. She is there when times are good and when times are bad.

—**Deidra Davis Alexis**

To the sister who has a calling to ministry but is being told because she is woman she cannot preach or pastor:

Jesus told us, "Many are called, but few are chosen." I would say this statement definitely applies to any woman who has a calling to minister. The Lord calls us into service, but we make the decision to be chosen when we accept the call to enlist in the fight.

Ministry is not easy, and pastoring is not a glamorous job. It is a fight from the moment we say yes to the Lord. The first battle you will have to win will be against the objections and arguments in your own mind. These you must settle if you are going to ever be effective in ministry. The outside challenges to your ministry suffer a deadly blow once *you* completely accept that the Lord has called you to ministry.

You do not need anyone's permission to fulfill the call of God on your life. Many people—men and women—are behind schedule in what God has commissioned them to do because they are waiting on approval and validation from others. You will stand before the Lord and give an account for every excuse that got in the way of your obedience.

If you are looking for a way around having to fight—forget it. The Bible calls us soldiers who must endure hardship, and God has given us a full suit of armor. Clearly the Lord expects us to be skilled warriors. As a woman in ministry, part of your warfare will be against the mindsets and prejudices of those who oppose the idea of women in ministry.

Prepare yourself to deal with the challenges of sisters in the church who consider themselves divas and who refuse to stop being superficial long enough to really be helped and healed through the ministry God has given you. You will also find that many women strongly resent being under the authority of another woman, and they will challenge, question, and rebel against your leadership each step of the way. Be prepared also to deal with the brothers in the body of Christ whose egos won't allow them to accept a woman in any leadership position at all. Both males and females tend to find it hard to receive from a woman, and as a woman in authority, you will find that those you are called to reach will often want you to pay the price for mistakes their own mothers and wives have made.

There are whole denominations who teach it is not right for a woman to preach or to pastor. To that my response is that I'm not interested in a title because more than anything I am a servant—just like Jesus. Call me whatever you like, but I *will* fulfill the assignment that God has placed on my life! You must have that same resolve.

Settle it in your heart and mind that it will always be a fight to preach this Gospel. The good news is the roles of men and women in the church are changing, and although there is still some resistance, women are striving for full participation in church leadership. *Never quit!* Be encouraged like the Apostle Paul who said, "At my first defense no one stood with me, but all forsook me. May it not be charged against them. But the Lord stood with me and strengthened me, so that the message might be preached fully through me, and *that* all ... might hear. Also I was delivered out of the mouth of the lion. And the Lord will deliver me from every evil work and preserve *me* for His heavenly kingdom. To Him *be* glory forever and ever. Amen!" (II Timothy 4:16-18).

—DR. RHONDA TRAVITT

"Even on my servants, both men and women, I will pour out my Spirit in those days, and they will prophesy" (Acts 2:18).

God has the power and authority to use whomever God wants to use. It doesn't matter what age, gender, limitations, or what's in your past. I am a living witness of how God transformed the weaknesses of a girl, who was afraid to allow God to use her, into a woman who knows that there is nothing impossible with God.

In 1990, upon entering seminary at the Interdenominational Theological Center (ITC) in Atlanta Georgia, we were given a survey questionnaire to fill out. One of the survey questions asked, "What is your family lineage into the 'called ministry'?" The second part of the question asked us to list them and their relationships to us.

The question baffled me because I couldn't name any relatives, maternal or paternal, past or present, who had been ministers of the Gospel. After pondering further about my family lineage in ministry, I decided to do some investigating into the matter.

My mother and her sisters informed me that their grandmother was known as an evangelist. She would preach on the street corners or anywhere she could. In addition, they had a sister and cousins who preached, prayed, and used their healing hands to pray for people. My lineage in ministry was passed through my maternal side of my family and through the females. These sisters of the Gospel were not allowed to minister in the church but worked for God in nontraditional ways throughout their lifetimes. If I had known their struggles with being called by God into ministry as women, perhaps my journey to accept being called to be a preacher would have been easier. Instead, it took a near-death experience for me to accept my calling from God.

In the fall of 1974, I was in my college dormitory room when I heard the voice of God speak to me about allowing God to use me to spread the Gospel of Good News. More than being frightened, I thought I must be going crazy because I knew God didn't use women to preach—at least this is what I had been taught. I laughed at this notion. How could I be hearing such foolishness? God went on to say, "If you will allow me to use you, I will place you with kings, queens, presidents, and leaders of the world!" I laughed even harder with that statement and vowed to myself that I would never tell anyone about my moment of madness. However, over the years, before accepting my calling, not a day went by when I didn't think about my encounter with God in my dormitory room. In addition, every day after hearing God's calling, I felt a tugging in my heart that God wanted to use me.

It wasn't until the spring of 1986 when once again I heard the voice of God speak to me in a hotel room in Seattle, Washington. God gave me the same commissioning orders: "Let me use you." This time, in spite of the same fear, I decided to pray, examine, and explore what this meant for me. I asked God to send me signs indicating I wasn't crazy. God did what God needed to do. Random strangers began telling me, "God has a divine purpose for your life." I spoke with a few sisters in ministry as well as with my mother.

The signs God sent me, the conversations with my sisters in ministry, and especially the conversations with my mother elevated me to partial acceptance. My mother shared that as a very young child, God used me to pray, prophesy, and heal. I didn't remember ever doing so. The only thing I could recall is everyone being in awe of me and saying I was different. I also remembered always desiring to be like everyone else.

However, the excitement was extremely short lived; fear crept back in quickly. I decided God had made a mistake. I wasn't strong, smart, or wise enough to preach because the world tradition said no. I had what I thought was my final conversation with God about my allowing God to use me. Late one night while driving home alone, I told God how I felt, that I was simply too weak, unskilled, and scared for my life. I also told God that I would leave God alone, and I wanted God to leave me alone! I said to myself that's it; I'm finished with God. And for a brief moment I was at peace with my decision.

Five minutes later, I was looking at a tractor-trailer truck coming directly toward me. I had no control over the car, and the steering wheel column had locked. To avoid what I had thought was a body in the expressway, I had driven over on the shoulder of the road. Once I had passed the item in the road, I had looked in the rearview mirror to see if I could move back into the northbound lane. It was clear, but what I hadn't seen in enough time were the sofa and dinette set in the expressway. I had hit the furniture and lost control of the car. I was now headed south in the northbound lanes of the expressway!

Prior to the truck hitting me, I had an out-of-body encounter with God. I exclaimed to God as I was traveling rapidly down a lighted tunnel that showed my life story, "Lord, forgive me for not doing what you asked, and please don't let me go to hell!" I didn't ask God to let me live, but I knew I didn't want to go to hell for being disobedient.

Then I heard a voice like thunder say, "Go back, not now, there's work for you to do." I entered back into my body, took my flight attendant posture for a plane crash, and by God's grace and mercy endured the impact of the truck, other vehicles, and the median wall as my car had become like a tennis ball before coming to a final rest. After the Jaws of Life released me from a totaled car and then doctors examined me at the hospital, I walked away without a scratch. That night, I said to God, "Thank you," with a grateful heart, and "I surrender my life unto you; have your will and way."

God has been true to His words of using me to do what I feel are amazing works in ministry. Today, I'm a preacher and senior pastor; I serve in a dean's role at ITC, and I'm a respected community leader. My work in ministry has allowed me the privilege of sitting with presidents of the United States and South Africa, with other influential politicians, and presidents of major corporations.

If God is calling you into ministry, don't risk your life in not trusting God. God can use you with all your faults, limitations, and weaknesses to do just what God said He would and what God wants you to do.

—REV. PORTIA WILLIS LEE

To the sister who is struggling with motherhood:

As mothers, our time is often divided into so many parts that it's hard to piece together even a semblance of wholeness. There are times when I wonder if I will ever move beyond the constant anxiety that accompanies symptoms of scatterbrain. That is, at any given moment, I can be thinking about critical theories of discourse analysis, what I can make for dinner in thirty minutes or less, and how to pull together a twenty-minute fun and exciting presentation that a group of toddlers will get, love, and award me the greatest mom accolade. Sometimes it works, and sometimes, truthfully, most times, not so much. I have found myself searching online chat groups and having long talks with my mom and other girlfriends about how to live in the dichotomy of Melva the mommy and Melva the scholar. The hard part is that in my scholarship I challenge specific dichotomies that seek to divide particular bodies and systems into incongruent parts. In theory, I'd like to think that I don't buy into competing notions that would have me succumb to a type of personality disorder where I perform one way at the kitchen table and another at the seminar podium. Yet, truth be told, balancing motherhood, the rigors of work, and intimate relationships has been one of the hardest feats to tackle.

The trick to such balance reveals a spiritual practice. On one end of the spectrum are those who would suggest that because women have fought so hard to gain equal civic, professional, and vocational footing that, which remains debatable, I should not take a deep breath but instead suck it up and work it out. At the other end of the spectrum lay those who argue on the side of tradition. This perspective aligns itself within the bifurcation of work and mothering wherein a mother's only job should be parenting.

I do not attempt to solve this contention or to even promote one view over the other. In search of wholeness, peace of mind, and the desire to raise womanish girls who question the status quo, know that their bodies are their own, and have an awareness of self, Spirit, and others, I often hang in the balance to maintain my sanity! I find comfort in the humility of motherhood. In doing so I find that I am not alone in my attempt to live out my dreams while trying to lay the groundwork for my daughters to discover their own. In moments of hanging in the balance, I submit my prayers to the universe: Grant me the ability to extend the same freedom of choice that I treasure daily; help me to honor the sound of the genuine in her, as I require others to honor the same sound in me. I don't claim to have the right answers. As a matter of fact, my response is about asking more than it is solving. I have grown enough to realize that my reprieve from holding it all together in a nicely coiffed and congealed chignon rests not in answers but in the ability to ask the questions. The weight of the question is oft too heavy for one inquirer to bear. Asking in community lessens the load and clarifies when and where I enter the spiritual practice of hanging in the balance. So hang on, sister, you are not alone. In moments of being deeply overwhelmed, remember that there is no playbook, and no one is keeping score. Do your best; be kind to yourself.

—MELVA SAMPSON

To a sister who is battling a sickness or disease:

"Very truly I tell you, whoever believes in me will do the works I have been doing, and they will do even greater things than these, because I am going to the Father" (John 14:12).

The Bible speaks often of Jesus being a healer. The Prophet Isaiah said in 53:5, "But he was pierced for our transgressions, he was crushed for our iniquities; the punishment that brought us peace was on him, and by his wounds we are healed."

Many of the miracles that Jesus performed were with those with infirmities of all kinds. The power of Jesus to heal is still available to us today through His Spirit, prayer, modern medicine, and the gift of healing that God has blessed many people with.

The Power of Prayer:
Prayer gives us the faith, hope, wisdom, and knowledge to believe that God has the power to heal our bodies. Prayer unlocks our mind, body, and spirit to receive the manifestation of our healing that may not be revealed instantly. Prayer gives us the strength to wait patiently for our healing to occur.

Modern Medicine:
Jesus said we would do even "greater works than he," and I'm always amazed at modern technology and medicine. With modern medicine and technology, the blind now see, the lame walk, and we can receive new hearts and other vital organs. We can be healed or live with all types of diseases such as cancer, diabetes, or hypertension, to name just a few.

Spiritual Healing:
Jesus also said that we "would do the works." Even today, in modern times, God still blesses and uses His people with the gift of healing to heal the sick.

For countless generations, on my maternal side of my family lineage, God has blessed and used the females as spiritual healers. That gift was passed on to me. Over the years God has used me to heal the bodies of God's people with all types of illnesses. And not just people, but animals as well.

A few years ago, my daughter Nina was given a beautiful and expensive dog, named Coco. After having Coco for a few weeks, I noticed that Coco was continuously running into things. I had never heard him bark, nor did he respond to sounds. I shared this insight with my daughter, and we didn't know what we would do with her dog because her beloved Coco was blind, deaf, and without voice. Nina cried, nodded her head, implying yes I know, as she took him in her arms and cradled him. She said, "We will love him and pray for him." Nina then said to me, "Mommy, you have healing hands; God has used you to heal a lot of people. You've even healed dogs and cats. Why don't you believe God and heal Coco?" Without waiting for my response, Nina placed my hands on Coco's eyes, his ears, and his mouth. Over the next weeks, Nina would cradle Coco in her arms; we would pray, and I'd lay my healing hands on his eyes, ears, and mouth. God heard our prayers and used my hands; today, Coco can see, his ears can hear extremely well, and he can even bark! Nina changed his named to Glen-Coco. Now, Glen-Coco holds his head up high and struts like President Obama. When God heals us, we are indeed a new creature.

If God healed a dog, then God has the power to heal you. Your responsibility is to believe, pray, and do what must be done for yourself to walk or strut out your blessing of being healed by God, no matter how God decides to give it to you.

—REV. PORTIA WILLIS LEE

To the sister who is thinking about suicide or who finds herself in a depression:

You must keep in mind that no one is perfect—not even you! There is always a solution to your problem, even if you do not see it right now. Give your cares to the Lord, and *He* will turn your hopeless situation into a glorious testimony. We have to look beyond ourselves and exercise our faith in *Him.* As women, we are accustomed to fulfilling so many roles on any given day—wife, mother, employee, friend, home manager, just to name a few. It is easy to begin to feel that we are self-sufficient and responsible for everyone and everything around us. As noble as that seems, it is really a lie from the enemy designed to make us put our trust in ourselves alone. Inevitably, we are going to fall short in some way, and when we do, the lies of the enemy are right there in our minds telling us to blame ourselves and to give up hope.

The real struggle is in our minds. The Lord commands us to bring our minds under subjection and to make every thought become captive and obedient to Jesus Christ. This is the real battle because we are so used to letting our thoughts go anywhere they want to go. It takes discipline and the power of the Holy Spirit to challenge every thought that comes across our minds, but this is where our victory lies. Look at yourself in the mirror and begin to declare to yourself everything God has said about you in His Word. You have to make a choice to fight thoughts of hopelessness, depression, and suicide with the weapons God has provided for us.

At one time in my life I had become so depressed that I spent my days sitting on the sofa, rocking back and forth, unable to silence the conversations in my mind. But I began to say to myself, "I am fearfully and wonderfully made!" according to God's Word in Psalm 139. In prayer, I began to see myself as a little girl sitting on my Father's lap, pouring out to Him the deepest thoughts of my heart. My testimony today is that I am free and that I have a sound mind—*unapologetically!*

You must quit looking for people to define you. You must know that destiny is stored on the inside of you, and it's not dependent on anyone else's opinion or validation. Guard your heart! Be diligent to watch what you let enter into your ears and who speaks into your life. Keep your mind on thoughts that are good and not negative. Use every little thing that is positive in your life to encourage yourself day after day. Most of all, *keep going* no matter what life is throwing at you.

—DR. RHONDA TRAVITT

To the high school teenager who is contemplating having sex for the first time:

Sex is a beautiful thing. However, one should always be cognizant of why it was created and for whom it was created. As a minister of the Gospel of Jesus Christ, it is my responsibility to share the truth from the Bible's perspective. That truth is that sex is to be experienced within the institution of holy matrimony. The reality, nevertheless, is that this is not always how it happens. Whether one is Christian or not, the temptation to have sex can be overwhelming. And it does not help when you see those around you engaging in sex when you know they are not married.

So, then, how does one face the contemplation to become sexually active? I would like to suggest considering the approach that I have shared with my children. First and foremost, I reminded them of their obligation, as Christians, to honor God's guidelines. This cannot be done without the guidance of the Holy Spirit. And even so, that's not to say that you won't become weaker than the temptation and give in, but you should at least try.

Second, I told them that this thing called *soul ties* is real! What, exactly, is a soul tie? A soul tie is a connection that is made when a person gives of themselves physically to another person. The exchange of bodily fluids, which happens when sexual intercourse takes place, is how soul ties are made. A piece of your soul is released with the bodily fluids, and it can have an effect on you emotionally. Every time you lay down with someone, a piece of you becomes a piece of them. This is why God ordained sex for marriage. Your spouse is the only person who should have that part of you. You see, when that "piece of you" and that "piece of them" come together, that is how the two become the one flesh that Genesis 2:24 speaks of.

This is also why people find themselves not being able to feel totally free and at ease with their spouse when the time comes for them to become intimate. There should be no sexual inhibitions in the marriage bed. That special feeling of intimacy that is to be enjoyed during lovemaking is a privilege your spouse should wholeheartedly enjoy. Many times, husbands and wives find themselves having slept with so many people that when it's time for them to truly connect with their spouse, they can't make the connection. Their soul is scattered here, there, and everywhere, and they become baffled because they can't figure out why they can't fully connect with their spouse. Not only that, the sweetness of making love can easily be chalked up to a quick screw (please pardon the language) if this is what they are used to. Your spouse is worth much more than a quick screw. The marriage place is *the* place to express your love for your spouse.

I want you to know that I do understand how real temptation is. I know it's not enough for me to instruct you to "Just say no." My hope is that you would always pray for strength, wisdom, and discernment on whom to share your precious body with. My own life's experiences have already shown me that a few moments of pleasure are not worth jeopardizing the beautiful bliss that God intends your marriage to be embodied by.

—**ALONIA JONES**

To the single mother whose children's father refuses to step up and be a father:

As a single mother, until someone walks a mile in your shoes, no one will completely understand all that you carry around to make certain that your children are cared for and are loved. Your children are a blessing, but when everything in life falls on you, it can at times be difficult to manage. I have been a single mother. I understand. It is a blessing that carries a heavy burden. Most single mothers are not looking for sympathy, just for people not to judge them. Single mothers are the foundations of many of our families since so many men have decided not to be present in the lives of their children.

A man who refuses to be a father to his child is a selfish coward. There is no excuse for a man not to be involved in the lives of his children. Although there are good fathers who don't get enough credit for being in their children's lives, in the African-American community, too many men are walking away from their children and refusing to raise them and be a part of their lives. In my opinion, it is the number one reason for the breakdown in the black family. It is also one of the contributing factors for the killing and violence that our young people are committing against one another. These children grow up angry and bitter. They want love from their fathers, and the men have walked away.

In large part, some women have allowed these fathers to get away with them coming in and out of their children's lives because they are just thankful for any attention they get. As such, the men are given permission to walk away from their responsibilities, or they are not held to a standard because they are allowed to do only the bare minimum when it comes to the rearing of their children. I am not suggesting that it is the fault of the woman as we cannot make a person do right. We can, however, set certain standards in our relationships even before the child comes into the world. If the man is no good to you before you get pregnant, you have to stop believing that a child will somehow change him and make the situation better. You know what you have in him long before a child comes into the world. You know his man's character or lack thereof. I hear stories time and time again where a man has several children by different women, but the woman believes that if she gives birth, her baby will be so special to him that somehow it will change him. It will only be another baby to him.

There are men who merely have sex with women, and when the child arrives, he feels because he is not with the woman, he bears no responsibility to the child. They have no sense of legacy or even what it means to be a man. A real man does not walk away from his children. A real man does not live a life of crime, go to prison, and not be there to lead and guide his children. A real man does not have multiple children by different women without marrying any of them. A real man does not have a million excuses why he can't father his children. I have little tolerance for fathers who do not take care of their children. It is shameful and disgraceful.

My mother was a single mother. As I have already alluded, it is difficult. The reason the African proverb states "it takes a village to raise a child" is because it is one of life's most profound truths. Raising a child by yourself has to be the most difficult job in the world. It is hard to raise a child by yourself because children need so much. My grandparents helped to raise me, and I don't know how my mother could have done it without them. My mother worked multiple jobs to make sure that her four daughters had the things we needed. She had and did little for herself, which explains why she died young.

I recommend that you implement a standard in your life as it relates to your child's father. You do everything in your power to make certain that this so-called father is made to take care of his financial responsibility with regard your son or daughter. File for child support, take him to court, do whatever legally you can do to make him pay for your child's financial needs. This is not about you, but you need this money to raise your child.

Secondly, never speak badly about the father to the child. Do not allow others to do so. Children want to be loved. They want their parents to love them. They don't care if their father is no good and, as my mother would say, not worth a dime. Children just want his love. It is not necessary that you make him look good to them. You are not to lie to your children, but you don't have to constantly put him down. Your son or daughter will grow to understand who he really is on his or her own. You need to take the high road.

If possible and there is no drama going on or abuse, try to make arrangements for your child to spend time with his or her father. Whether he is paying child support or not, it is important that they have some contact with each other. Perhaps the father and your child can speak over the telephone. The children need to interact with their father. If their father has made bad decisions in life, you can point those out as a fact if asked. I advise you not to speak negatively about him because as they grow up, they will see him for who he really is anyway. Understand this—your children will love their father no matter what. Children are pure in that way. They give love to people who have not earned it or who don't deserve it.

Be careful with the father substitutes. You may think that bringing another man around will help with the issue of an absent father, but in some cases it can make circumstances even more difficult for your children. Mentors are great to have, but in this day and time, you have to make certain that you find someone you can trust because these predators are looking for single women who have children whose fathers have no presence in their lives. You are a target. Your children are targets. Please be reluctant and careful about whom you bring into your children's lives.

It breaks my heart every time I have to hear on the evening news that a child has either been abused or murdered at the hand of a single mother's boyfriend. Never leave your children with your boyfriend. I don't care who a man is that you are dating, go get a babysitter, or leave your children with a family member you can trust. Find an elder who loves children or someone from your church—but don't you allow a boyfriend to keep your kids when you are not around. Please do not trust him in that way. It is not worth the risk of what could happen to your children.

Stay strong and keep doing the best you can for your kids. As long as you have done the best you can do to make certain that the father is held responsible for the financial well-being of your children, you cannot make him do right. All you can do is create an atmosphere whereby if he wants to be in a relationship with his child, he can do so.

—JUDGE PENNY

To the sister who is not satisfied with her body image and has given up on life:

Everyone has something to be proud of: your smile, cheeks, dimples, legs, hips, breasts, butt, etc. If none of those work, I'll bet you have a winning, funny, or witty personality, or you're extremely smart! Find one thing, one little thing, to build on. It's an art to accentuating the parts you like about yourself and downplaying the parts you don't. You can also ask a friend or loved one you trust what they like about you. Keep note of their answers and try to focus on that positive aspect. People are generally attracted to positive, confident, and genuine people.

—SHIRLEY LANGLEY HENRY

To the sister who is going through a divorce:

One of the most painful experiences to face in life is that of a divorce. I know because I have been there. After twenty years of marriage (twenty-one by the time the divorce was final), birthing three children, and raising a fourth child, facing a divorce was actually the most painful experience I have ever had to face outside of losing my daddy. On top of that, I had spent more than a decade preaching the Gospel of Jesus Christ. As part of that journey, I had ministered to countless people by telling them that God could fix anything. I had been waiting for years for Him to fix my marriage for me. It was devastating to realize what I desired to be fixed was not meant to be fixed from the beginning. Whew! What? God, are you for real? Yes, He was.

The details of what led to my divorce are not the most important information to share right now. What is most important is that God still loves you and that He can heal you of your brokenheartedness and disappointment. I really don't believe anyone enters a marriage intending to get a divorce. It bothers me when I often hear people say, "Go ahead and get married. And if it doesn't work out, you can always get a divorce." That's not God's way. He intends for marriage to be a lifelong commitment. When things go awry, it can be beyond excruciating. Indeed, it can. But be encouraged, my sisters. There is good news: you can make it. There is life after divorce!

I want you to know that you don't have to hold on to the guilt or the shame that divorce may have brought upon you. Take some time to reflect on your situation. What role did you play? What role did he play? Good or bad on either end, don't run from it; you absolutely must deal with it. But how, you may be wondering. Think about the roles each of you played and consider the lessons learned. Then, ask God to help you understand the situation in its totality and to heal you from it. Forgive yourself, forgive your spouse, and move on. It's going to hurt, but I'm a witness that there is a mender of broken hearts. His name is Jesus Christ. If He did it for me, I know He can do it for you.

—**ALONIA JONES**

To the sister who wakes up depressed:

Hey, sis! Are you awake? Get up girl! I need to chat with you for a minute. I'm going to get straight to the point because I need you to move off of Depression Street ASAP! Listen, when depression walks through your door, it will make you shut down, withdraw, turn around, and walk back to those places of despair. When you let depression grip you, and you go into seclusion and shut the world out, you will be right where the devil wants you. Now, get your pad and pencil. I want you to ask yourself three questions: 1) What am I doing down here? 2) How did I get down here in the first place? 3) What/who caused me to get stuck in this downward spiral? Find yourself a quiet place where you will not be interrupted. Sit at God's feet and start writing. Make sure to turn off all electronic devices because you are about to *take off!* After this exercise, I believe that you will be on your way to soaring like an eagle. God wants you better … not bitter!

—**DEETTA M. WEST**

To the sister who dreams of going back to school:

The best advice I can give to the sister who is going back to school is encouragement. Going back to school is a great undertaking that requires determination. Have you ever felt that you wanted more or that you have more to give to the world? Are you the sister who started the process and somehow found yourself at a crossroad and abandoned your dreams for a better life? I must say yes to both.

Sometimes we don't understand or even realize the greatness others may see in us. My mentor is the very person who helped me understand my potential and further encouraged me to go back to school. I am ever so grateful to her.

Going back to school requires you to envision yourself at the finish line. However, you will be faced with life challenges in the midst of your educational journey. Do not be discouraged! Please understand that it is a great sacrifice. You may even encounter those close to you who may not understand your plight, but continue to persevere. Why? Because you were designed for greatness.

Create realistic goals, define your worth, and fulfill your dreams. Always remember all things designed for greatness require work. You were built for this journey no matter what. Do not defer your dreams any longer. There are people waiting on the sidelines to cheer you on who cannot wait to see or hear about your success story. Be that motivation to help the next generation understand that education is and has always been our ticket out!

—MICHELLE LIPPITT

If you are dreaming of going back to school, make sure you have a good support system. You need loved ones who are happy for you and will always be there, near or far, cheering you on for your success. Only have people around you who are positive with and for you and who are never negative about what you believe in. Be around others who give you strength during hard times. Most importantly, never look back; continue to keep walking in the right path until your dreams are fulfilled.

—**KEISHA BROWN**

I encourage you to go back to school. Education provides a way for you to change your life, to design it to look the way you want it to look regardless of your circumstances or the life cards you have been dealt. My father passed away when I was eleven, leaving my mother to raise three young children on her own. Seven years later, we lost everything in a house fire. Despite these adversities, I remained focused on my goal to become a lawyer. When it came time for me to go to law school, I had no idea how I was going to pay for it. I contemplated not going. And then, I decided I was not going to worry about the "how"; instead, I focused only on ensuring that I had done my part to get into school and believed with all my heart that everything would somehow work out. Once I was accepted, I made my mind up that I was going to work harder than I had ever worked before in school.

I attended Howard University School of Law, and by the end of my first year I was awarded a scholarship that I continued to receive during my matriculation at Howard. As a second-year law student, I was awarded the Kirkland & Ellis Diversity Fellowship, making me the first student at Howard to receive the honor. This fellowship provided me with a $15,000 stipend and a paid summer associate position at Kirkland & Ellis, LLP—one of the top ten most prestigious law firms in the United States. I graduated in the top five percent of my class and went on to work as an attorney at Kirkland & Ellis.

You see, it was not for me to worry about the hows, such as, how was I going to pay for law school or how was I going to pay my rent once in law school. Just like it is not for you to worry about any of the hows that may get in your way. Your responsibility is to claim your desire and to go after it with all your might. God always handles the hows, but we have to do the work.

—Raina Jones

To the sister who just found out her husband has been having an affair:

To the sister who just found out her husband has been having an affair, I say *stop*; take the time to find a quiet place, close your eyes, place your face in your hands, bow your head, and call on your God. Ask God to calm your spirit and soothe your soul. Express your love, faith, and trust in Him; tell God how much you need Him right now. Then tell Him you firmly believe He will get you through this. Don't question Him, don't doubt Him, and don't challenge Him. Just simply tell God you need Him. Though adultery is not a rare illness, there is no science, and there are no doctors with a magic prescription that can heal this gut-wrenching pain; this requires a God treatment.

Like a tornado, your mind is spinning so fast you cannot put your thoughts in order. Who, what, when, where, how, *why*? The searing pain of a two-edged sword pierces your heart; like oozing blood from that wound, tears flow uncontrollably. A roller coaster of emotions strips you of all sanity—through betrayal, guilt, shame, hate, vengeance, embarrassment, hurt. Either you want to die, or you want to kill, maybe both.

Just stop; *pray*. Then, from your posture of prayer, go to the sink, lather and massage your face in warm soapy water, then rinse with cool water. Gently pat dry. Pause and take a soothing breath. Make your movements slow and methodical. Look up into the mirror at God's creation—God's child. He has not and He will not leave you alone to handle this challenge. Though you can think only about what you are feeling right now, you are not the first, and you won't be the last. As you peer into your own eyes, you must embrace being a survivor of this betrayal and not a victim. You and only you must decide to get over and beyond this. Stay with him, forgive him, and work it out, or walk away. Don't make a decision in haste—tomorrow you will feel differently. Next week will present a whole new set of feelings, thoughts, doubts, questions, and ideas. You will never see your husband as you once did—not ever again. You both stood before God and man and took vows to love only each other, to be faithful till death do you part. An extramarital affair may or may not suggest that love is gone, but one thing is for certain; the vow has been broken. You also vowed to be with your husband through better or worse; this affair is worse. If your husband wants to reconcile, if he wants forgiveness, is your love the kind of love described in 1 Corinthians 13:8—"a love that never fails"? Ask for divine guidance and do not lean on your own understanding (Proverbs 3:5)

To the sister who just found out her husband has been having an affair, this is the devil at work. Don't let the devil win and don't grant him any overtime in your life. Put God to work in your life and ask Him to guide your thoughts, your heart, and your mind. When God does His job on your behalf, you can take a vacation.

—SCARLET PRESSLEY-BROWN

It's his loss! He doesn't deserve you! Don't wait for him to do it again. Take the children and leave.

—SHIRLEY LANGLEY HENRY

To the sister who finds herself living in a shelter:

My dear sister, I am sorry that you have to be in a shelter. I know how it feels to not have a place to call your own. I never had to live in a shelter, but I did have to sleep in my car for a time when I had no place to live. Circumstances have come upon you, and I know you have to be asking yourself how your life could have turned out the way that it has.

First, remember you are not defined by where you lay your head at night. This is a temporary situation, and don't you believe for an instant that living in a shelter is your permanent future. You merely find yourself in a bad way. I am just happy you are not on the streets. The greatest battle that you have is not to become discouraged and stuck. You cannot be paralyzed and do nothing to change your outlook.

Develop an exit strategy. Agencies and groups, such as the Salvation Army, can assist you in developing a life plan. I wrote about it in the chapter to the homeless sister. Create goals for yourself. Take everything one step at a time. When you accomplish one step, you move to the next. You don't have time to constantly beat yourself up. You have to keep your eyes on what is ahead of you and putting your life back together. There are people out there who want to help you. You are not alone.

Don't be hard on yourself. Learn from your mistakes and walk out of the shelter learning the lesson of a lifetime. Make a vow that you will never have to return and spend every day putting the pieces together that will allow you to be independent and self-sufficient.

Let go of the shame and find something to be thankful for each day. Where you are is not who you are.

—JUDGE PENNY

To the disabled teenager coping with wanting to be accepted:

I am a teenager with a hearing impairment. I have never had problems with being accepted by my peers. When I told them about my hearing aid, the more they were interested in me. I never had a problem with wearing a hearing aid or had a problem of letting it show because I know who I am as a person. I am grateful that I have a hearing aid and just accept how God created me.

Don't let the small things stop you as a person. Continue to be you; never be ashamed of a disability. If others have problems with it, then you should move on. Be sure to become involved in extracurricular activities. Just because one person does not accept you, doesn't mean others will not. Always be yourself, and don't despair because of another's negative re-action to your disability. Stay focused on your educational pursuits. Sometimes, you may feel as if you are alone, but don't let it affect you. There are others who understand what you are going through.

—Nia DeJoie

To the sister who just got a brand new job in corporate America or a major law firm:

First, you have an obligation to do well. As an African-American, you must always remember that your role is larger than you. Our ancestors gave and suffered tremendously so that one day you would be where you are today. When you do well, you help build a narrative that people who look like you will also do well. Therefore, it is incumbent upon you to do your very best in whatever position you fill and to reach back and pull others up as you go.

Second, you are often only as strong in a working environment as your reputation. So, prior to starting your new job, gather as much information as you can about what your work environment values, determine how you want to be perceived, and also decide what adjectives and action verbs you want people to use when your name comes to mind. Once you start working, with each task you complete, do so with your list in mind. At a minimum, you want to be thought of as someone who has a strong work ethic, who is a creative problem solver, who is committed to being reliable, and who values consistently getting the job done accurately and on time.

Lastly, know that you are well prepared to fill the position you will soon move into, and you will succeed as long as you put the work in to do so. So, give every task all you've got, and when you begin to feel you have nothing left, then find a way to give it some more!

I remember when I was a summer associate at Kirkland & Ellis (K&E) in Washington, D.C. K&E is one of the top ten most prestigious law firms in the United States, and I was just a girl from Birmingham, Alabama, who didn't know the first thing about working at a big law firm. But, I knew that hard work and a commitment to accuracy had always paid off for me in the past. So, that summer, I put my head down and worked as hard as I could to turn in quality work by every deadline I was given. At the end of the summer I was offered a full-time permanent position as an attorney upon graduating law school. Hard work always pays off!

—Raina Jones

To the sister who has been married for a week:

To the sister who has been married for one week, I say embrace and cherish every moment of newness in your marriage. What you feel right now you will never ever feel again. Even if you are blessed enough to be with a man whom you feel you are falling in love with all over again, every day, the newness of that love as his new wife is once in your lifetime.

My prayer is that the two of you are together as husband and wife until the end of time. However, time won't always be your friend in marriage. Time breeds familiarity, casualness, and informality. What is special today will be commonplace tomorrow. A long passionate kiss in the morning as you depart from each other for the day will become a quick peck on the cheek and well wishes for a great day. The deep conversations about life, politics, people, will become short snippets, repeating thoughts based on news reports. These gradual changes that creep their way into your marriage do not mean it's the end of the world—but it is the world that awaits every marriage.

I say to the sister who has been married for a week, take control and be the navigator of the happiness you want and need in your marriage. Be a bride every day; dress, speak, act, smell, and taste like the woman he met and wanted to be with for the rest of his life.

Marriage is one hundred percent surrender. To get to that, each party, in his or her own mind, must commit to giving ninety percent and expecting ten percent. Relationships usually stem from the spirit of giving, but as human beings, we innately need to feel valued and appreciated. Giving isn't the issue; being appreciated is—especially for females. Our society doesn't customarily mold and influence males to shoulder the responsibility of leadership in nurturing and appreciation. Therefore the onus is on us, the women/wives, to ensure our marriage has the elements of acknowledgment, profundity, and gravity that we need for success. Your man—your husband—is open and up for the challenge, but you will have to set the stage. Though this first week has been la-la land, marriage is not a fairy tale. Marriage is a never-ending, constant work in progress. The reward is a strong bond withstanding the test of time. Marriage is two imperfect people joined together, committed, and dedicated to build a perfect life. Life—hopefully—is a very long time. The fact that your marriage can last a lifetime and that this commitment can work is real. More importantly, know this: marriage is real lifetime work.

—SCARLET PRESSLEY-BROWN

To the sister whose child was just murdered:

My only child was murdered in 2012 at the age of 19. When you lose a child, there's no other pain to compare it to. I've had people say they know how I feel because they lost a parent or sibling, and I would get so angry because there is no comparison. Only a parent who's suffered the loss of a child knows the devastation and despair. My heart and spirit were broken, and many days, I didn't want to live. The hurt was so deep, there were times when I couldn't catch my breath. I no longer saw the world or people the same. I prayed for my son every day and trusted God to protect him, so I was mad at God for allowing my child to be murdered and for leaving me alone and with no hopes of ever having grand-children. I hated the ones who killed my son. I went to a very dark place in my life, and there I realized I had a choice to ei-ther live or die. I knew God loved me and had a purpose for my life, so I had to live. I had many questions without answers, and if I was going to survive, I had to trust God and allow him to bring some healing to my life. After a three-year trial, both boys were convicted for the murder of my son.

I say to the sister whose child was murdered, you will never get over losing your child, but you can choose to live through it. Share your pain with family and friends because they have suffered a loss as well. Don't allow yourself to be-come isolated. Educate yourself on the grief process and know what's happening to you. You will not lose your mind even though there are times you feel like you will. Let grief take its course, seek help by getting counseling or joining a support group, and most of all, don't stop praying!

—MONICA COLEMAN

To the sister who has been betrayed by her best friend:

I don't know a woman today who has not at some point

been betrayed by a friend. If it has never happened to you, God bless you. But for those of us who have lived through the pain of a best friend's betrayal, it is a pain like no other. The betrayal shocks you at your core. You question everything about the friendship. It is realizing that what you thought was real turns out not to be real at all. I remember feeling disoriented and totally vulnerable. I held her secrets, and once the betrayal occurred, I knew mine were no longer safe. The secrets that friends hold have to do with feelings. It has to do with having your guard down and trusting that the person really cares about you. The moment the betrayal occurs, you realize the trust is gone.

I encourage you to grieve the loss of the friendship and the loss of the person who was in your life. It is a process. It takes time. However, you have to understand that it is necessary to go through the grieving steps because loss is loss. You cared for this person, and her betrayal does not diminish how you felt. If you are like me, I ignored the signs of who this person really was. I refused to be honest with myself. Even when others tried to warn me, I refused to listen because I thought she was my true friend.

I found myself having to hide from her many of the good things that were happening for me so that she wouldn't get jealous. I didn't mind it because I felt I understood that she was a competitive person, and I did not want her to feel badly. Can you believe I did that? The very fact that I had to hide my joys from her should have shown me this person was incapable of being a true and committed friend. Her betrayal to me was inevitable because you can't be in friendship with someone you are competing against. I don't even believe that deep down inside she was ever my friend.

Don't become isolated. Don't cut yourself off from others. Come to an understanding of what friendship is all about.

The next time you enter into a friendship, make certain that you both have the same understanding and expectations. Never change to be a person's friend. She must accept you for who you are. A friend wants only the best for her friend and will never do anything to hurt her.

Forgive. Forgive. You must forgive. Forgiveness allows you to be free. There will come a time when you will be able to smile about the good times you shared with your friend. Let it go. You will miss the friendship, but you will accept that life goes on. People come into our lives for a reason and a season. Pray for them and move on with your life. Allow yourself to enter into friendships again, but this time you will be a little wiser.

—JUDGE PENNY

To the sister who is unemployed and looking for a job:

Never become discouraged about being unemployed, but always be proactive. Most job opportunities, or the types of jobs you want most, are discovered by word of mouth or in-depth research. Sometimes it takes months to find a job that aligns with your current circumstances or desires. During this time, it is important to take advantage of as many chances to meet people and network as much as possible because you never know what you can discover from simply having a conversation with another person. When the process of finding a job becomes tough, it is important not to shut down or develop the belief that no one wants to hire you. If you do not get the job, then it was never the right job for you, and there is something better in store.

Do not always chase after the Fortune 500s or large corporations, as you'll find more value in the smaller places that will in turn value you. If you must lean on a temporary job for support, never lose sight of the kind of job you want and never stop networking.

One of the most valuable lessons I've learned in finding a job is to never wait for the job to present itself to you. There may not be a "wanted" sign for the job you're interested in, but there can be an opportunity if you seek after it. Be proactive and inquire about every job. Email or visit any company you may be interested in because many of them may be looking for someone they never knew they wanted. You'll never know how much value you can bring to a job until you actively strive to go after one. Be fearless in your approach and take any rejection as an opportunity to find something better.

—MAYA DEJOIE

To a sister who is thinking about joining a sorority:

I am a proud member of Alpha Kappa Alpha Sorority, Incorporated. I pledged in undergraduate in 1991. It was a dream come true for me. I was not able to go to college right after high school. My best friend at that the time, Michelle Simon, left and went to Xavier University in New Orleans. While there, she pledged AKA. Although she left for college, and I was left in my small town working and raising a son, she continued to stay in contact with me, and she never really left me behind. I love her even today for that. She later married, and all the girls in the wedding were her sorors, except for me and her little sister. When they sang the AKA sorority song, I remember feeling like an outsider. I later left the wedding feeling down and out. I cried most of the night because I was filled with deep regrets that I was not able to be in college. I finally realized how much I had lost in not going to college straight from high school. I made the best of my life, but I knew at that very moment that it would be a season in time I would never be able to recapture. I hated that because of my mistakes in life, I was not able to live the joy and adventure that comes from leaving home for the first time and going off to college. I vowed while listening to them sing that song that day and witnessing the tremendous sisterhood they shared, that one day I would pledge and become an AKA. My little cousin Cabrini pledged while attending Xavier, as well as my sister Monica while she was in undergrad. When I finally made it to college in my late twenties, after years of working, being a mother, and constantly dreaming, it was at the top of my wish list of dreams. I was determined to make my dream come true.

I encourage anyone who is thinking about joining a sorority to do so. It is about sisterhood. It gives you lifelong sisters. You can go all over the world and find someone you get to call your sister.

While in college, joining a sorority gives you support, both academically and socially. You become a part of an institution with legacy. You are in an organization that not only focuses on personal development of its members, but service is the cornerstone of everything the organization does. You learn how important it is to serve others, and you get opportunities to do so. It helps to understand what true leadership is all about. As a professional, it provides a wonderful networking vehicle. However, with all of those reasons, the greatest reason to join a sorority is about the sisterhood; it's about friendship; it is about love.

—JUDGE PENNY

To the sister who just graduated from college:

Congratulations! You are among those who hold a degree, and you have much to be proud of. I will not revisit all that you likely had to go through to get where you are now. But, through it all, you did it. You made it! You are grown now. Thanks to President Obama, you get to stay on your parents' insurance until you're 26. Other than that, you are now on your own. Some parents give you one year of care after college, while others give you two months or less. Some allow you time to get a job, while others say you are own your own. Either way, you have some decisions to make.

You can further your education—head off to graduate school—or you can start working. Either way, you need to get a job so you can start taking care of your financial responsibilities. You will not feel like a grown-up living in your parents' house until you do. I encourage you to have multiple revenue streams. Even if you get a day job, do something that is connected to your purpose and dreams. Make it about your passion, and it will be easy to do as you work to put a roof over your head and have a car to drive.

I recommend, if you can, to move forward with going to graduate school, medical school, or law school. Getting additional education beyond a college degree gives you an advantage. It is always best to get your education completed before you have to deal with a husband and/or children and the responsibilities of being our own adult.

Stay away from credit cards. Learn delayed gratification. It is easy to get into debt, but it takes years to get out of it. Your credit score is the key for everything you wish to acquire in the future. I strongly recommend that if you have debt, always pay your bills on time. You will have to make some debt to establish credit, but you should do so wisely and never be late making your payments. Save money and always pay yourself. Don't spend based on emotions. Have self-control when you shop. Start a retirement account now, while you are young. Because of your age, you don't have to put a lot of money into a retirement account because time is on your side. You can put a small amount over time, and twenty or thirty years from now, you will reap the benefits of being a wise steward over your resources. If you don't do anything else, please do this.

I recommend that you embrace a relationship with God. During college, you likely didn't spend a great deal of time in a worship experience. No excuses now. Your life cannot be successful if God is not first. Find a place to gather once a week to worship and serve God.

Finally, find who you are first before you connect with someone else. Stop worrying so much about rushing into getting married. Stay focused on your personal development, getting into a good relationship with God, getting additional education, healing the pains of your past, building a career, and seeing the world. Once you have all those pieces in place, it will be time to share your life with someone. But do you first! Enjoy these years, as they will pass by quickly.

—JUDGE PENNY

To the sister who is jealous of women:

Jealous women are everywhere. It's sad but true. Thinking about it reminds me of the famous words of police brutality victim Rodney King, "Can't we all just get along?" I find it hilarious to see the many reality television shows featuring women because I already know that it is only a matter of time before they will be going at each other like animals. The cattiness, being two-faced, the lies, and manipulation are just way too much. As I see it, it's nothing short of foolishness. But it is real, nevertheless.

For various reasons, women getting along is a lot easier said than done. I think there are at least two factors that this can be attributed to. One is the problem of perception, and the other is insecurity. As it relates to perception, we see things one way, but what we see may not be the true reality of the way things actually are. In other words, everything that glitters just may not be gold after all.

Women have a wealth of responsibilities. As wives, mothers, daughters, and sisters, we are nurturers. As leaders, we find ourselves in the marketplace, in institutions of faith, government, education, and so many other arenas. We are expected to do so much, but there are only twenty-four hours in the day. As we go through our daily routines of doing what we have to do, it's natural to not avoid our surroundings; we can't help but observe those who are around us. So when we look around and see a sister who seems to have it goin' on or have it all together, and we're going through our own set of struggles, for many, it is natural for envy to set in.

While this may be true, it doesn't have to be that way. I had to get to a point in my life where I realized that my God wants to see everybody blessed and that He has the capacity and ability to make it happen. It took me a while to grasp this understanding, but when I did, He went on to show me that it would be wise for me to sincerely rejoice with others when they rejoice because what He had done for them, He could do the same for me.

God also showed me the importance of not judging a book by its cover. A sister who may be doing well in one area of her life may be suffering or struggling miserably in an-other. The beautiful smile she flashes could be a major cam-ouflage for a lifetime of pain. Don't envy her. Love her. For she is just a girl like you, one who is made of flesh and blood and emotions, and one who has a desire to be loved and ac-cepted.

The other factor I mentioned was insecurity. Regardless of what you look like, what you've been through, where you're from, what you don't have, or what others say about you, you have to be able to love yourself. You are not the sum total of what others say and think of you. What you are is everything God says about you. The only way to know that is to seek His Word on your own and then have a conversation with Him about it. When I read my Bible, God speaks to me. I speak to Him when I get down on my knees and talk to Him. Then, when I allow myself to get away from the hustle and bustle of my daily obligations, I can hear that still, small voice contin-uing to speak words of love and life into my spirit.

When I begin to fully understand how much He loves me and how precious I am in His sight, I find a freedom that causes me to not be concerned about what others think about me. I find a freedom to walk into any room and command it. I find the strength to smile through my tears, to push past my pain, and to triumph over my tragedies because I know that sooner or later, my dearly beloved Heavenly Father is going to perfect everything that concerns me. With this kind of freedom, there is no room or reason to envy anybody. And so it is. Selah.

—ALONIA JONES

To the sister who feels greatness is in her life, but she cannot get the world to see it:

"Work hard in silence. Let success be your noise."
—FRANK OCEAN

It can be frustrating to feel as though you are capable of something great, yet no one sees it except you. It can be frustrating to be passionate about something that no one sees the same level of passion in. Living in a society that is heavily centered on validation, social media has impacted the way in which we learn if what we're doing is deemed "acceptable." As a society, we measure our success and ourselves by the types of photos we share and the number of "likes" we get. The more likes there are, the more popular we become, and the less likes there are, the more we feel as if we are doing something wrong or need to do something of more shock value to gain more attention. Suddenly, the validity of our actions is determined by strangers instead of by us, and it is deemed not acceptable to satisfy only a handful of people.

More importantly, we lose sight of satisfying and being happy with ourselves.

If there's anything I've taken away from my experience, it's that the harder you work at something, the more others will pick up on your potential for greatness. The more authentic and true you are to yourself, the more others will respect you and what you have to offer. Never succumb to the pressure of what other people want you to be, but rather continue to do exactly what you want to do, and that commitment to yourself will bring more greatness and validity than any other person could present to you.

Success does not always come in the form of big numbers, nor does it have a universal definition. Sometimes, impacting and knowing that you've impacted only one person is more meaningful than attempting to impact thousands. In the midst of possessing greatness and wanting others to see it, continue to work hard and embrace being a student. Take this time to observe your surroundings and learn as much as possible because it all applies to the greater vision of your life that people will eventually see. Always keep your head up and strive to prove a supporter right rather than prove a critic wrong.

One of my favorite quotes is, "The good news is that the moment you decide that what you know is more important than what you have been taught to believe, you will have shifted gears in your quest for abundance. Success comes from within, not from without," by Ralph Waldo Emerson.

—MAYA DEJOIE

Favor isn't fair! You don't need the world's permission to be who God has destined you to be! God gives us gifts according to His will. He doesn't give us the same gifts at the same time or in the same amount. God gives us different gifts. Your gift might be the gift of song. Another might have the gift of dance. Another gift might be the gift of counsel. Another gift might be the gift of money. Another gift might be the gift of a wonderful husband and mild-mannered children. Your gift of greatness is for you! You can't expect small minds to understand great gifts.

—SHIRLEY LANGLEY HENRY

To the sister who has been raped or abused:

I asked a young lady I worked with about her relationship with her boyfriend. She said, "My man loves me even when I don't want him to love me." I asked her what that meant, and she stated her boyfriend likes to have sex, but sometimes she doesn't want to but she does anyway. I asked her, "Do you tell him no, and he convinces you to have sex?" She said, "No, I tell him no, and he pushes me on the bed and puts it in." I told her, "You're being raped." She said, "No, that's not rape, that's my boyfriend." I said, "Sweetheart, you can be raped by a stranger or boyfriend. If the sex is forced, if you tell him no, then he needs to respect that, otherwise it's considered rape." I informed her she was repeatedly being raped every time he forces her to have sex.

It's your body, and you have a right to not want to have sex with anyone. There is no girlfriend manual that says you have to have sex with your boyfriend. Start loving yourself to know that you are important and loved. You don't deserve to be abused, and you don't deserve to be treated this way. Remember, no means no!

—TYISKA DEMERY

To the sister who just got out of prison:

You are out now. Let it go. Let your captivity go. As soon as you possibly can, let the past and what you did that landed you behind prison walls go. You have a future ahead of you that requires you to be positive. If you stay focused on what happened while you were in prison, you might as well go back. It is my prayer that you learned something while you were there.

You enter a society where your family, and perhaps your children, will be happy to welcome you home. No one will truly understand what you have been through. But, this one thing is for sure: You are forgiven once you have served your time, and you must hit the restart button on your life.

The main thing to remember is to stay away from the people and circumstances that put you there in the first place. No one is going to hold your hand to get your life back in order. In fact, employers don't want to hire someone who has spent time in prison. Therefore, you will have to become educated or get a trade or start your own business. Someone will give you a chance, but you are going to have to learn to hear no before you get to a yes. There are agencies that will assist you, and I am sure you were told about them upon your release. I recommend that you get a job, but use this as an opportunity to do something that is about your purpose in life.

It is never too late to start your life over. You made a mistake. Work hard every day to not make it again. Repair broken relationships every day. You left somebody behind. And for every day you were in prison, so were they. It was a different prison, but nevertheless, it was bondage. Help your children develop a future so they don't believe that they are only worthy of going in the path that you took. Make things right by giving them a future and allow them to dream.

You keep dreaming, and, above all, keep believing in you. Go talk to someone like a counselor so you can get your self-worth and your self-esteem back. Your life has been on pause. Now is the time to let the regrets go, let the anger go, let the resentment go, let the excuses go, and start living.

—JUDGE PENNY

To the sister who has been hurt by those in the church or mosque:

Just like there's no place like home, there's no hurt like church hurt. After all, people don't go to church to get hurt. They go there to be healed. If there is no other place one can expect to be a place of refuge and peace, the church should be it. More often than not, this is simply not the case.

I have experienced my own extreme measures of church hurt. It's almost indescribable. I have also encountered others who have experienced the same. As a result, many of them resolved to never set foot inside another church. They have said that since the church is in their heart, they are content to nurture their faith on their own, outside the church's walls. Others have even gone as far as to denounce their faith altogether.

This is painfully sad. Although I have had my own experiences, I am grateful that I did not allow my disappointments to stunt my spiritual growth. So why did I continue going to church? Why did I keep the faith? Was it out of habit? Was it out of fear that my family would hound me until I came back? No. It was neither. Rather, it was my revelation of the importance of having a personal relationship with Jesus Christ. This relationship caused me to understand that it was not about the individuals who hurt me. People, because they are human, are prone to err. It does not matter if they are in a position of authority or not. Yes, leaders are held to a higher level of accountability, and the expectation for them to err less than others is real. The truth of the matter, though, is that people do fall short. But at the end of the day, I have to know that any service that I render is not rendered unto man; it is rendered unto the Lord. God wants our worship in every way. I know for myself that the closer I get to Him, the stronger my faith is. Never will I allow any person or situation to separate me from His love.

—**ALONIA JONES**

The church experience is a combination of worshipping and praising God, a place for spiritual healing and fellowship with other believers. However, it's not always a place of refuge. I went for counseling about a personal situation with a pastor whose church I was attending. He questioned me like I was on trial. He had minimal compassion, and he judged me. I was wounded again. I continued to attend church but soon left because I wanted to expose him to the congregation. However, I knew it was not the best way to handle the situation. I felt so lost because I enjoyed going to church. I didn't trust pastors or anyone else in the church.

Finally, I found my way to another church, which brought me healing and deliverance from the incident with the pastor and many other things. Looking back, I would have dealt with the problem differently. I would have confronted the pastor and told him how he made me feel in hopes that he would never treat another woman the way he treated me. I also realized it was time for me to leave that church because I was not growing spiritually. So, sister, if you have been wounded, pray for healing and wisdom on how to deal with it. There will always be someone in church who is capable of hurting you, so guard your heart and mind and stay focused. Use discernment when dealing with church folk because they can be some of the most dangerous people. Most importantly, don't stop attending church. It's not about them—it's about God.

—MONICA COLEMAN

To the sister who has lost her way and is not connected to God:

My sister, God has a love for you that is unimaginable. He is always there and is just waiting for you to call His name. God has never left you, nor has He forsaken you. Ask yourself, why am I not connected with God? What has God done to make me leave Him? The answers to those questions are nothing. God doesn't disconnect from us; we disconnect ourselves from Him. When things go wrong, we want to blame God. When we are unhappy, we want to blame God. God allows things to go wrong in our lives; He allows us to be unhappy and sometimes suffer. God does this for us so that we can give our testimony of how good God is and how God brings us through difficulties. My sister, you have to learn to praise God during the bad times as well as the good times. To reconnect with God, all you have to do is acknowledge that He is God and that He is Ruler of your life. We all fall short of the glory of God, but He still forgives us. Romans 10:9-10 states, "If you confess with your mouth the Lord Jesus and believe in your heart that God has raised Him from the dead, you will be saved. For with the heart one believes to righteousness, and with the mouth confession is made to salvation." My sister, save your soul and welcome God back into your heart. His spirit is real, it is true, and it is pure love. He loves you, and so do I. There is nothing my God won't do for you.

—DEIDRA DAVIS ALEXIS

To the teenage girl who has dreams but has no one in her life to support her:

First and foremost, I am so proud of you for having a dream—so many people do not. Many are blind, confused, conflicted, and stuck, but you have a vision, a way out and up.

The vision that was addressed to you was given for a specific reason. It is precious, and there is no one else who can handle it but you. Ideally, you would have someone to share it with, someone to help you nurture it and prepare you, but if you do not, then what? Sister, I encourage you to know that everything you need to survive is inside you.

You are learning at a young age that you will not always have support, whether financial or emotional. It's a good thing support is not a primary ingredient of success. Develop strength to be your own support system, and add value to your dream by spending time researching and resourcing information that makes you an expert in your field. After you become an expert on your dream, begin to express it. You will be surprised at how many people have similar interests and goals, and they would love to support you based on like-minded missions.

Understand that your situation is blind. Regardless of your environment, whether it is crowded with noise or silenced with emptiness, your vision lives on. Your environment needs your vision; the people around you need your ideas. This is your setup; embrace the independence and executive role you have in your life, and begin to be the support to others that you would love for yourself.

—CHELSI GLASCOE

**To the sister who knows her man is no good,
but she cannot let him go:**

Letting go of a relationship is difficult. However, it is necessary when ultimately it will lead to a destructive place for you. When you know that your man is no good, and you allow him in your life, you have basically walked away from yourself as a woman. You no longer have true self-worth because you are giving him permission to disrespect you and your womanhood. Everything he does to you chips away at something deep in your soul. You will never be your best self as long as you tolerate and keep holding on to a man who is incapable of doing right by you. He is selfish and manipulative and, frankly, is not worthy of your love.

You may be keeping him around because of the potential you see in him. Many of us fall in love with the potential. This so-called potential never manifests into the man that you dream of. You may even keep him for the financial benefit he brings to the table. But the stress and the drama he brings comes at an enormous cost. Is it really worth it?

Our God wants the best for us. No one has the right to mistreat you or not do right by you. You have to find the strength deep down inside and do right for yourself. He will continue to treat you the way he does because you gave him permission to do it. You gave permission because you allow it.

Let him go. I want you to understand that this is more about you than him anyway. Repair the brokenness that is in you and begin to live your life, albeit by yourself.

—JUDGE PENNY

To the sister who is in an abusive relationship:

Tell someone! You need help and obviously can't get out of the relationship by yourself. Let someone who truly loves you help you. Love yourself enough to get out of that relationship. Know that you don't deserve to be abused.

—SHIRLEY LANGLEY HENRY

My dear sister! If you are reading this, I want you to go and look in the mirror and say to yourself, "I love me better than that." This is the title of a song recorded by the amazing gospel recording artist Shirley Murdock. See, I was in an abusive relationship for two years, so I am coming from a place of experience, and I understand how difficult it is to get out. The operative phrase is "*get out!*" Okay, I know that you say you love him, but are you loving him, or is it you think that you can't do any better? Maybe it's because you are afraid to leave because of the fear that he has instilled in you? Maybe it is because you feel that you have no place to go and that you are trapped because you do not have the finances needed to move on. Maybe you have allowed him to tear down your self-esteem so badly that you feel you could never love again or that no one could love you. Lastly, you may even be in a place where you feel that *you* have done something wrong and that you deserve this abuse. I could go on and on, but I pulled out a few of the questions and thoughts that ran through my mind when I was living in hell. I say to you, my dear sister, don't give up when you still have something to give. If you are living in hell right here on earth, it's time for you to throw your shoulders back, lift up your head, and make a quality decision that you are going to give God the

fragments of your broken life. I heard someone say, "It's wonderful what God can do with a broken heart if He gets all the pieces." Don't hold back. You have to pull yourself up by your bootstraps and know that what's inside of you is good no matter how you may be feeling right now. You can live again. You can be set free from the hands of the enemy. You need to "bust a move" and bust out of prison! The Potter wants to put you back together again. Let God do it this time.
—DEETTA M. WEST

To the sister who is having difficulty with a son or daughter:

Raising children is difficult. If you are having problems with your son or daughter, there is likely something going on in their lives, and the acting out is their way of dealing with it. This is one of those moments when it is truly not about you. Your child is in pain, and your job is to find out what is going on.

At the first sign of trouble, you need to try to have an open and honest conversation where you keep your mouth closed and allow him or her to talk. If the situation is so bad that the child does not want to communicate with you, bring in a third party such as a therapist, pastor, or someone the child respects. Be prepared to hear anything your child has to say. Do not take it personally. As I have said, this is not about you.

Try and remember the last time things were going well for your child and attempt to pinpoint circumstances or situations that may be the cause for the change that has occurred. Become observant and listen more than you complain or demand.

Counseling for your child is important. They must be given a safe space to work out the issues that are causing their pain. Children today have to deal with a lot. Bullying is a problem. Many kids believe they can handle it on their own. Someone could be abusing your child, yet he or she will never come out and tell you. This is why it is important for you to be observant. It may be something simple, or it may be a challenging issue the family needs to deal with. Either way, sweeping it under the rug will not solve it.

For those dealing with teenagers, they need your attention. They may act indifferent, but deep down inside they need to know that you care about them. They want you to treat them with respect. They want a parent and not a friend. Continue to spend time with them. Don't allow them to go to their rooms every evening and be on the computer or their phones. Make your family a priority and go to their middle and high school activities. Stay connected to your children. Try to eat together, if not every night, a least few times a week.

Get off your telephone when you are dealing them! Stop the texting while you are talking to them. When you take them to the store, get off the phone while you are shopping. They need your attention.

As a parent, you have one opportunity to get it right for them. If you don't fix this now, when they grow up, they will not be able to go back in time and fix it for themselves. Take this seriously and do something. Your children are counting on you to give them a good life with a good future. They need good memories, and you are the only one who can make that happen for them.

—JUDGE PENNY

To the single and lonely sister:

The best advice I can give to the sister who is single and lonely is coming from a place of experience. My perspective is from the view of a sister who was married and has now found herself divorced and single again.

The question that I often ask is how did I get here again? Well, it is simple. I fell for the "happily ever after" fantasy that we all were taught as little girls. You will one day meet Prince Charming, and he will whisk you away, and you will live happily ever after. Wrong! Wrong! Wrong! That is not how the story truly ends. Often, we don't look at how our relationship and courtship began. We often are not honest about what we want and what we need in a relationship and a marriage. Therefore, we sometimes end up in relationships that send us backward.

In your time of singlehood, work on you. If you truly want a mate, there is a mate for you. But sisters, I need you all to put the brakes on for a moment and take care of yourself—body, mind, and soul. We are always saying we want a good man, but what are we bringing to the table? Let's be honest with each other. We could use some self-time to just get our act together as God works on developing our Prince Charming into to the man he has wholeheartedly created exclusively for us. In other words, stay out of God's business worrying about a man and let God send you someone worthy of your love.

—MICHELLE LIPPITT

Enjoy your single life. Go out and meet people. Join some organizations or social groups. Don't allow just anything to come into your life. Maybe this is your time to get your life together. Stop looking at what everyone else has and is doing. You can't compare your relationships to others. Everything that looks good on the outside may not be. Sometimes we are so desperate to have someone that we will settle for anything. When it's time for him to come, he will show up. Work on you. Don't settle!

—CHRISTI HECTOR

Webster defines *single* as one individual not part of a group or one thing.

Latwanda Anderson defines *single* as one individual working through life's intricate details expanding one's knowledge, power, and enlightenment. Singleness is not a disease; it's not a handicap or a shameful place to be in your life. Singleness is a time to find out who you really are in life, to search your fears, to find your strengths, and to test your limits. Life is a wonderful thing, but if you do not know who you are in this life, it's time to find out. Society deems single people as outcasts who are loveless, depressed, sad, and incomplete. The number one is a power number meaning priority, never to be divided, unity, freedom, specific individuality, etc. Only you can define who you are. Never allow society, friends, or family the privilege of identifying who you are. Life is a journey, so find your path.

Get out and find other individuals like you. Social media

is a great way to find likeminded people. Get involved in that hobby or hobbies you love. Find that political or social consciousness you believe in and get involved. Find that organization and start helping people who need your expertise.

Never allow depression to take over your life. Depression is a trick. Never fall for something or someone that will blind or destroy you mentally. The world is a great place for education, exploration, and experiences. All these things we need as individuals to grow.

Trust and believe there are other people, be they male or female, who have your life's answers. Go out and find them. Help never knocks on your door and says, "Hi, I'm here." Finding one's self is a journey of love, hate, exploration, limits, and convictions, but most of its truths will be found. Never underestimate the power of one! Always remember in your explorations you never know whom you will find.

Open that locked door of the unknown to find the life you have been searching for. In the walk of discovery, life as you know it can always be changed; there are no limits.

—LATWANDA ANDERSON

My sister, I've been there. What you have to realize is that God is working on a mate for you, and He is also working on you for your mate. Instead of thinking about being lonely, embrace what God has done for you already. You are a beautiful, loving, kind, and amazing sister. Doing things alone is not the end of the world. It's a new world of discovering yourself. It may be hard at first, but you will get through this.

Don't stop trusting or believing in God and His Word. You are single because this is exactly where God needs you to be right now. Maybe God wants you to focus on your relationship with Him. Are you giving God your all? A man cannot make you happy unless God allows it.

If you believe you are lonely, then you are lonely. You behave lonely. Loneliness is a feeling; it is a choice to feel lonely. Today, my sister, choose to not be lonely because you are not alone. God is with you. He is better than a mother, father, sister, brother, or friend. You have the power to change your life around with the help of God. Fall down on your knees and pray that God removes that feeling of loneliness and replaces it with a joy that only He can give you. Enjoy being you, all of you. Being single is only for a season, and being lonely is a feeling that you can choose not to have. The songwriter says, "Speak into the atmosphere." Speak it into the atmosphere: "I refuse to be lonely." Make it your mantra; say it as many times as you have to change your mind about being lonely. Be ready when God blesses you with your mate because God is working on you and him.

—DEIDRA DAVIS ALEXIS

To the sister who is caring for her elderly parent:

Caring for your elderly parent is the most selfless act you can do. It also screams "I love you!" without you opening your mouth. You're also sowing seeds. You too will need assistance as you age

—SHIRLEY LANGLEY HENRY

To the sister who cannot say no:

It's a brand-new day. While I know it is a day filled with a world of opportunities, I still seem to feel so overwhelmed. I have a million things to get done, and before I know it, here comes someone else with yet another request. I know my plate is full, but why in the world do I find myself saying yes again? I hang up the phone and beat myself up. Dang, I've done it again!

This was me for years. Well, truthfully, it was me until recently. I just could not say no! Why was this my plight? I'm still trying to figure it out. So far, I have concluded that, whether we will admit it or not, there is an innate desire for everyone to feel needed. Many people will not admit this either, but there is also a tendency to want to be people pleasers. I was included in that number, but now I have a different outlook on life. Let me tell you why. I was recently having a conversation with my husband and my 10-year-old son. We were talking about hobbies, and I realized that I really don't have any because I'm always busy. It's almost like everything I do is done because I just have to do it. There has been little room for me to just sit back and "do me."

My 10-year-old, in his pure innocence, said, "Mama, yes, you do have hobbies."

Out of shock and curiosity, I asked, "What are my hobbies, Manny?"

He looked at me like I was a complete idiot and said, "Ma, your hobbies are cooking and going to the ATM."

Naturally, my husband and I looked at each other; it took all we had not to just holler in laughter. I do realize that I cook a lot. I like to cook, but it is most definitely not a hobby. I cook out of necessity: it's cheaper, and it's healthier. But God used my baby to help me realize that I am constantly running to the ATM to keep my finances balanced. The business that I am running is much more than the perceived hustle that Emmanuel brought to my attention. The most amazing thing is that he did it without realizing what he was doing.

That was a real eye-opener for me. With this revelation came the knowledge that I cannot be so busy doing this and doing that for others that I cannot do what I need to do for myself. Yes, it's good to help. But you've got to be able to help yourself first, and you must be able to find balance. I have been a servant my entire life. My dues have been paid. Now it is time for me to live. Does that mean I have totally given up on helping others? Absolutely not. What it does mean, how-ever, is that I am taking authority over the battles that I choose to fight. I, under God's direction, am now the navigator of my life's destiny. Wow! What a feeling!

—ALONIA JONES

"No" is a complete sentence! Once you say no, learn not to give an explanation when *no* will do. My sister often tells me, "You can't argue with a stop sign." Stop trying to explain when *no* is the answer and will do all by itself. When you learn to do this, it's powerful! Girl, get your power back.

—SHIRLEY LANGLEY HENRY

To the sister who is an elected official about the issues that matter to women:

Once you are elected to public office, you have a responsibility to all your constituents regardless of gender, race, or nationality. It is my hope that a component of your agenda be about issues that are important to women and children. Equal pay for women is important. Affordable health care and economic avenues for opportunity where the government has programs and contracts should be made available to women. Women are the heart and soul of the American family.

We are concerned about voter restrictions enacted by many state legislatures. As Americans, we are given the right to vote. No public official should have the right to suppress or restrict our fundamental right to vote. Too many people marched and died for our right to vote. This should be an important issue for all elected officials.

We are concerned about the poor, and we believe the government should sponsor programs that help those who are marginalized and disenfranchised. Poor people are not looking for a handout, but a helping hand to allow them access to the American dream. As a business owner, I support tax breaks for businesses to help with job creation, but I also support developing programs that work to allow people to move from poverty to the middle class. This is the group of people whom everyone seems to have forgotten about.

We care about the inequalities in our criminal justice system. It is a good system that is seriously flawed. Sentencing should only be in the hands of judges. There are important opportunities to make changes in this area.

We care about public education. Every child should have the opportunity to attend a good school. Education makes the difference in how one's future turns out. As an elected official who cares about the future, education should be on your list of priorities. Please support initiatives that allow young people to go to college free of charge. This is a game changer. We owe it to the children to give them a chance to dream and have their dreams come true.

We care about the environment. This is God's creation, and we have a duty to take care of this planet for the next generation.

There are countless issues you can focus on. Just remember that you were elected to make a difference. If you refuse to do so, get out the way and allow someone else to do it. We are counting on you.

—JUDGE PENNY

To a sister who is not happy in her job or career:

Never settle. When we commit to a job, we are often doing it out of an obligation to live a financially stable life. As young adults, it is the logical next step in our lives to find a job or career that we believe will not only build our income but satisfy those around us who instill the belief that jobs nowadays are hard to come by and should be taken advantage of at the first opportunity. While I believe in taking advantage of opportunities and learning from them, I do not believe in settling for a job that makes you unhappy. I believe that you have two options: make the most out of your current job and use what you've learned to your advantage, or chase your dream.

When you find yourself unhappy with your job, it inevitably affects not only how you work but also how others around you work. No one wants to be surrounded by negative energy or a person who makes you feel as if your positive energy is ineffective. Negative energy is a contagiously powerful entity that decreases morale and increases apathy toward everyday life. The less you desire to be at your job, the more others around you will start to feel the same vibe.

The best advice I can give to someone who dislikes his or her current job is to continue to look forward but do not settle for the first opportunity that comes just because it is not your current job that you dislike. If you settle for "anything but this job," then you will follow the same cycle that will lead you to another unsatisfactory work experience. From my experience, it is important to work less toward settling for another "opportunity" and more on focusing on your dream. Ask yourself important questions that you should never lose sight of. What opportunity will align with what I want most in life? How can I use this opportunity to set me up for success and not failure? Will this opportunity help me grow into the kind of person I want to become rather than degrade me to a person I don't recognize? Even if this opportunity isn't exactly what I want to do, how can I get the most out of it and apply what I've learned to what I want to do next?

The next time you find yourself unhappy with your job, remember to take something away from the experience that will help define a clearer path toward where you actually want to go in life. In the long run, settling for something you do not love will only negatively impact your morale and relationships with others inside and outside work. When transitioning out of this state of dissatisfaction, remember to make the most out of the opportunity you have, but take the time to find something you can put passion behind. In the words of Ralph Waldo Emerson, "Nothing great was ever achieved without enthusiasm.

—MAYA DEJOIE

Pain is inevitable, but misery is optional!

Pain does not discriminate! We all experience the pain that accompanies defeat and disappointment that are often the lows that come with occupying professional space that no longer serves our future. However, with each moment that we chose to sit in the pain of occupational boredom or vocational amnesia, we invite misery to pull up a chair and make her abode. Yes, it was painful when we were overlooked for the promotion. Yes, it was painful when we then had to train the person to do the job that he/she was not as qualified to do. It is painful to know that our gifts are not being recognized in our current position. Do not allow the pain that often materializes as fear to paralyze your movement. Misery is like yeast to complacency. It expands feelings of doubt and despair and is combatant to the necessary change required to propel us forward.

Our lives are characterized by transitions and transformations, by necessary losses and unexpected gains, and by an unyielding sense of passages. Life is change. When we fail to have the courage to change, we neglect the calling we were born to accomplish. When we are not happy, we must ask ourselves: Who moved our vision? We must not be alarmed when the response points back at us. We fear change because we fear the unknown. Looking for a new job, starting our own business, or going back to school is an unknown. How will we pay for it? How will we pay our bills? We don't know anyone in a particular city, et cetera. While change is inevitable, the misery that travels alongside uncertainty is debilitating. When discerning next steps, a former student and friend shared with me the following:

Your calling, existence, passion, and purpose are not subject to change. Your mind, feelings, friends, and route are subject to change. Some people can't move past the latter to even realize the former. Don't get stuck in the wishy-washy-ness of the mind, of feelings, friendships, and routes such that you can't realize that your calling, existence, passion, and purpose will never change or shift. The route may change, but your purpose will not. Your feelings may change, but your passion will not. Your friends may change, but your calling will not. Your existence is why you live. Your calling is what you do. Your passion is what your soul feels. Your purpose is who you are. These things were embedded in you before you were even born. Everything else, people and routes, will change. Don't be afraid of what will change. Focus on what will not change while being flexible on what will change. People change, time changes, things change, and when they do—let them. Be honest about your challenges, but focus on your greatness. Your truest and deepest dream is God's will for your life.

If you're not happy in your current job, then change it! The lesson that life is trying to teach us is that when we exchange change for complacency, we resist an even greater work and forgo Divine vision. Every transition is a part of a continuum of being. How do you choose to be? Pain is inevitable, but misery is optional!

—MELVA SAMPSON

If you are unhappy with what you are doing in your job or career, you are likely not being the best *you* that you can be. It is up to you to make your life look the way you want it to look. Typically, we remain in the same job or career because we are afraid of the unknown. However, it is not for us to know what is going to happen or, for that matter, how it will happen. Instead, claim your goal. Write it down and own making it happen. God will do the rest.

—RAINA JONES

To the sister who is estranged from a family member:

Tomorrow is not promised. There is no deeper pain than the loss of a family member whom you have not spoken to in years because of some minor or stupid misunderstanding. Don't wait another day. Call that family member, repair whatever is wrong, and live life. If it's pride that's keeping you from calling, remember that pride goes before a fall. Make the call today. Tomorrow is not promised.

—SHIRLEY LANGLEY HENRY

To a sister who is pastoring a church:

The honest truth is that being a female pastor in a male-dominated profession is a real struggle. Quickly you will realize there is a double standard when it comes to how men and women are perceived and received in the ministry. Men experience far more leniency in the ministry, and congregations are much more willing to forgive or overlook the flaws and even the sins of male pastors. A woman called to minister must be prepared to be misunderstood often, especially if she is a strong woman with a "by any means necessary" approach to fulfilling her calling. You will likely be labeled a "Jezebel" by women and men alike who are unaccustomed to seeing women in leadership positions. You can expect that many men will find it difficult to receive from you simply because you are a female. Sadly, you must also brace yourself against the sabotage and competitive behavior you will experience from other women who see you as a threat because you are operating in a position of authority and influence that they themselves have not had the courage to strive for.

The Bible tells us plainly that jealousy is crueler than the grave. In other words, envious people have an agenda of murder in their hearts. You must be prepared for the unmerciful treatment that you will receive from people who will hate you without any cause—no matter how much you love and try to help them. Never forget that Jesus had a Judas in his camp and that Judas was motivated by jealousy and an offended heart to plot against the Lord. A servant is not greater than her master, so you will also experience the deep pain of betrayal in ministry.

The jealousy and disrespect you will experience within the pastoral community can become a chokehold that refuses to let you go if you allow them to penetrate your heart. This you must fight against at all costs. Humility comes before honor, so as a minister of the Gospel you must make it your constant aim to remain humble before the Lord who called you and not give in to the temptation to retaliate or to vindicate yourself in the eyes of people—even when they are clearly in the wrong.

I had to come to terms with the fact that people are not going to change just because I want them to or just because I try my hardest to effectively minister to them and love them. I am not God, and I cannot change anyone. When I realized that, I found the strength within me to continue teaching and preaching the Gospel of Jesus Christ. I live by my own saying: "Warriors fight because they love to. We are 'ride or die' people—but dying is *never* an option!"

—DR. RHONDA TRAVITT

To a teenager getting ready to start high school:

My name is Nia Dejoie. I am a 17-year-old high school student. I can tell you that high school is different from middle school because of the workload. You must cope with late-night homework and preparing projects for the following day. Teachers are available for assistance if you are having problems, but you will have to speak up first. High school also presents challenges that require you to become independent and more responsible. These experiences help you evolve into a well-rounded person. If you are nervous on your first day of high school, that is to be expected. Take some time to find your way around the school, and keep in mind that others are probably as nervous as you. Always remember that high school changes people. You will make friends during the first year, but you can have an entirely different circle of friends by the third year. High school offers many kinds of extracurricular activities. There are clubs, sports, musicals, and sometimes free time. There will be good times and bad times. Just make sure that you are focused because high school is the next step before college. Always make it a point to be on time for classes. Be sure to stay organized and have your assignments completed on time. Also, study hard so you will be prepared for tests and quizzes that are sure to come along. Remember, if you are focused, responsible, and willing to ask questions, you'll be on the road to success.

—NIA DEJOIE

I would tell a young lady entering high school to stay focused. You should start thinking about what you would like to do later in life. Don't worry about fitting into the crowd. Be social. Get into sports, activities, or organizations. Don't fall for peer pressure. The decisions you make now will follow you, whether they're academic or behavioral. Make good decisions. College is not for everybody, but you can also learn a trade. Start working on these things now so that when you graduate you will already have some direction. Enjoy these years of your life. Prepare for your future

—CHRISTI HECTOR

One of my favorite quotes is "If I had an hour to chop down a tree, I'd take forty-five minutes to sharpen the blade." I love it because it shows how gravely important it is to use your time wisely. You have only four years, but here are three Tools for Time and Success that may help.

Baseball players say that the hardest ball to catch is the one coming straight at you. Just like your future: clearly visible, but difficult to grasp. You see the vision for yourself—graduating, becoming a world-renowned author, owning your own studio—but fear reminds us of past failures. Don't be intimidated by your own future; instead, invest time into your dreams.

The first challenge is to find your passions and pursue your purpose. Get involved in activities that will give you tools to follow your dreams and help you meet people you can build a team with. Look fear in the eye and tell it to get out your way so you can try new things

I say get involved, but not too involved, and I tell you to try new things, but not try everything. You see, when you get to school, you'll find your access to things, places, and people will open, and you'll be like a kid in the candy store. With so many options, so much could be lost deciding if you like dark, caramel, or white chocolate that you forget your original goals to be healthy and fit.

So the next challenge is to destroy your distractions. We all have them. Light and dark chocolate may not be your thing, but for the rest of your life something will always try to deter you from your destiny. This includes stress, boys, girls, family, friends, finances, etc. The most potent weapon you can have is discipline, which starts with denial. Just say no.

The beauty about distractions, however, is that you won't

even see them if you are focused. The word *focus* comes from Latin and means fire; a common synonym for focus is heart. So we put the two together and understand that focus means to be fiercely passionate, which means that focus originates in your heart, and wherever your heart is your head will follow. And whatever your heart wants, your heart will get. So the original charge was to stay focused, but the more specific charge is to guard your heart. Because if your heart starts to long for popularity, attention, stress relievers, it will manifest in your decision-making, and you will find yourself in the wrong places with the wrong people. But if you fall in love with your future, you will focus on everything that contributes to you being your best self. So be careful with the things that you love.

High school will present you with 1,001 experiences and opportunities, but be picky in choosing the ones that maximize your time. You have only one hour to chop down the tree and forty-five minutes to sharpen your blade, so time must be used wisely. Don't waste this next phase in your life. Instead, think of what your future will look like when you arrive

—Chelsi Glascoe

To a sister about forgiveness:

Forgiving someone isn't for them; it's for you. Saying I'm sorry for something you've done or forgiving someone for something they've done releases you and cleanses your mind, heart, and spirit. There's a guilt that goes along with an un-forgiving attitude. Don't wait for someone to ask for forgive-ness. Forgive and live freely.

—SHIRLEY LANGLEY HENRY

To the sister who is raising a special needs child:

The best advice I can give to the sister who is raising a special needs child comes from a place of hope. I am the voice and the face of a mother with a unique blessing: a child with special needs.

A child with special needs is special not by virtue of a medical diagnosis or even a label provided by the world. These miracles were simply created by God, out of His love for us, and they remind us all to stay humble and nonjudgmental, and to be a person of vision and courageous as a lion in a world of many injustices.

The journey is not easy because you have the awesome responsibility of being the mother, the caregiver, the advocate, spokesperson, and, ultimately, the voice for a population of children who are often criticized, stigmatized, traumatized, bullied, marginalized, and isolated from society. They have been written off medically, educationally, and, in some cases, legally.

The tasks are many, and the road can be exhausting. The reality is that your norm is not ever going to be everyone else's norm, but do not give up, give in, or even think about giving out. Stay positive, surround yourself with those with like minds, ask for help when you need it, and learn as much as you can about your child's special needs, rights, and re-sources. Join support groups. I did, and it made a big difference to be able to share freely with others about my child and her journey without feeling that others either did not understand or would judge me. Most importantly, please take care of yourself—physically, spiritually, and mentally—because your child depends on you!

When you are faced with opposition or unfavorable news, as you often will be, continue to fight. Be determined to make things right for your child. God chose you. It is not anything so terrible or terrific that you did to be given this assignment. However, He has equipped you and only you to do a task that requires a special type of sister's endurance. Because of your faithfulness and love, your child will be able to turn nonbelievers into believers based on the mere fact of their existence.

Always be clear that your child's exceptionality is not a burden, but a blessing.

—MICHELLE LIPPITT

To the sister whose husband has just passed away:

Time is a great healer. Talk about your husband, the times you had together, how much he loved you, how much you loved him, and laugh and cry as much as you need to. The passage of time will aid in removing the pain you now feel given the loss of your husband. Don't be silent and hold your feelings in. Expressing yourself releases the stress and tension

—SHIRLEY LANGLEY HENRY

"… weeping may endure for a night, but joy *cometh* in the morning" (Psalm 30:5, KJV)

The death of a husband is an extremely heart-wrenching experience for a wife. With a spouse's death, there is also the death of the dreams, visions, aspirations, and hopes that you've made as a couple.

After the death of my husband, Julian A. Lee, I sought out the wisdom of other young widows. I asked each of them the same question, "Will I ever feel joy and happiness again?" I could see the sun shining, but there was a cloud there that prevented me from seeing the rays of hope. Each one said, "Yes, you will feel again, and you will see the hope."

In spite of the numbness, pain, sorrow, and doubt, I chose to forge my life forward instead of surrendering completely to the hopelessness. To grieve as one who has hope, I needed the love and support of God, family, and friends.

The Love and Support of God:

Initially, I was furious with God about my husband's death. It was heart-wrenching that he had to die and leave our only child fatherless. After all, I had surrendered to my calling to ministry; I was in seminary, and I was working diligently in the church. I was angry because all my life all I wanted was to be married and have a family. Now, he was dead. However, prior to my learning that my husband had died, God spoke to me saying, "I will be with you and see you through this." And God did just what He said He would do. The love of Jesus gave me strength when I didn't think I could endure another day of pain. The Holy Spirit comforted me.

The Love and Support of Family:

If I could have, I would have grieved in isolation, but that would not have been good grief. Being alone would have sunk me deeper into isolation. Without understanding the significance of embracing the love and support of family, I welcomed them to sit with me in my pain. And that's what they did. There were times when we did little talking, but they were there to do whatever needed to be done.

Our daughter, Nina Yvette, was almost three years old when her father died. She loved and adored him. In fact, she was with him at a college homecoming when he had a car accident and died. Because, Nina was so young, she didn't understand at all what was going on or why her father was not there. Her need for me gave me the strength to receive the hope that God was offering.

If you are reading this article because you have lost a loved one, please be assured that God is with you and that God has blessed you with those who will share with you on the journey of grief and that "weeping may endureth for the night, but joy will come in the morning."

—Rev. Portia Willis Lee

To the teenager who is being bullied:

I would tell her to be strong. It's not easy when people mistreat you without knowing anything about you. I would advise the teen to talk to someone—a counselor or a person she trusts. Bullying is never easy to understand. Sometimes, it has little to do with the person being bullied. In many instances, the bully suffers from low self-esteem and believes pushing others around will make her feel better about herself. No matter what a bully says to you, keep believing that you are beautiful inside and out. You also should learn to walk away from bullies. It is up to you to take control of the situation. Let them know that they cannot control you. Focus on the positive things in life, and realize that you are not alone.

—Nia Dejoie

YOUR TRUTH

How did this chapter speak to you?

_____

_____

_____

_____

_____

_____

_____

_____

_____

_____

_____

_____

_____

_____

_____

YOUR TRUTH

What is your truth?

_____

_____

_____

_____

_____

_____

_____

_____

_____

_____

_____

_____

_____

_____

_____

_____

_____

_____

YOUR TRUTH

Plan of action to deal with your truth:

_____

_____

_____

_____

_____

_____

_____

_____

_____

_____

_____

_____

_____

_____

_____

_____

_____

ACKNOWLEDGEMENTS

I thank God for the gifts and talents that I received when I was allowed to come into this world. Thank you, Deforest Marie Brown.

This book would have been impossible to write without the help of any number of people.

I want to thank my devoted husband Edward who for over twenty years has loved, supported and prayed for me. I am grateful to my son Michael who has never left my side and to Fela who always has encouraging words. Thank God for Pelly-Marie, she is the reason I wrote the book in the first place.

I am grateful for my real sisters, "The Brown Girls," Monica, Ayango and Keisha, we finally managed to get it right and we will never be separated again. I am grateful for my real sister Deborah, who has never been an "in-law" but rather my beloved sister. I am thankful to my number one cheerleader, my Aunt Blanche, whose love is unconditional and wisdom is always in abundance. I want to thank my Midway family and especially the Sisters in Faith Women's Ministry who have walked this spiritual journey with me, including Rev. Mother Dorothy and all the wise women who spoke life into my spirit. The young women who have allowed me to serve as a mentor have blessed me through the years. They have helped me to become a better human being, especially Michelle, the one who never left. I am grateful for Jared, who is looking down from heaven, Aeisha, Joshua, Shelby Divine, Nia, Maya, and Erica. I thank God for my spiritual son, Brandon, for whom I am well pleased. I am grateful for my friend Charles W. for his continued encouragement and getting me to Nancy.

I want to thank the thousands of women and teen girls who join me every year for *Judge Penny's SisterTalk Women's Empowerment Conference* and for allowing me to pour into their womanhood. Also, to the millions of devoted fans of, *Family Court with Judge Penny*, you understood the moment you watched what was really going on in that courtroom.

I am grateful to the twenty real sisters who contributed to this book. They embraced the vision and shared a part of themselves so others could be blessed.

Chelsi Glascoe, Maya DeJoie, Latwanda Anderson, Janice and Davida Mathis, Keisha Brown, Melva Sampson, Scarlet Pressley Brown, Shirley Langley Henry, Deetta M. West, Christi Hector, Tyiska Demery, Monica Coleman, Deidra Davis Alexis, Rhonda Travitt, Portia Willis Lee, Alonia Jones, Michelle Lippitt, Raina Jones, and Nia Dejoie

Finally, my life was changed forever when a mentor and friend, Dr. Michael Dash, whispered these words to me, "You are enough." It was his departing gift as he made his way to his eternal home. I believed him.

Please visit www.judgepenny.com.

CPSIA information can be obtained at www.ICGtesting.com
Printed in the USA
LVOW10*1930010916

502360LV00003B/4/P